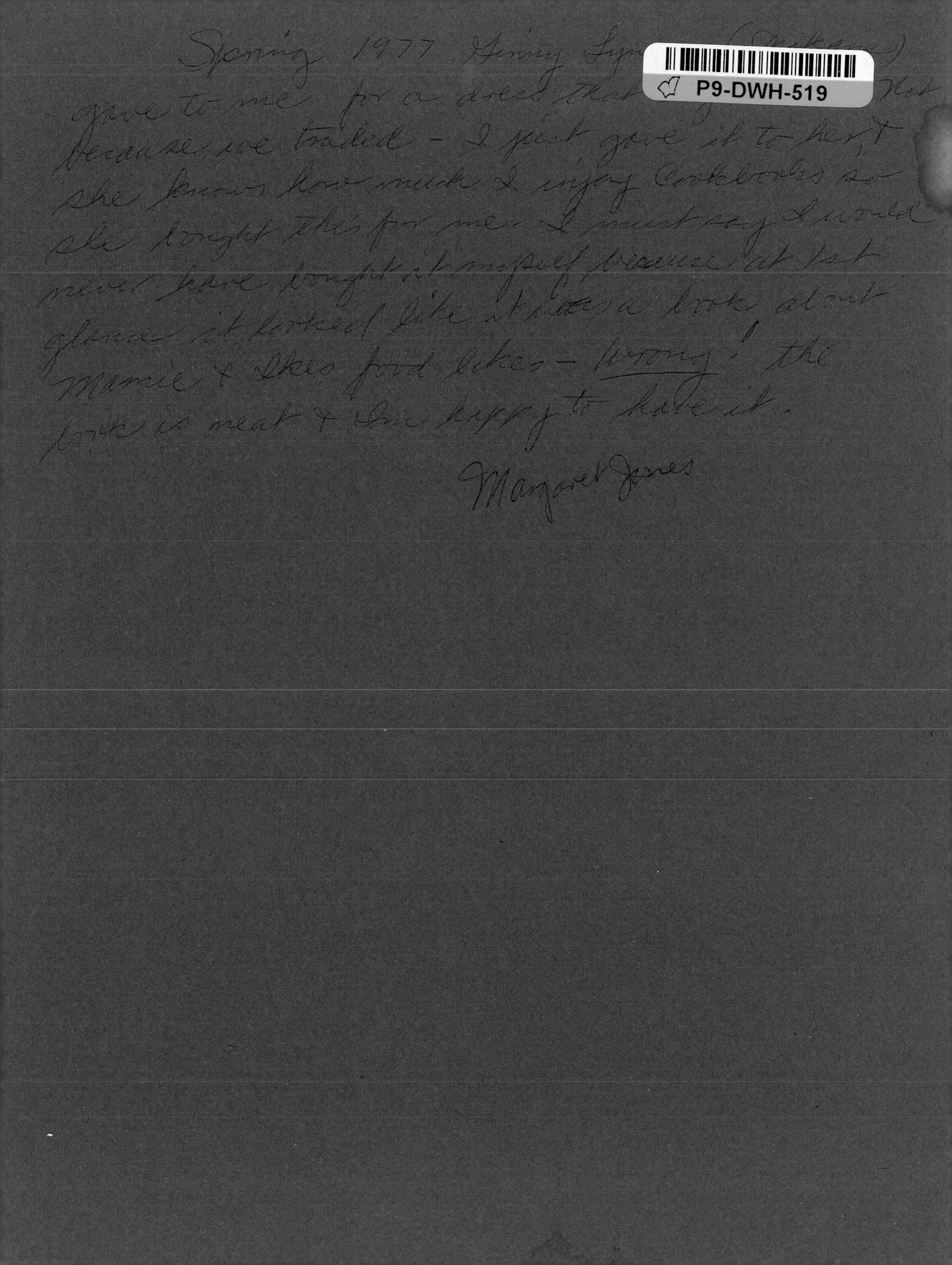

Spring 1977 Ginny Lyn[illegible] ([illegible])
gave to me for a dress that [illegible] Not
because we traded - I just gave it to her, &
she knows how much I enjoy Cookbooks so
she bought this for me. I must say I would
never have bought it myself because at 1st
glance it looked like it was a book about
Mamie & Ikes food likes - wrong! the
book is neat & I'm happy to have it.

Margaret Jones

Five-Star Favorites

Five-Star Favorites

RECIPES FROM FRIENDS OF MAMIE AND IKE

Golden Press New York
Western Publishing Company, Inc.
Racine, Wisconsin

ART DIRECTOR: Remo Cosentino
ASSISTANT: Constance T. Doyle
PHOTOGRAPHY: Victor Scocozza

Produced in the United States of America.

Library of Congress Catalog Card Number: 74-82071

Foreword

Our original idea for *Five-Star Favorites* was simple enough: to compile a cookbook as a fund-raising project for the Eisenhower Medical Center. Then, as the enthusiastic response from friends, associates and admirers of General and Mrs. Eisenhower mushroomed, so too did the plans.

We are not dieticians nor home economists—and neither are any of the members of the Committee. But all of us like to think that we know good food, and we do enjoy preparing it for our families and friends.

We discovered that favorite recipes do not come with a built-in balancing mechanism, and so you will find more cookies than cakes, more beef than lamb. Similarly, there are two gazpachos, three spoon breads and other seeming duplications—but each was so special in its own way that we let no artificial rule of numbers be our master.

The recipes on the following pages are the result of our efforts. We hope you will enjoy them. It has been a privilege to present them to you in this special tribute to two great Americans.

Chairmen, Cookbook Committee
Eisenhower Medical Center Auxiliary

Mrs. William O. Fleetwood
Mrs. Wilford H. Gonyea
Mrs. Harrison H. Roberts
Mrs. William R. Yancey

Acknowledgements

The chairmen wish to express their gratitude to the members of the Cookbook Committee, Eisenhower Medical Center Auxiliary:

Mrs. Dwight Babcock, Mrs. Leland Baker, Mrs. Joseph E. Bell, Jean M. Benson, Mrs. George Berkey, Mrs. William Demarest, Mrs. Samuel Jaggar, Mrs. N. Joe Jared, Mrs. Paul Jenkins, Mrs. Frank M. MacFall, Mrs. Howard D. McGrew, Mrs. Woodfin H. McMorries, Mrs. Earl E. Pinnell, Mrs. William Sorrentino, Mrs. John B. Suggs, Mrs. Ellsworth Vines, Mrs. Paul K. Yost, Jr.

A special note of thanks to Mollie Porter Cullum, Ambassador at Large, Eisenhower Medical Center Auxiliary.

MAMIE DOUD EISENHOWER

Gettysburg, Pennsylvania
September 3, 1974

To the Reader—

I am very grateful to the members of the Auxiliary for carrying through this wonderful project to benefit the Eisenhower Medical Center.

The recipes I have contributed have been used and served in the White House, Columbia University and my own home. I hope you enjoy them as much as my husband, my family and my friends have in the past.

I understand that all recipes have been tested, so you can be sure they will be successful in your own kitchen.

Thank you for selecting "Five-Star Favorites—Recipes from Friends of Mamie and Ike." I am sure you will find many interesting foods to serve and enjoy.

Sincerely
Mamie Doud Eisenhower

Contents

APPETIZERS & DRINKS

First Things First

First courses are a welcome gesture—a good sign of the
hospitality ahead. And to prove the point,
here is a happy collection of appetite-whetters
for any occasion. An elegant opener at the table,
to launch a memorable company meal.
A "little something" before dinner, to go along with drinks.
An array of nifty nibbles, to serve as cocktail-party fare.
You'll find the perfect prologue here—
plus some famous beverages to serve with snacks
or to offer as a finale.

Mushroom Roulade

¼ cup butter
½ cup flour
Pinch of salt
2 cups milk
4 eggs, separated
1 tsp. sugar
Toasted fine bread crumbs

MUSHROOM FILLING
2 medium onions, chopped
¼ cup olive oil
1 lb. fresh mushrooms, trimmed and finely chopped
3 tbsp. sour cream
3 tbsp. chopped green onions
2 tbsp. lemon juice
Salt and pepper

SAUCE
Lightly salted sour cream
Chopped chives

SERVES 8–10

Line a 10x15-inch jelly roll pan with waxed paper. Oil the paper and dust with a little flour. Set aside.

Melt the butter in a saucepan. Stir in flour and salt. Cook, stirring, over medium heat several minutes. Gradually beat in milk and cook, stirring constantly, until smooth and very thick. Remove from heat and stir in egg yolks and sugar. Let cool.

Beat egg whites until stiff, then fold into the cooled sauce. Spread mixture evenly in the prepared pan. Bake in a preheated 325° oven 40 to 45 minutes or until top is golden and edges shrink from sides of pan.

Meanwhile, make Mushroom Filling. Sauté onions in oil until tender and golden. Add mushrooms and cook mixture over low heat, stirring frequently, until juices have been absorbed. Remove from heat and stir in 3 tablespoons each of sour cream and chopped green onions. Add the lemon juice and salt and pepper to taste. Keep hot.

Arrange two overlapping sheets of waxed paper on counter and sprinkle with bread crumbs. Remove pan from oven and invert on the paper, then lift off. Peel away the paper used to line pan. Spread roulade with hot Mushroom Filling. Beginning at one of the narrow ends, roll up roulade with the aid of the waxed paper, lifting and rolling the roulade gently onto itself. Slice and serve hot, with a sauce made by combining the salted sour cream with chopped chives.

GENERAL and MRS. LAURIS NORSTAD
Toledo, Ohio

Caviar Pie

5 hard-boiled eggs
1 jar (3 oz.) lumpfish caviar, drained
½ small onion, finely chopped
1 tsp. lemon juice
1 cup sour cream
Paprika
Parsley

SERVES 8

Rice the eggs into an 8-inch pie plate. Mash down with the bottom of a spoon, covering bottom and side of plate to form a "crust." Spread caviar evenly over eggs. Add a very thin layer of chopped onion and sprinkle with lemon juice. Top with a smooth layer of sour cream. Garnish with paprika and parsley. Chill at least 2 hours. Cut into wedges to serve.

SYDNEY WHITE
New York, New York

Avocado with Hot Sauce

4 tbsp. butter
4 tbsp. catsup
2 tbsp. water
2 tbsp. vinegar
3 tsp. sugar
⅓ tsp. salt
2 tsp. Worcestershire sauce
Dash of Tabasco sauce
2 avocados

SERVES 4

Heat all ingredients except avocados in the top of a double boiler. Halve the avocados lengthwise and remove stones. Serve each half on a lettuce leaf, and garnish with water-cress. Pass the hot sauce. Serve as a first course.

Cover any leftover sauce and store in the refrigerator.

AMBASSADOR and MRS. JAMES SCOTT KEMPER
Chicago, Illinois

Melon Appetizer

1 melon (cantaloupe, honeydew or crenshaw)
Marsala or sherry to fill cavity, about 1 wineglass
Ginger (optional)
Thinly sliced prosciutto (optional)

Cut out a small round plug on end of melon. Scoop out seeds and pour in wine. Place in freezer; remove when flesh of melon is almost frozen. To serve, remove rind and cut melon into small cubes. Spoon some of the wine over fruit. If desired, sprinkle ginger on cubes, or cut unpared melon into wedges and top with thin slices of prosciutto.

MRS. DEAN TUMMEL
Palm Desert, California

Old English Hot Cheese Dip

2 jars (5 oz. each) very sharp cheese spread
1 can (7 oz.) minced clams, drained (reserve liquid)
2 tbsp. finely chopped green pepper
3 or 4 green onions, minced
Dash of hot pepper sauce

Combine all ingredients except reserved clam liquid in a saucepan over medium heat. While heating, thin mixture gradually with reserved liquid, stirring until desired consistency. Pour into serving dish and keep hot on a warming tray.

MRS. GERALD WELLS
Palm Desert, California

Chile con Queso

4 large onions, finely chopped
2/3 cup butter
4 cans (4 oz. each) peeled green chiles, rinsed, seeded and chopped
1 can (28 oz.) tomatoes, drained and chopped
1/2 tsp. sugar
Salt
4 lb. aged cheddar cheese, grated
5 tbsp. Worcestershire sauce

Sauté onions in butter over very low heat until clear, about 30 minutes (do not brown). Stir often. Add chiles and cook about 10 minutes. Add tomatoes, sugar and salt. Simmer about 5 minutes. Add grated cheese little by little, stirring constantly until cheese melts. Stir in Worcestershire sauce. Transfer to a chafing dish and keep hot over low heat.

Serve with corn chips, plain Melba toast or crackers.

MRS. FRANK WATERFALL
Indian Wells, California

Hot Shrimp Dip

2 cans (4½ oz. each) shrimp
1 package (8 oz.) cream cheese, softened
6 tbsp. butter, softened (do not use margarine)
8 green onions, sliced (include a small amount of the tops)

Drain shrimp; rinse and chop. Blend cream cheese and butter. Mix with onions and shrimp.

When ready to serve, heat in a chafing dish, stirring occasionally.

MRS. JOHN KING
Denver, Colorado

Hot Crab Fondue

1 jar (5 oz.) Kraft Old English cream cheese
1 package (8 oz.) cream cheese
1 package (6 oz.) frozen Alaska king crab, thawed
¼ cup light cream
½ tsp. Worcestershire sauce
¼ tsp. garlic salt
¼ tsp. cayenne pepper

Combine cheeses in top of a double boiler. Place over hot water and stir until smooth. Add remaining ingredients and heat through. Stir as needed to blend well. Serve hot in a fondue pot or chafing dish, with chunks of crusty French bread on the side. If mixture thickens while standing, stir in more cream.

MRS. JOHN ROSS
Indio, California

Hot Chipped Beef and Cream Cheese Dip

2 tbsp. butter
½ cup chopped pecans
Salt
1 package (8 oz.) cream cheese, softened
2 tbsp. milk
1 jar (2½ oz.) dried beef, minced
1 cup sour cream
2 tbsp. minced onion
2 tbsp. minced green pepper
½ tsp. garlic salt
½ tsp. pepper

Melt butter in a small skillet and sauté pecans. Add salt to taste. Remove from heat and reserve.

Blend cream cheese and milk in a bowl. Add remaining ingredients and mix well. Turn into a lightly buttered small casserole. Cover with the pecans and bake in a 350° oven 20 minutes. Serve hot, with crackers, corn chips or toast strips.

MRS. WINSTON NEWELL
Santa Monica, California

Crab Dip

1 can (6½ oz.) crabmeat, shredded
½ cup sour cream
1 tsp. lemon juice
½ tsp. Tabasco sauce
¼ tsp. prepared horseradish
½ tsp. salt

Combine crabmeat and sour cream; mix well. Blend in remaining ingredients.

Serve with crackers, potato chips or crisp celery and carrot sticks.

MRS. CLYDE SKEEN
Dallas, Texas

Ensenada Guacamole

2 ripe avocados
¼ cup finely chopped onion
½ can (4-oz. size) diced green chiles
½ can (7-oz. size) green chile sauce
1 small tomato, finely chopped
2 tbsp. lemon juice
1 tbsp. salad oil
Garlic salt

Peel and pit avocados, then mash with a fork. Combine with remaining ingredients and mix well. (If you like a very hot guacamole, use the whole can of diced chiles. And if you don't have a tomato handy, just add more green chile sauce.)

Serve in a dip dish and accompany with tortilla chips.

MRS. JACK MOREY
Desert Hot Springs, California

Curry Dip

1 package (8 oz.) cream cheese, softened
3 heaping tbsp. sour cream
2 heaping tbsp. chutney (Major Grey's), finely chopped
1 tbsp. syrup from chutney
1 tsp. curry powder

Place all ingredients in a blender and mix for 2 minutes. Serve with Melba toast or crackers.

MOLLIE PORTER CULLUM
La Quinta, California

Artichoke Dip

2 cups sour cream
1 package (8 oz.) cream cheese, softened
5 tbsp. white wine
½ tsp. garlic salt
½ tsp. salt
Freshly ground pepper
2 jars (6 oz. each) marinated artichoke hearts, drained

Mix sour cream, cream cheese, wine and seasonings. Chop artichoke hearts (a blender may be used); stir into sour cream mixture. Chill thoroughly. Serve with fresh vegetable dippers, such as cucumbers, cauliflower, carrots, celery, zucchini, squash and radishes.

MRS. DONAVAN BROWN
Cathedral City, California

Caviar and Blue Cheese Dip

1 package (8 oz.) cream cheese, softened
1 package (3 oz.) blue cheese
1 tsp. Worcestershire sauce
¼ cup mayonnaise
Dash of Tabasco sauce
3 oz. caviar

Combine all ingredients except caviar and blend thoroughly. Pack into serving bowl and frost top with caviar.

To serve as a spread, dip through caviar into cheese mixture. Serve with toasted bread rounds or Melba toast.

MRS. ELTON HALLETT
Corona del Mar, California

Eggs and Caviar

6 hard-boiled eggs, chopped
½ cup butter, softened
¼ to ½ cup mayonnaise
½ cup chopped green onions
Lemon juice
Salt
1 cup sour cream
1 jar (6 oz.) caviar (preferably beluga)

Combine all ingredients except sour cream and caviar. Mix well. Line a small bowl with plastic wrap. Pack mixture firmly into bowl and chill overnight.

When ready to serve, unmold onto serving platter and peel off plastic wrap. Frost evenly with sour cream and top with caviar. Serve with party rye rounds.

MRS. J. LEWIS DANIELSON
Palm Springs, California

Pâté Provençal

- 1 can ($10\frac{1}{2}$ oz.) condensed beef broth
- 1 tbsp. unflavored gelatin
- 2 cans (3 oz. each) liver paste
- 1 can ($4\frac{1}{2}$ oz.) deviled ham
- 1 tsp. lemon juice
- 1 tsp. grated onion

Pour broth into a saucepan. Add gelatin and soften, then warm over low heat until gelatin dissolves. Pour ¾ cup of the broth into a 2-cup mold or a round pan about 8 inches in diameter and at least 3 inches high. Chill until set.

Combine liver paste, ham, lemon juice, onion and remaining broth. Mix thoroughly. Remove mold from refrigerator and carefully spoon in meat mixture. Chill.

To serve, unmold onto a serving platter.

MRS. CLARENCE FRANCIS
Bronxville, New York

Canapé Santa Barbara

- 1 tbsp. unflavored gelatin
- 1 can ($10\frac{1}{2}$ oz.) condensed beef consommé
- ⅓ cup sherry
- 1 small jar pimiento-stuffed green olives, drained and sliced
- 1 can ($4\frac{3}{4}$ oz.) liver paste

Dissolve gelatin in a small amount of consommé. Heat remaining consommé and add softened gelatin and sherry. Stir well. Pour into a mold (or muffin tin, small glasses or loaf pan). Add olives. Chill until partially set.

Spread liver paste on top; chill until firm.

When ready to serve, unmold onto serving plate and surround with small round crackers.

MRS. PAUL F. MURPHY
Lake Oswego, Oregon

Steak Tartare

2 lb. lean round steak
2 eggs, beaten
½ cup capers
½ cup minced onion
2 tsp. salt
Freshly ground pepper
Worcestershire sauce
Fresh parsley
Capers for garnishing

SERVES 12

Put meat through grinder only once (your butcher can do this for you). Mix eggs, ½ cup capers, the onion and seasonings with the freshly ground meat. Chill.

When ready to serve, mound the raw meat on a serving platter and garnish with fresh parsley and additional capers. Accompany with thinly sliced pumpernickel or Swedish rye bread.

Steak Tartare can also be served as an entrée; this recipe would yield about 4 servings.

MRS. CARLETON COVENY
Palm Springs, California

Ham Log

X add green grapes on topping—

2 cans (4½ oz. each) deviled ham
½ envelope dry onion soup mix
1 package (8 oz.) cream cheese, softened
1 cup chopped unsalted pecans

Mix ham and soup mix. Chill until firm enough to handle, about 1 hour.

To make the "log," spread a third of the cream cheese in a long rectangular layer on a serving dish. Mound ham mixture on top, shaping a "log." Chill until firm. Frost with remaining cream cheese and cover evenly with pecans. Serve with crackers.

MRS. HAROLD TARLETON
Palm Desert, California

Clam Roll

1 can ($7\frac{1}{2}$ oz.) minced clams, drained
2 packages (8 oz. each) cream cheese, softened
2 tbsp. finely chopped onion
2 tbsp. lemon juice
Garlic salt
Dash of Maggi liquid seasoning or Worcestershire sauce
$1\frac{1}{4}$ cups chopped toasted nuts*

Mix clams and cheese. Beat in onion, lemon juice, garlic salt and Maggi seasoning; stir in $\frac{1}{2}$ cup of the nuts. Shape mixture into a log and roll in remaining nuts, coating well. Chill thoroughly. Serve with crackers.

*If using walnuts, remove shells and drop into boiling water. Boil 3 minutes. Drain well and spread in a shallow pan. Toast in a preheated 350° oven until golden brown, 15 to 20 minutes, stirring occasionally.

MRS. DANIEL TOMLINSON
Cathedral City, California

Eggplant Caviar

1 large eggplant
$\frac{1}{4}$ cup olive oil
1 clove garlic, crushed
1 large onion, chopped
$\frac{1}{2}$ cup diced green pepper
$\frac{1}{2}$ cup diced celery
1 can (15 oz.) Italian tomatoes, broken up
$\frac{1}{2}$ cup halved ripe olives
5 tbsp. garlic wine vinegar
1 tsp. capers
2 tsp. oregano
1 tsp. basil
$\frac{1}{2}$ tsp. salt
$\frac{1}{2}$ tsp. pepper

Place unpeeled eggplant in a preheated 350° oven and bake about 1 hour until very soft. Let cool, then cut open. Remove pulp and reserve; discard skin.

Heat oil in a large skillet. Add garlic, onion, green pepper and celery. Cook until onion is golden. Stir in eggplant and remaining ingredients. Simmer, uncovered, 20 minutes. Let cool, then chill.

Serve cold on Melba toast or toasted bread fingers.

MRS. WILLIAM GARLAND
Indian Wells, California

Chutney Cheese Spread

- 2 packages (3 oz. each) cream cheese, softened
- 1 cup shredded cheddar cheese, at room temperature
- 2 tbsp. dry sherry
- ½ tsp. curry powder
- ¼ tsp. salt
- MSG
- ½ cup chutney (Major Grey's), chopped
- ½ cup thinly sliced green onions

Blend cheeses thoroughly. Add sherry, curry powder, salt and MSG; beat well. Spread mixture in a layer ½ inch thick on serving dish. Chill.

Spread chutney over cheese layer and sprinkle with green onions. Serve with Triscuits or wheat crackers.

MRS. DWIGHT BABCOCK
Hot Springs, Arkansas

"Oh So Good!"

- 1 lb. very lean bacon
- ½ lb. cheddar cheese
- 1 medium onion, cut up
- Triscuits or party rye bread

Combine bacon, cheese and onion. Put through grinder (with medium plate) twice. Spread on Triscuits or party rye bread. Place under broiler, with tops of canapés about 6 or 7 inches from heat. Broil until browned.

The uncooked spread can be kept for weeks in freezer. Cover cooked canapés in refrigerator and store for snacks.

MRS. VIRGIL SCOTT GLASS
Shaker Heights, Ohio

Riveredge Sardine Canapés

- 1 tsp. lemon juice
- 1 can (3¾ oz.) boneless sardines
- ½ tsp. onion juice
- Mayonnaise
- 12 toasted, buttered bread rounds
- ¼ lb. good cheddar cheese, cut into small square slices

MAKES 1 DOZEN

Sprinkle lemon juice over sardines and mash. Stir in onion juice and bind with a little mayonnaise.

Pile mixture on toasted bread rounds. Top each canapé with a small square of cheese and heat under low broiler flame until cheese is melted. Serve at once.

MOLLIE PORTER CULLUM
La Quinta, California

X

Pie Sandwiches

1 hard-boiled egg, finely chopped
Mayonnaise
Dash of dill
Salt
1 can (4½ oz.) deviled ham
1 tsp. prepared horseradish
1 tsp. prepared mustard
1 package (8 oz.) cream cheese, softened
2 tbsp. crumbled blue cheese
2 medium cucumbers
1 unsliced round loaf rye bread, about 6 inches in diameter
1 jar (2 oz.) caviar

MAKES 3 "PIES," EACH SERVING 4 OR 5

Make three fillings as follows—Egg filling: Combine egg, 1 tablespoon mayonnaise, the dill and salt. Ham filling: Combine deviled ham, horseradish and mustard. Cheese filling: Combine cream cheese and blue cheese; beat until fluffy.

Score rind of cucumbers with a fork and halve them lengthwise. Cut the halves into thin slices and set aside.

Horizontally cut 3 half-inch-thick slices of bread from center of loaf. Spread each slice with mayonnaise. For each "pie," spread egg filling in center of slice. Ring with ham filling, then cheese filling. Overlap cucumber slices on top of cheese filling. Add a band of caviar between cucumber and ham. To serve, cut into wedges.

MRS. JOSEPH SHEFFET
Indian Wells, California

Palos Verdes Hot Shrimp

1½ cups olive oil
1½ cups wine vinegar
1 cup Dusseldorf mustard (use yellow mustard if you enjoy a sharper flavor)
¾ cup minced parsley
¾ cup finely chopped green onions
½ cup minced celery
½ cup cayenne pepper
2½ tbsp. salt
5 lb. shelled cooked shrimp

Combine all ingredients except shrimp in a large bowl. Mix thoroughly. Stir in shrimp, making sure all are covered with the sauce. Marinate at room temperature at least 3 hours, turning occasionally.

Serve with toothpicks—and lots of strong, cold drinks to put out the fire!

MRS. THEODORE E. JUNG
Palm Desert, California

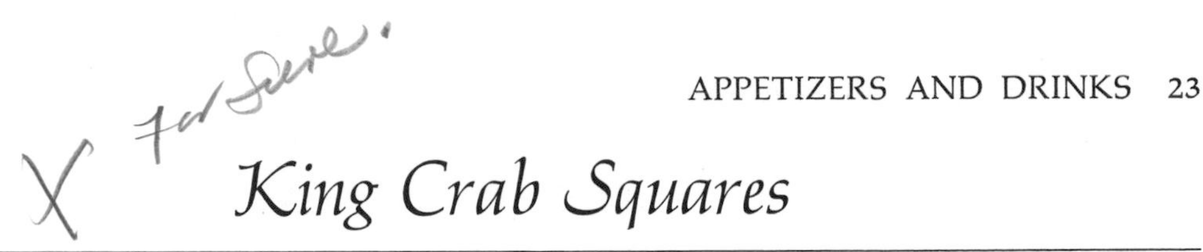

King Crab Squares

- 1 can (7½ oz.) king crab or ½ lb. frozen crabmeat, thawed
- 1½ cups grated cheddar cheese
- 3 tbsp. minced green onion
- 3 tbsp. finely sliced ripe or green olives
- ¼ cup mayonnaise
- 1 egg, slightly beaten
- 2 cups buttermilk biscuit mix
- ½ cup white cornmeal
- ⅔ cup water
- 3 tbsp. butter, melted

MAKES 36–40

Combine crabmeat, cheese, onion, olives and mayonnaise. Add egg and mix well.

In another bowl, combine biscuit mix, cornmeal, water and butter. Blend well. Spread in a greased baking pan, about 13x9x2 inches. Cover with crabmeat mixture and bake in a preheated 375° oven 20 to 25 minutes.

To serve, cut into small squares.

MRS. ALBERT CHILDS
Birmingham, Michigan

Deluxe Clam Cakes

- 1 can (7½ oz.) minced clams (undrained)
- 2 eggs
- ½ cup cottage cheese with chives
- ¼ cup sour cream
- ¾ cup sifted flour
- 1 tbsp. oil or melted shortening
- 2 tbsp. dried sweet pepper flakes
- ⅓ tsp. salt
- ¼ tsp. MSG

MAKES ABOUT 3 DOZEN

Combine all ingredients in a bowl and stir until thoroughly mixed. (For thicker consistency, add more flour.)

Grease and heat a griddle. Pour just enough batter to make silver-dollar-size patties. Cook each side until brown.

Serve as finger food, hot or cold. Especially good with sour cream.

MRS. W. H. McMORRIES
Palm Desert, California

Baked Frankfurters

4 tbsp. salad oil
1 medium onion, chopped
1 cup catsup
1 cup water
½ cup vinegar
2 tbsp. Worcestershire sauce
2 tsp. dry mustard
2 tsp. paprika
Salt and pepper
24 lean top-quality frankfurters

Heat oil in a skillet and sauté onion until golden. Combine remaining ingredients, except frankfurters, and add to pan. Simmer, uncovered, 15 minutes. Split frankfurters and cut into 1-inch pieces. Place cut side down in an ungreased shallow baking dish. Cover with hot sauce and bake in a preheated 350° oven 30 minutes, basting several times. Pour into a chafing dish and serve with toothpicks.

Try these for lunch or supper sometime—split as directed but do not cut into pieces.

MRS. WILLIAM O. CAUSIN
Tacoma, Washington

Mrs. Causin is Mamie Eisenhower's niece.

Mexican Fireballs

1 lb. ground chuck
1 cup seasoned bread crumbs
1 egg, beaten
¼ cup minced onion
3 tbsp. diced green chiles
3 tbsp. tomato paste
2 tbsp. Worcestershire sauce
½ tsp. MSG
½ tsp. garlic salt
1 cup grated Parmesan cheese

MAKES ABOUT 40

Combine all ingredients except cheese and mix well. Form 1-inch balls. Stuff each with one of the following: sliced ripe or green olives, pineapple tidbits, sliced water chestnuts, sliced mushrooms, raisins or anything you wish. Coat balls with Parmesan cheese. Place on a broiler pan and bake in a preheated 425° oven 15 minutes.

These may be frozen in a plastic bag. Thaw before baking.

MRS. DON ACKERMAN
Las Vegas, Nevada

Artichoke Nibbles

2 jars (6 oz. each) marinated artichoke hearts
1 large onion, finely chopped
1 clove garlic, minced
4 eggs
¼ cup fine dry seasoned bread crumbs
½ tsp. salt
⅛ tsp. pepper
⅛ tsp. oregano
⅛ tsp. Tabasco sauce
½ lb. sharp cheddar cheese, grated
2 tbsp. minced parsley

MAKES ABOUT 6 DOZEN

Drain marinade from 1 jar of artichokes into a skillet. (Drain other jar of artichokes, discarding marinade.) Chop artichokes and set aside. Sauté onion and garlic in marinade until onion is limp, about 5 minutes. Beat eggs until fluffy, then add bread crumbs, salt, pepper, oregano and Tabasco sauce. Stir in cheese, parsley, artichokes and onion mixture. Mix well and pour into a greased 11x7-inch baking pan. Bake in a preheated 325° oven 30 minutes. Let cool in pan and cut into 1-inch squares.

Serve warm or cold. Good either way! (These can be reheated in oven 10 to 12 minutes.)

MRS. HOWARD BAGLEY
Indian Wells, California

Quesadillas

Salsa de jalapeño or a hot, Mexican-style tomato sauce*
3 corn or flour tortillas
½ cup coarsely grated sharp cheddar cheese
½ cup coarsely grated Monterey jack or Muenster cheese

SERVES 6

"I have a lot of different teasers like this because of the land office business done at Dinah's Bar and Grill during the cocktail—after tennis—post meetings—name your mission—hour."

Brush sauce thinly over surface of tortillas. Mix cheeses and sprinkle heavily over tortillas. Place on a cookie sheet and bake in a preheated 400° oven until cheese is melted and tortillas are crisp. Cut into wedges and serve immediately with a cold drink.

*These sauces are easy to find in Southern California. If they are unavailable, you may substitute tomato sauce to which you've added a few drops of Tabasco sauce.

DINAH SHORE
Beverly Hills, California

Chiles Rellenos

- 1½ tsp. butter
- 1 can (7 oz.) whole green chiles, drained, split and seeded
- ½ lb. Tillamook or Monterey jack cheese, sliced
- 5 eggs
- ¼ tsp. salt

Melt butter in a 9x9-inch baking pan. Place chiles in pan and cover with cheese slices, leaving about ½ inch between slices. Beat eggs with salt and pour over cheese. Bake in a preheated 325° oven until cheese has melted and eggs have set, about 25 minutes. Remove from oven. Let set 20 minutes, then cut into small squares.

This can be baked ahead of time, then reheated.

CHARLES ANGER
Palm Springs, California

Stuffed Mushroom Caps

- 24 fresh whole mushrooms
- ¼ cup melted butter
- 1 tsp. seasoned salt
- 2 envelopes toasted onion dip mix (Lawry's)
- 2 cups fresh bread crumbs
- 3 tbsp. sherry
- ½ lb. ground beef, cooked (optional)

Wash and drain mushrooms. Pluck out stems (reserve), leaving caps hollow. Dip caps in melted butter and place on a cookie sheet, hollow sides up. Chop stems and sauté in a little butter. Add seasoned salt, onion dip mix and bread crumbs. Toss lightly and moisten with sherry (add meat, if desired, at this point). Spoon stuffing into mushroom caps and bake in a preheated 425° oven 10 minutes.

MRS. COY FARRAR
Palm Springs, California

X Brunch.

Suzie's Delectables

- 1 lb. fresh mushrooms, cleaned and sliced
- ¼ cup butter
- ½ lb. bulk sausage
- Salt
- ¾ cup heavy cream (or more)
- Dry sherry
- Tiny tart shells

Sauté mushrooms in butter with a little salt. Remove from skillet and reserve. Brown sausage, then drain off fat. Return mushrooms to skillet and add cream. Reduce liquid over high heat, stirring carefully. Add a little sherry. Taste for additional salt. Serve hot, in tiny tart shells.

MRS. PETER SCHAUS
Stanford, California

Cheese Wafer Hors d'Oeuvres

- 1 cup butter or margarine, softened
- 1 lb. New York cheddar cheese, grated
- 2 cups flour
- 1 tsp. salt
- ½ tsp. (scant) cayenne pepper
- 4 cups corn flakes, crushed

Blend butter and cheese thoroughly. Add flour, salt, cayenne pepper and corn flakes; mix well. Shape into balls about the size of a walnut. Place on an ungreased cookie sheet and flatten with a fork. Bake in a preheated 325° oven 20 to 30 minutes, until dry.

These keep well in a tin box.

MRS. WILLIAM C. STROUBE
Corsicana, Texas

Cheese Bread Cubes

- 1 unsliced loaf day-old bread
- 1 cup butter
- ½ lb. cheddar cheese, diced
- 2 packages (3 oz. each) cream cheese
- 4 egg whites

MAKES ABOUT 3 DOZEN

Remove crust from loaf and cut bread into 1½-inch cubes. Melt butter and cheeses together in top of a double boiler. Blend well. Beat egg whites until stiff but not dry. Fold cheese mixture into egg whites. Dip bread cubes into mixture and place on cookie sheet. Cover and refrigerate at least 8 hours.

To serve, bake in a preheated 375° oven 13 to 15 minutes. Serve hot.

May be prepared ahead and frozen; bake when needed. Good served with soup or salad for lunch.

MRS. WINSTON NEWELL
Santa Monica, California

A Different Brandy Alexander

1¾ tsp. unflavored gelatin
⅓ cup heavy cream
2 egg yolks
¼ cup sugar
⅓ cup brandy
⅓ cup dark crème de cacao
1 cup heavy cream, whipped
Flavored whipped cream for garnishing

SERVES 6

In a small bowl or pan, sprinkle gelatin over ⅓ cup heavy cream. Let stand 5 minutes to soften, then stir over hot water until dissolved. Let cool (do not let congeal).

In a small mixer bowl, beat egg yolks until frothy. Gradually beat in sugar. Continue to beat several minutes, until mixture ribbons when beater is lifted. Stir in brandy, crème de cacao and gelatin mixture. Chill until slightly thickened. Just before serving, fold in whipped cream. Pour into shallow champagne or sherbet glasses. Top with whipped cream flavored with brandy or crème de cacao.

MRS. FRANK RIEHL
Newport Beach, California

Tex's Li'l Darling

1½ oz. bourbon
1½ oz. sweet vermouth
10 dashes aromatic bitters
Pernod
Lemon peel

SERVES 1

"This drink is for the morning after, or when you just can't get started. It sounds so simple, and it is—but it does the trick."

Combine bourbon, vermouth and bitters in an old-fashioned glass. Add several ice cubes and stir until cold. Remove ice cubes and add several drops of Pernod. Twist lemon peel over but do not drop in.

"Down the hatch," then sit back—and wait!

GEORGE "TEX" GREGG
Racquet Club
Palm Springs, California

NOTE: George Gregg, better known as "Tex," was the only professional mixologist asked to contribute recipes to this cookbook. This recipe and all of those on the facing page are some of his favorites. Tex has tended bar at Charlie Farrell's world-famous Racquet Club since 1937, when Mr. Farrell hired him on a temporary basis, while searching for the "ideal" English pub bartender. The "temporary" job lasted 27 years; in 1964 Mr. Farrell decided his search was unnecessary, and he officially hired Tex. As wine improves with age, so bartenders improve with seniority—we consider Tex THE authority.

Folding Farrell

3 oz. tomato juice (use a premium brand)
2 oz. vodka
1 oz. catsup
½ oz. lemon or lime juice
2 dashes Worcestershire sauce
2 dashes Tabasco sauce
5 good shakes each celery salt, salt and pepper
Cracked ice (about 1 cup)

SERVES 1

"Here's a variation on the Bloody Mary. It's a favorite of Racquet Club founder Charlie Farrell, who named it. Sounds crazy, but it comes on strong; hence the name!"

Combine all ingredients in a blender or malt mixer. Give it a short whirl and strain into a chilled champagne goblet.

Peligrosa

1 oz. light rum
1 oz. dark rum
½ oz. 151-proof rum
1 oz. passion fruit juice
1 oz. lime juice
½ oz. Falernum
Piece of fresh pineapple (the size of a golf ball)
Crushed ice (about 1 cup)
Pernod

SERVES 1

*"This is an original drink from the Racquet Club. The taste is great, but be forewarned—*peligrosa *means 'dangerous' in Spanish."*

Combine all ingredients except Pernod in a blender and mix well. Put *one* drop of Pernod over ice cubes in a large brandy snifter. Pour (do not strain) the rum mixture over the ice.

Pasa Doble

2 oz. vodka
1 oz. passion fruit juice
1 oz. lime juice
½ oz. Galliano
Piece of fresh pineapple (the size of a golf ball)
Crushed ice (about 1 cup)

SERVES 1

Combine all ingredients in a blender and mix well. Pour (do not strain) over ice cubes in a *quart* brandy snifter.

Cuidado: Substitute Falernum for the Galliano.

"21" Club Southside

2 oz. gin or vodka (or any beverage of your choice)
Juice of ½ lime
1 tsp. confectioners' sugar
Crushed ice
5 fresh mint leaves
Sprig of mint (optional)

SERVES 1

Combine gin, lime juice, sugar, ice and fresh mint leaves in a cocktail shaker and shake well. Strain into a glass, over ice cubes. (If serving straight up, shake with ice cubes.) Garnish with a mint stub.

If one wishes mint leaves to show, snip the fresh leaves into very fine pieces so that they will go through the sieve.

JERRY BERNS
New York, New York

"21" Club Sour

2 oz. Ballantine Scotch, Ezra Brooks Bourbon or Hine Cognac
Juice of ½ lemon
1 tbsp. warm honey (or more or less, to taste)
Crushed ice

SERVES 1

Combine all ingredients in a cocktail shaker and shake with vigor. Strain into a glass, straight up or on the rocks.

JERRY BERNS
New York, New York

Aunt Tess

1 can (6 oz.) frozen lemonade concentrate
6 oz. milk (use lemonade can)
6 oz. vodka or gin
Dash of orange-flower water
2 cans crushed ice (about 12 ice cubes)

SERVES 4

Combine all ingredients in a blender and whirl 30 to 40 seconds.

Great for Sunday brunch!

MRS. JOHN NEUKOM
Hillsborough, California

Pineapple Daiquiri

Juice of 4 limes
1 small can (6 oz.) unsweetened pineapple juice
4 jiggers white rum
12 sugar cubes
Shaved ice

SERVES 4

Combine all ingredients in a blender and mix briefly. Cheers!

BOB HOPE
North Hollywood, California

The Gatsby

2 oz. vodka
1 oz. Rose's lime juice
Soda water
Orange wedge

SERVES 1

Pour vodka and lime juice over ice cubes in an old-fashioned glass. Fill glass with soda water. Serve with an orange wedge.

MRS. JOHN BASH
Palm Desert, California

Eggnog

⅞ cup good bourbon
1 tbsp. unflavored gelatin
1 dozen eggs, separated
¾ cup sugar
Pinch of salt
1⅓ cups whipping cream, whipped

SERVES 8

Pour ½ cup of the bourbon over gelatin in a cup. Let stand 5 minutes to soften, then stir over hot water until dissolved. (Do not let congeal; if it does, melt again.) In a bowl, beat egg yolks until lemon-colored. Very slowly add gelatin mixture and remaining bourbon, beating constantly. Beat in ¼ cup of the sugar.

Put egg whites in a large bowl. Add salt and beat until stiff. Slowly add remaining sugar, beating constantly. Combine whipped cream, egg whites and egg yolk mixture; fold together.

May be served at once or stored, covered, in refrigerator.

MRS. ROBERT HAYNIE
Hillsborough, California

Cognac Frappé

1 scoop vanilla ice cream
1 oz. cognac (Hennessy, by all means)
½ oz. Tia Maria
1 tbsp. coffee
½ cup crushed ice

SERVES 1

Combine all ingredients in a blender and mix.

MRS. JACK HENNESSY
North Hollywood, California

Coffee Liqueur

2 cups water
4 cups sugar
1 jar (2 oz.) very strong instant coffee (such as Yuban)
1 bottle (4/5 qt.) vodka
1 vanilla bean

MAKES ABOUT 1½ QUARTS

Combine water, sugar and coffee in a large saucepan and bring to a slow boil. Remove pan from heat and cool. Add vodka and vanilla bean; stir and pour into a half-gallon bottle. Cap loosely and let stand at room temperature 15 to 30 days.

MRS. WILLIAM JUVONEN
Indian Wells, California

Spiced Tea

5 tbsp. tea leaves
20 cloves
5 cups boiling water
2 cups sugar
¾ to 1 cup lemon juice (or to taste)
7½ cups cold water

SERVES 12

Combine tea and cloves. Cover with boiling water and steep, covered, to strength desired. Strain. Stir in sugar, lemon juice and cold water. Chill.

MRS. MAX D. ORR
Lake Forest, Illinois

SOUPS

Just a Soupçon of Genius

A chowder bubbling over an open fire, a potage simmering on the stove. Always and everywhere a good soup marks the expert cook. This collection reads like a travelogue: exotics from the Orient, sophisticates from the Continent, plus some all-American favorites. Hots and colds, blender-quickies, hearties to eat like stew. To start a meal or make a meal, dip into these pages whenever a soup is called for.

Gazpacho

3 ripe tomatoes, peeled and chopped
1 cucumber, peeled and chopped
1 green pepper, chopped
1 medium onion, chopped
1 clove garlic, chopped
1½ cups tomato juice
½ cup milk
¼ cup olive oil
¼ cup vinegar
Dash of salt
Dash of cayenne pepper
1 egg, well beaten
Garnishes

SERVES 8

Combine all ingredients except egg in a blender. Mix until thoroughly blended. Mix in the egg and taste for seasoning. Chill.

Serve with the following garnishes, each in its own bowl: croutons, diced cucumber, chopped green onions, chopped green peppers and chopped ripe tomato.

OVETA CULP HOBBY
Houston, Texas

Gazpacho La Quinta

2 large tomatoes, peeled and chopped
1 large cucumber, peeled and chopped
1 medium onion, chopped
½ medium green pepper, chopped
4½ cups tomato juice
⅓ cup olive oil
⅓ cup red wine vinegar
¼ tsp. Tabasco sauce
1½ tsp. salt
⅛ tsp. coarsely ground pepper
2 cloves garlic, minced (optional)
Minced chives
Croutons

SERVES 6–8

Place *half* the quantities of the first four chopped vegetables in a blender with ½ cup of the tomato juice. (Reserve remaining vegetables for garnishes.) Blend at high speed 30 seconds. In a large bowl, combine this mixture with the remaining tomato juice, the oil, vinegar, Tabasco sauce, salt, pepper and garlic. Mix well and chill.

To serve, mix the reserved chopped vegetables and put a small amount in the bottom of each soup cup. Pour in the soup and sprinkle with chives and croutons.

ELEANOR B. SCOTT
La Quinta, California

Iced Cucumber Soup

1 small onion, diced
2 cucumbers (unpeeled), chopped
Butter
1 cup light cream
1/8 tsp. thyme
Salt and pepper
4 cups homemade chicken broth
Chopped fresh tarragon
2 egg yolks
6 to 8 lemon slices
Toasted sliced almonds
Sour cream

SERVES 6–8

Sauté onion and cucumbers in a small amount of butter until tender. Stir in cream, thyme and salt and pepper to taste. Simmer 5 minutes.

Put 3 cups of the chicken broth in a pot. Using the back of a spoon, force the cucumber mixture through a sieve into the broth. Add tarragon and heat.

Beat egg yolks with the remaining cup of cool broth. Slowly pour 1/2 cup of the hot broth mixture into egg yolk mixture, beating briskly. Add another 1/2 cup, still beating. Stir egg yolk mixture into pot with other ingredients and allow to thicken over lowest heat, stirring constantly. Do not boil. Cool, then chill.

Garnish each cup of soup with a lemon slice, almonds and 1 teaspoon sour cream.

ELLIS D. SLATER
North Palm Beach, Florida

Crème Senegalese

4 cups rich chicken broth
2 tsp. curry powder
3 egg yolks, beaten
2 cups heavy cream
1 cup minced cooked chicken breast
Salt and white pepper
6 tbsp. chopped apple
Toasted coconut

SERVES 8

Simmer broth and curry powder together 15 minutes. Beat 2 to 3 tablespoons of hot broth into the beaten egg yolks. Stir in cream, then whisk this mixture into the broth, stirring constantly over very low heat until slightly thickened. Do not boil. Stir in chicken. Add salt and white pepper to taste. Cool, then chill.

Serve cold, garnished with chopped apple and toasted coconut.

MRS. LEONARD ETTELSON
Chicago, Illinois

Cold Avocado Soup

1 avocado
2 cups chicken broth
1 cup sour cream
1 jigger rum
Juice of ½ lemon
1 tsp. curry powder
½ tsp. seasoned salt
4 slices lemon

SERVES 4

Peel and pit avocado. Mash and put in a blender with all ingredients except lemon slices. Blend until smooth. Chill at least 2 hours.

Serve cold, with a slice of lemon on each serving.

MRS. PAUL JENKINS
Bermuda Dunes, California

Easy Vichyssoise

2¼ cups chicken broth
3 leeks (white part only), sliced
2 potatoes, peeled and sliced
½ medium onion, sliced
½ tsp. salt
½ cup half-and-half
½ cup sour cream
Chopped chives

SERVES 4

Combine broth, leeks, potatoes, onion and salt in a saucepan and bring to a boil. Reduce heat and cook gently 45 minutes.

Mash the mixture and force through a sieve. Add half-and-half and sour cream, stirring until smooth. Add more salt, if necessary. Heat to just below boiling and remove from heat. Cool, then chill. Serve cold, garnished with chives.

MRS. PATRICK RYAN
Palm Desert, California

Quick Clam Vichyssoise

1 can (10¾ oz.) condensed New England clam chowder
1 cup chicken broth
1 tsp. minced fresh dill
½ cup sour cream

SERVES 4

Combine chowder, broth and dill in a blender. Blend until smooth. Chill thoroughly.

Just before serving, stir in the sour cream.

MRS. JOSEPH RAPKIN
Milwaukee, Wisconsin

Jellied Consommé

3 lb. beef shanks
¼ to ½ lb. beef liver
1 medium onion, quartered
1 stalk celery, sliced
3 tbsp. salt
3 tbsp. Worcestershire sauce
3 tbsp. Maggi liquid seasoning
2 to 3 tbsp. Kitchen Bouquet seasoning
3 tbsp. unflavored gelatin

SERVES 8–10

Place beef shanks, liver, onion, celery and salt in a large pot and cover with cold water. Bring to a boil and skim. Reduce heat and cook slowly until meat is tender. Stir in Worcestershire sauce, Maggi seasoning and Kitchen Bouquet seasoning. In a very large bowl, soften gelatin in a small amount of cold water. Remove bones and strain hot liquid through a cheesecloth-lined sieve over gelatin. Stir thoroughly. Cool, then chill. Slip solidified fat from top before serving.

This soup keeps well.

MRS. OSCAR G. MAYER
Madison, Wisconsin

Cold Soup Casuarina * Use my icers Pretty-

2 cans (10½ oz. each) consommé
¼ cup tomato juice
3 tbsp. lemon juice
2 tbsp. Worcestershire sauce
Salt and pepper
Chopped celery
Chopped crabmeat
Curry- or mustard-flavored mayonnaise

SERVES 4–6

Mix consommé, tomato juice, lemon juice and Worcestershire sauce; add salt and pepper to taste. Pour into a bowl and chill 3 hours or more.

Place a little chopped celery and chopped crabmeat in each chilled soup cup. Spoon jellied consommé on top and garnish each serving with a heaping tablespoon of flavored mayonnaise.

MRS. NICHOLAS R. duPONT
Palm Beach, Florida

Black Bean Soup

2 cups dried black beans
3 qt. water
¼ lb. salt pork or ham
1 onion, minced
2 cloves garlic
Dash of salt
Dash of cayenne pepper
¼ cup dry sherry
3 hard-boiled eggs, sliced
1 lemon, sliced

SERVES 8–10

Rinse and pick over beans. Soak 8 hours or overnight, following directions on package.

To cook, drain beans and place in a large kettle with the 3 quarts water, salt pork, onion, garlic, salt and cayenne pepper. Cover and cook slowly 3 hours or until beans are very soft. Remove meat; dice and set aside. Press beans through a sieve and return purée to kettle. Reheat and pour into a tureen. Stir in the meat and sherry. Garnish with egg and lemon slices.

MRS. GEORGE BERKEY
Palm Desert, California

Fresh Corn Soup

3 ears corn
3 cups water
3 tbsp. butter
2 tbsp. minced onion
Salt and pepper
1 can (14 oz.) evaporated milk

SERVES 4

Husk and clean corn. Hold over a saucepan and, using the tip of a sharp knife, slit through center of each row of kernels (do not cut off kernels). With the back of the knife, press out the pulp, leaving hulls on the cob. Discard cobs.

Add the water, butter, onion, salt and pepper. Bring to a boil, reduce heat and simmer, uncovered, until tender, about 10 minutes. Just before serving, add evaporated milk and stir until heated through. Do not boil.

MRS. ROBERT BREMSON
Shawnee Mission, Kansas

Cream-Carrot Soup

4 tbsp. butter
6 carrots, sliced
2 medium potatoes, peeled and sliced
1 onion, chopped
1 cup chicken broth
½ tsp. salt
Pepper
1 cup heavy cream
Freshly ground nutmeg
Paprika
Minced parsley

SERVES 4–6

Melt butter in a saucepan. Add vegetables and cook over low heat, stirring, for 15 minutes. Add broth and salt and pepper to taste. Cover and cook slowly 45 minutes. Pour into a blender and purée. Return to saucepan and reheat over low heat. Stir in cream, a pinch of nutmeg and a pinch of paprika. Sprinkle each serving with minced parsley or additional nutmeg, or both.

MRS. AMORY HOUGHTON
Corning, New York

Lettuce Soup

1 medium to large head lettuce, chopped
1 large onion, chopped
2 eggs
3 tbsp. butter
1 cup grated aged Parmesan cheese
3 cups chicken broth
Salt and white pepper

SERVES 6

Purée half the lettuce with half the onion 90 seconds in a blender. Place purée in a *heavy* cooking pot. Purée remaining lettuce and onion 90 seconds. Add eggs, butter, cheese and broth; blend. Pour into the pot and cook 30 minutes over *very* low heat, stirring frequently. Do not boil. Season to taste with salt and white pepper. Serve with additional grated Parmesan cheese, if desired.

MRS. JOHN FRAIM
Indian Wells, California

Zucchini Soup

3 lb. zucchini (unpeeled), cut up
4 slices bacon, fried and crumbled
3½ cups water
1 can (10½ oz.) condensed beef or chicken broth
1 small clove garlic
1 onion, chopped
Salt and pepper

SERVES 6

Combine all ingredients in a saucepan. Cover and cook over low heat until tender, about 1 hour. Pour into a blender and blend until smooth.

To give the soup more color, add a drop or two of green food coloring before blending, if desired.

MRS. MARK R. KELTNER
Los Angeles, California

Creole Gumbo

2 tbsp. shortening or butter (or a combination of both)
1 chicken,* cut into serving pieces
2 cups diced cooked ham
1 cup chopped onions
Juice of 1 tomato
¼ cup minced parsley
1 tsp. thyme
1 tsp. salt
Cayenne pepper
3 qt. boiling water
2 tbsp. filé powder

SERVES 8

Melt shortening in a soup kettle. When hot, add chicken and ham. Cover and cook slowly 10 minutes, turning once. Add onions. Cook, stirring frequently to prevent sticking, until ingredients are well browned. Add tomato juice (this imparts a superior flavor), parsley, thyme and salt. Add cayenne pepper to taste. Add boiling water and stir; simmer, uncovered, about 1 hour.

Remove from heat. Sprinkle with filé powder, stirring slowly. (*Never* add filé powder while gumbo is on the heat: boiling causes it to string.) Pour into a tureen and serve with boiled rice.

*Crab, shrimp or rounds of beef may be substituted for the chicken.

MRS. CHARLES S. JONES
Pasadena, California

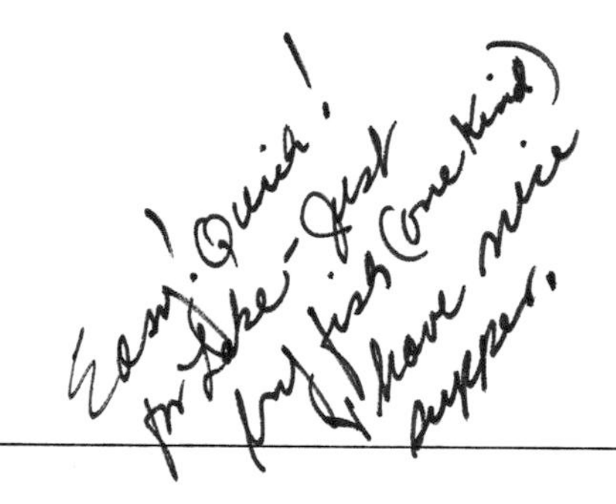

Fish Chowder

2 to 3 lb. cleaned white fish
Boiling water
½ cup chopped carrots
½ cup chopped celery
½ cup chopped onions
½ cup chopped potatoes
1 cup butter
3 to 4 tbsp. flour
2 cups milk
Salt and pepper
Light cream or half-and-half (optional)
1 to 2 tsp. Worcestershire sauce (optional)

SERVES 4

Cover fish with boiling water and simmer until flesh falls away from the bones. Remove fish and set aside. Reserve liquid. Discard bones and skin.

Sauté the chopped vegetables in half the butter until tender. While vegetables are cooking, melt the remaining butter in a saucepan and stir in the flour to make a roux. Blend in reserved fish broth and the milk. Stir over low heat until thickened.

Mix the fish and vegetables into the sauce and season with salt and pepper to taste. If desired, stir in a little cream and the Worcestershire sauce.

ROBERT W. WOODRUFF
Atlanta, Georgia

Garbage Soup

One of the rare delicacies of the civilized world. It is an old French, Scandinavian, Yugoslavian, Icelandic, German, Dutch, Italian, Mohammedan, Irish, Jewish custom to have a big pot on the back of the stove where you throw all the "useable" garbage.

Today so many vitamins go down the drain. We Americans have the healthiest drains this side of the Mayo Clinic! We throw away the juice from cans, the water we've cooked vegetables and meat in, etc., etc.

Now, here's the way to make Garbage Soup:

You cozy up to your butcher (I hope he looks like Cary Grant, but he probably doesn't) and ask him for a soup bone. This will thrill his body. Nobody asks for a soup bone. How many people own a Great Dane??? You take this home, and this is the beginning of Garbage Soup for the week.

Fill a huge pot half full with water; add salt, cracked pepper, salad lift, grated Parmesan cheese, chili powder and a pinch of poultry seasoning (optional). Drop in the bone. (Forget the Great Dane—let him find his own butcher.) Add chopped onion, chopped parsley, chopped carrots, chopped celery, chopped potato and chopped green pepper (all of it fresh). Simmer endlessly. Then add 1 large can tomatoes, cut up, and 2 cans kidney beans.

From this point on, all leftovers (with the exception of pickles and Jello) go into the soup. Make sure you chop leftovers fine, and be sure to keep adding juice from all cooking or cans opened, including salad leftovers with dressing! And after frying any kind of meat, rinse skillet with water and throw it in the Garbage Soup. (Remember, anything boiled is germless.) And the flavor is fantastic!

PHYLLIS DILLER
Los Angeles, California

Phyllis Diller is one of Bob Hope's favorite caddies. She's toted for him in the Desert Classic.

Oyster Stew

6 raw oysters
2 tbsp. butter
½ tsp. Worcestershire sauce
Dash of Tabasco sauce
Salt and pepper
2 cups half-and-half
1 tsp. chives

SERVES 1

Combine oysters, butter and Worcestershire sauce in a saucepan or skillet. Heat about 5 minutes, stirring occasionally, until edges of oysters curl. Season with Tabasco sauce and salt and pepper to taste.

In another pan, heat the half-and-half. Add the oysters with pan juices and cook until mixture reaches a boil. Add chives and remove from heat.

MRS. WILLIAM POWELL
Palm Springs, California

Beef Shank Supper Soup

4 lb. meaty beef shanks, cut into pieces 1½ inches thick
1 large onion, finely chopped
2 stalks celery, finely chopped
1 can (28 oz.) whole tomatoes
1 tbsp. oregano
1 tsp. thyme
¼ tsp. ground cloves
1 bay leaf
1½ tsp. salt
6 cups water
½ cup pearl barley
4 large carrots, cut into 1-inch chunks
1 package (9 oz.) frozen cut green beans
1 cup finely chopped parsley

SERVES 6

In a large kettle (about 8 quarts), brown shanks in their own fat over medium heat. Transfer meat to a bowl. Add onion and celery to drippings in kettle. Cook and stir over medium heat until onions are limp. Add tomatoes and their liquid. Stir in oregano, thyme, cloves, bay leaf, salt and the water. Return meat and any juices to kettle. Cover and bring to a boil. Reduce heat and simmer gently 1½ hours.

Remove kettle from heat and cool until meat can be handled. Pull meat off bones and cut into 1-inch pieces. Discard fat and gristle. Return meat and any bones with marrow to kettle. Chill the soup until surface fat has solidified. Lift off fat and discard. Bring soup to a simmer. Stir in barley and simmer, covered, 50 minutes. Add carrots and cook, covered, 10 minutes. Add beans and cook, uncovered, 10 minutes. Correct seasoning. Stir in parsley.

This recipe can be doubled and frozen. Omit the parsley and add after soup is reheated.

MRS. WILLIAM C. STROUBE
Corsicana, Texas

MEAT

A Who's Who of Main Courses

For a family supper or a company buffet, the meat course
always takes center stage. And here is a treasury
of recipes worthy of the brightest spotlight.
A stroganoff rich enough to please a czar,
peppery south-of-the-border chilis, piquant veal dishes
from Italy, classic American roasts and stews,
intriguingly seasoned casseroles from almost everywhere.
Whatever your purpose, whatever your pleasure,
you'll find the just-right recipe for a starring role.

Foolproof Roast Beef

1 standing or rolled rib roast (2 to 4 ribs) of any weight
Salt and pepper
Flour

The roast must be at room temperature. Rub lightly with salt, pepper and flour.

Place in a roasting pan (rib side down if bones are in) and roast, uncovered, in a preheated 325° oven exactly one hour. Turn off oven, but do not remove roast from oven. Do not open oven door at any time during this roasting period or while roast is "resting" in oven. This can be done early in the day.

About an hour before serving, set oven again at 325° and continue roasting as follows: 2-rib roast, about 25 minutes; 3-rib roast, about 30 minutes; 4-rib roast, about 35 minutes. The beef will be medium rare throughout.

MRS. FRANK DIXON
Chicago, Illinois

Beef Filets for a Buffet

Beef filets
Soy sauce
Butter
Worcestershire sauce
Sour cream
Prepared horseradish

Buy filets of beef weighing 3 to 4 pounds each. Allow ¼ pound per person if other meats are being served, but if the filets are the only hot meat, allow at least ½ pound.

Marinate filets in soy sauce 8 hours, turning several times. On the morning of the day of the party, brown filets in butter with Worcestershire sauce. (These steps give color and flavor to the meat.) Set aside.

After the party has started (and about 45 minutes before serving time), place a filet in an open roasting pan. Roast one filet at a time in a preheated 450° oven about 45 minutes (each filet). The beef will be medium rare. Slice *very* thin and keep warm. Serve with a sauce composed of equal portions of sour cream and horseradish.

MRS. ALOYS D. HEYEN
Rancho Mirage, California

Tenderloin Deluxe

1 beef tenderloin (2 lb.)
2 tbsp. butter, softened
1/4 cup chopped green onion
3/4 cup dry sherry
2 tbsp. soy sauce
1 tsp. Dijon mustard
Dash of freshly ground black pepper

SERVES 4–6

Spread meat with all but about 1 teaspoon of the butter. Place on a rack in a roasting pan. Roast, uncovered, in a preheated 400° oven 20 minutes.

While tenderloin roasts, cook onion in remaining butter in a small saucepan. Stir in sherry, soy sauce, mustard and pepper. Heat and pour over meat. Roast 20 to 25 minutes longer, basting frequently. Serve remaining sauce with the meat.

MRS. JAMES P. HEALEY
Indian Wells, California

Stuffed Beef or Pork Tenderloin

1/4 cup butter or margarine
1 medium onion, chopped
1/2 cup diced celery
1 can (4 oz.) sliced mushrooms, well drained
2 cups soft bread crumbs
1/2 tsp. basil
1/8 tsp. chopped parsley
1/2 tsp. salt
1/8 tsp. pepper
1 beef or pork tenderloin (3 lb.)
4 slices bacon

SERVES 8

Melt butter in a small skillet over low heat. Sauté onion, celery and mushrooms until onion is soft and transparent, about 10 minutes.

Mix bread crumbs, basil, parsley, salt and pepper in a bowl. Add cooked vegetables and toss lightly until well mixed.

Make a lengthwise cut in the tenderloin, cutting three-fourths of the way into the meat. Lightly stuff mixture in the pocket. Close pocket by fastening meat together with wooden toothpicks. Place bacon slices diagonally across the top, covering the toothpicks and seam.

Place meat in a baking dish or roasting pan. Roast, uncovered, in a preheated 350° oven 1 hour for medium-rare beef; 1 1/2 hours for pork.

MRS. SOLLE MANASSE
Palm Springs, California

Ike's Steak

"I talked to General Eisenhower's cook, who often watched the General grill a steak. He told me that Ike preferred a 3-inch New York cut, and did not marinate the meat. Here is his recipe."

Buy a good piece of beef—for instance, a New York cut, 3 inches thick. Put a great quantity of salt and some pepper into a small pan. Dip both sides and all edges of the steak into the pan until it is completely covered with the salt and pepper.

The fire should burn for some time, until the coals are white-hot. With a pair of tongs, lay the steak *directly on top of the coals.* After about a minute, you may turn it over to get the other side started. A 3-inch steak may need 7 to 9 minutes on one side and 5 to 6 minutes on the other, depending on the heat of the coals.

The only way to tell if the steak is done is to take it off the fire after it has cooked about 4 to 5 minutes on each side. Make a small incision in the meat to determine how it is doing. Put it back on the coals if it is not done enough. After it has reached medium rare, or however you like it, lay the steak on a board. Using a wire brush or a stiff bristle brush, rub the meat hard to take off the salt and the ashes. Then transfer it to a clean board and cut it diagonally across the grain in slices about ¾ inch thick.

NOTE: A "New York cut," or shell steak, is also known as strip steak or Kansas City strip steak in various parts of the country.

"I have seen General Eisenhower grill a steak this way and can assure you that it is delicious. I might add that the first time friends would see him put the steak directly on the coals, they would think he possibly had gone berserk. But the steak always came out in great shape."

FREEMAN F. GOSDEN
Beverly Hills, California

Cognac Steak à la Flambé

3 tbsp. butter
4 small beef filet mignons, 1½ to 2 inches thick
Salt and pepper
1 oz. cognac (preferably Hennessy's!)
½ cup heavy cream

SERVES 4

Melt butter in a heavy skillet or a French brass or copper pan. Season steaks with salt and pepper and cook over medium heat about 10 minutes on each side (less for rare and more for well done).

Pour cognac over steaks and ignite. Immediately spoon juices and flaming cognac over steaks. Remove to a heated platter. Stir cream into pan juices. Pour sauce over steaks and serve at once.

MRS. JACK HENNESSY
North Hollywood, California

Braised Swiss Steaks

1 large onion, sliced
2 to 4 tbsp. corn oil
¼ tsp. thyme
6 beef round steaks (8 oz. each)
Seasoned salt
Flour
1 cup vegetable cocktail juice (V-8)
1 cup beef broth
1½ cups mixed julienne strips of carrots, leeks and celery
2 tbsp. chopped parsley

SERVES 6

In a large ovenproof skillet, sauté onion in 1 tablespoon of the oil until golden. Remove from heat and add thyme. Set aside.

Sprinkle steaks on both sides with seasoned salt and flour. Heat remaining oil in an iron skillet and brown steaks on both sides. Transfer to pan with onions. Pour vegetable juice and broth over steaks. Cover and simmer very slowly 1 hour in the oven or on top of the stove. Turn steaks, sprinkle with the vegetable julienne and continue to cook 30 minutes longer.

To serve, arrange steaks on a serving platter. Spoon sauce and vegetables over steaks and sprinkle with parsley.

MRS. RICHARD M. NIXON
San Clemente, California

Pepperoni Steak Sorrentino

Olive oil
1 clove garlic, minced
1 large green pepper, cut into thin strips
½ lb. fresh mushrooms, sliced
1½ lb. beef tenderloin, trimmed and cut into bite-size cubes
Salt
Coarsely ground black pepper
Pinch of oregano
3 oz. red wine, warmed
Chopped fresh parsley

SERVES 4

Heat olive oil in a heavy skillet and sauté garlic, green pepper and mushrooms.

Sprinkle meat with salt and pepper. Heat a small amount of oil in another skillet and sauté meat quickly until brown but still rare. Transfer to skillet with vegetables and add oregano. Pour red wine into skillet used to sauté meat; heat and then flame. (It *will* flame.) Pour wine over meat and sprinkle with parsley. Serve with rice.

MRS. WILLIAM SORRENTINO
Palm Springs, California

Beef Rouladen

1 bunch parsley, chopped
2 onions, chopped
Cooking oil
6 lb. sirloin tip, cut into ¼-inch-thick slices
Salt and pepper
1 lb. bacon, diced
Flour
2 cups boiling water

SERVES 16–18

Sauté parsley and onions in 1 tablespoon oil. Cover and steam 2 minutes. Cut sirloin into 5-inch squares. Sprinkle with salt and pepper. Place a little of the onion mixture and some bacon in center of each piece of meat. Roll up meat and wrap with thread to hold stuffing inside. Dust with flour.

Heat cooking oil in a very large, heavy skillet. Add several *rouladen* (do not crowd) and brown. When all have been browned, remove from skillet. Add boiling water and make a thin gravy. Return *rouladen* to gravy, cover and cook 1½ hours. Remove threads before serving and thicken gravy, if necessary.

MRS. THOMAS CARTER
Bermuda Dunes, California

Come for Cocktails—Melon Appetizer (page 13), Hot Crab Fondue (page 15), Ensenada Guacamole (page 16), Pâté Provençal (page 18), Pie Sandwiches (page 22). And a new drink—Aunt Tess (page 30).

The Pluperfect Picnic—A bountiful spread that's as easy as it is elegant: Danish Tomatoes (page 172), Gazpacho La Quinta (page 34), Margo's Italian Rice Salad (page 166) and cold Tenderloin Deluxe (page 45).

Sliced Beef Chinese Style

2½ lb. very lean beef tenderloin
Oil for deep-frying

MARINADE
¾ cup cold beef broth
5 tbsp. soy sauce
5 tbsp. oil
5 tbsp. cornstarch

SEASONING SAUCE
¾ cup cold beef broth
6 tbsp. catsup
2 tbsp. Worcestershire sauce
2 tbsp. dry sherry
1½ tbsp. sugar
1 tbsp. cornstarch
1½ tsp. salt

SERVES 6

"This dish was created by Mr. Tze Yang Chen, who learned to cook in Taiwan and served as chef in a number of embassies before coming to the United States. We believe this is one of his best creations."

Cut meat into 2x2-inch pieces, ¼ inch thick. Combine ingredients for the marinade. Add beef and marinate 2 hours at room temperature, turning every 30 minutes so that each piece is well soaked.

Mix all ingredients for Seasoning Sauce and set aside.

Heat 3 cups oil to 350° in a deep skillet. Deep-fry sliced beef, turning occasionally until done. Remove meat and set aside. Drain the oil from the skillet. Heat 2 tablespoons fresh oil in same skillet. Pour Seasoning Sauce into the skillet and bring to a boil, stirring occasionally, until thickened. Add beef slices and heat. Mix well and serve.

ROBERT B. ANDERSON
New York, New York

Beef Stroganoff à la Russe

2 lb. beef (top sirloin, round steak or filet)
Butter
2 large onions, chopped
1 lb. fresh mushrooms, sliced
2 cups sour cream
3 tbsp. tomato paste
2 tbsp. slivered seeded cucumber slices (matchstick size)
½ tsp. dill
¼ tsp. dry mustard
Salt and pepper
2 tbsp. Burgundy

SERVES 6

Cut meat into short thin strips. Sauté in butter until nicely browned. In a separate pan, sauté onions in butter. Add mushrooms and cook briefly. Reserving 2 tablespoons of the sour cream, mix remainder with the onions, mushrooms, tomato paste, cucumber, dill, mustard, salt and pepper.

Combine with meat in a casserole. Cover and bake in a preheated 350° oven 1 hour or until meat is tender. Ten minutes before serving, stir in wine and reserved sour cream.

MRS. CLARENCE BROWN
Beverly Hills, California

Sauerbraten and Spaetzles

2 cups water
2 cups vinegar
1 medium onion, chopped
3 to 4 bay leaves
12 peppercorns (more or fewer, to taste)
2 tsp. salt
4 lb. beef pot roast (round, rump, chuck or shoulder)

SPAETZLES
2 or 3 eggs
½ tsp. baking powder
About 1 cup flour
6 to 8 cups boiling water

SERVES 4–6

"The spaetzles in this dish are made like my mother, grandmother and great-grandma made them. There doesn't seem to be a printed recipe for these particular dumplings, where the only liquid used is eggs."

Combine water, vinegar, onion, bay leaves, peppercorns and salt. Bring to a boil and pour over meat. Cover and marinate in refrigerator from 3 to 24 hours. Remove meat from marinade. Wipe off and dry well. Brown meat in fat in a Dutch oven. Heat the marinade and pour over meat. Cover and simmer 3 to 4 hours or until tender.

A short time before meat is done, make spaetzles. Mix eggs and baking powder with enough flour to make a batter almost as stiff as dough. Using a sharp knife, cut off small pieces (about ¼ to ½ teaspoon) and drop into boiling water. (Dip tip of knife into the water and the dough will come off cleanly.) Add a small amount at a time so dumplings in pan will cook uniformly. Boil until bits of dough come to the surface. Remove dumplings with slotted spoon.

When meat is done, remove from pan. Strain liquid and make a gravy. Serve meat in the gravy, with the spaetzles. Accompany with stewed prunes and vegetables or a salad.

MRS. REX PRUETT
Indian Wells, California

Liver à la Parmesan

Calves' liver, sliced very thin
Grated Parmesan cheese
Butter
Sour cream, lightly salted
Green onion tops, chopped

Dredge liver with Parmesan cheese, shaking off excess. Sauté gently in butter. When done, remove from pan and top each slice with a spoonful of sour cream. Sprinkle with chopped onion tops.

MRS. THOMAS A. PAULSON
La Quinta, California

Barbecued Beef Brisket

1 beef brisket (3 to 4½ lb.)
Celery salt
Garlic salt
Onion salt
Unseasoned tenderizer
1 bottle (3 oz.) liquid smoke
½ bottle (5-oz. size) Worcestershire sauce
½ bottle (16-oz. size) barbecue sauce

SERVES 6

Sprinkle both sides of beef brisket with salts and the tenderizer. Place in a baking dish and pour liquid smoke over meat. Cover and marinate overnight in refrigerator.

When ready to cook, pour Worcestershire sauce over meat. Cover and bake in a preheated 250° to 300° oven 5 hours. Remove pan from oven. Pour barbecue sauce over meat and bake, uncovered, 1 hour longer, turning once or twice. Remove from oven and cover pan. Let stand 30 minutes.

To serve, cut across the grain into very thin slices. Good hot or cold.

MR. and MRS. TOMMY JACOBS
Rancho Santa Fe, California

Tommy Jacobs was the winner of the 1964 Bob Hope Desert Classic.

Barbecued Short Ribs

1 large onion, diced
1 can (8 oz.) tomato sauce
2 tbsp. cider vinegar
2 tbsp. molasses
1½ tsp. salt
1½ tsp. pepper
4 lb. lean beef short ribs
Wide noodles

SERVES 4

Combine all ingredients except beef in a saucepan and bring to a boil. Place meat in a roasting pan and pour sauce over meat. Cover and bake in a preheated 275° oven 4 hours. Cool and skim off fat.

When ready to serve, heat ribs and serve over freshly cooked wide noodles.

MRS. BERNARD H. CHERNIN
Palm Desert, California

✳ Arnie's Favorite Beef Stew

2 to 3 lb. good beef, cut into 1-inch cubes
Oil
1 to 2 cups vegetable cocktail juice (V-8)
½ cup red table wine
1 can (10½ oz.) condensed beef broth
1 can (10½ oz.) mushroom gravy
Cut-up fresh vegetables

SERVES 6–8

Brown beef slowly in a small amount of oil. Add vegetable juice, wine, broth and gravy. Simmer, covered, 2 hours, then add fresh vegetables. (We like onions, carrots, potatoes and mushrooms.) Cook 1 hour longer. Liquid ingredients may be increased, if necessary.

MR. and MRS. ARNOLD PALMER
Latrobe, Pennsylvania

Arnold Palmer was the winner of the Bob Hope Desert Classic five times: in 1960, 1962, 1968, 1971 and 1973.

Brown Beef Stew

- 1½ to 2½ lb. stewing beef, cut into 1½-inch cubes
- 4 tbsp. flour
- 3 tbsp. chopped onion
- 1 clove garlic, finely chopped
- 1½ cups boiling water
- 1½ cups canned tomatoes
- 1 bay leaf
- 4 tsp. salt
- ⅛ tsp. pepper
- 4 potatoes, peeled and quartered
- 6 medium carrots
- 6 small onions
- 1½ cups cut-up green beans (1-inch pieces)

SERVES 6

Trim excess fat from meat and fry it out in a large kettle until you have about 2 tablespoons liquid fat. Remove any browned bits of fat from pan. Dredge meat in flour, shaking off excess. Place in kettle with chopped onion and garlic and brown slowly on all sides over medium heat. Slowly add boiling water, tomatoes, bay leaf, salt and pepper. Cover tightly and simmer over low heat 1½ hours.

Add potatoes, carrots and onions. Cover and cook about 35 minutes longer, until vegetables and meat are tender. Add green beans and cook 15 minutes longer.

MRS. CARLTON BARRETT
Los Angeles, California

General Eisenhower's Old-Fashioned Beef Stew

- 2 lb. prime beef round, cut up for stewing
- 5 cups beef broth
- 1 lb. small Irish potatoes, peeled
- 1 bunch small carrots
- ¾ lb. small onions
- 2 fresh tomatoes, chopped
- Bouquet garni
- MSG
- Salt and pepper
- Beef roux (for thickening)

SERVES 6

Stew meat in broth until tender. Add vegetables and bouquet garni; season with MSG, salt and pepper to taste. Cover and cook until vegetables are done. Strain 1 cup broth from the stew and thicken slightly with a roux. Pour back into stew and simmer, covered, 30 minutes. Correct seasoning.

NOTE: To adapt this recipe for a very large gathering (60 portions), multiply the ingredients by 10.

MAMIE DOUD EISENHOWER
Gettysburg, Pennsylvania

Dreier's Devil Delight

¾ cup beef or chicken broth
2 tbsp. soy sauce
1 tbsp. dry sherry
2 tsp. cornstarch
1 lb. cooked or uncooked beef, chicken or pork (leftovers may be used)
Oil
2 to 3 green onions, diagonally sliced
1 stalk celery, diagonally sliced
¼ lb. fresh mushrooms, sliced
2 to 3 thin slices gingerroot, minced
1 tomato, peeled and sliced
Salt and pepper
Hot cooked rice or toast

SERVES 2

Combine broth, soy sauce, wine and cornstarch; blend and set aside.

Cut meat into thin slices. Heat 1 tablespoon oil in a wok or heavy skillet. When very hot, add meat and stir-fry until done (if already cooked, until heated through). Remove from pan. Add 2 to 3 teaspoons oil to pan and heat. Add onions, celery, mushrooms and gingerroot and stir-fry until lightly cooked but crisp, about 2 minutes.

Stir the reserved sauce into the vegetables. Add meat and tomatoes and cook, stirring until sauce thickens. Season to taste and serve on rice or toast.

ALEX DREIER
Palm Springs, California

Applesauce Meatballs

1 egg
½ cup milk
1½ cups packaged seasoned stuffing croutons
1½ lb. ground beef
⅔ cup applesauce
3 tbsp. finely chopped onion
1½ tsp. salt
⅛ tsp. pepper
¼ tsp. sage
1 can (10¾ oz.) condensed tomato soup
½ cup water

SERVES 6

Beat egg with milk. Add croutons and let stand until soft, about 5 minutes. Beat until smooth and fluffy. Add beef, applesauce, onion, salt, pepper and sage. Mix thoroughly.

Shape mixture into 24 balls. Place in a shallow baking pan. Combine soup and water and pour over meatballs. Bake in a preheated 350° oven about 45 minutes.

Serve in a heated dish with sauce. Accompany with rice or noodles.

MRS. ROBERT S. CALLENDER
Indian Wells, California

Maxwell's Meat Loaf

2 lb. ground beef (chuck, round or rump)
2 cups crushed saltine crackers
1 large onion, finely chopped
¼ cup chopped green pepper
4 large stalks celery, finely chopped
2 small eggs, beaten
1 can (about 16 oz.) stewed tomatoes
1 tsp. garlic salt
1 tsp. celery salt
1 tsp. seasoned salt

SERVES 4

Combine all ingredients and mix thoroughly but lightly (mixture should have a soft, fluffy consistency). Shape into an oval loaf and place in a baking dish. Bake in a preheated 325° oven 1½ to 2 hours.

MR. and MRS. BILLY MAXWELL
Jacksonville, Florida
Billy Maxwell was the winner of the 1961 Bob Hope Desert Classic.

Try!

Beef and Sausage Loaf

2 cups chopped celery
3 onions, chopped
2 tbsp. butter
4 lb. ground beef (round or sirloin)
1 lb. ground sausage (Jones)
2 cups bread crumbs
4 eggs
1 cup sour cream
1 cup chopped parsley
1 tsp. pepper
1 tsp. salt
4 beef bouillon cubes, crumbled
2 tbsp. Worcestershire sauce
4 tbsp. catsup
2 small cans condensed beef broth
2 cans (8 oz. each) tomato sauce

SERVES 10

Sauté celery and onions in butter until soft. Mix thoroughly with all remaining ingredients except broth and tomato sauce. Shape into a loaf in a baking dish. Bake in a preheated 350° oven 1½ hours. Pour off fat.

While loaf bakes, combine beef broth and tomato sauce and cook until thickened. Pour over loaf before serving.

MRS. REX A. BARTLETT
Incline Village, Nevada

Beef Loaf on Finn Bread

FINN BREAD
- 1 package dry yeast
- 1/2 cup warm water (105° to 115°)
- 1 1/2 quarts milk (105° to 115°)
- 5 tbsp. sugar
- 4 tsp. salt
- 3 tbsp. melted shortening or oil
- 12 to 15 cups flour

BEEF LOAF
- 1 egg
- 1/2 cup milk
- 1 cup fine bread crumbs
- 1 cup tiny cubes Swiss or cheddar cheese
- 3 tbsp. minced onion
- 3 tbsp. minced parsley (fresh or dried)
- 1 tsp. salt
- 1/2 tsp. dried dill
- 1/4 tsp. pepper
- Dash of smoke salt or liquid smoke
- 1 lb. ground chuck

SERVES 6–8

To make Finn Bread, soften yeast in the water. In a large bowl combine milk, sugar, salt, shortening, the softened yeast and 6 to 7 cups flour. Mix well. (If you are using a mixer, beat several minutes.) Continue to add flour until the dough can be handled. Turn out on a floured board and knead until smooth and elastic. Place in a greased bowl and allow to rise until doubled in bulk. Punch down and let rise again until doubled in bulk. (This will all take about 1 1/2 to 1 3/4 hours). Divide dough into 6 pieces and form into circles 1 inch thick. Pierce each loaf 6 times with a fork. Let rise 1 hour, then pierce again. Place immediately in a preheated 325° oven and bake 30 minutes. (Makes 6 round wheels, 2 inches thick.)

To make Beef Loaf, combine all ingredients except meat and mix well. Add beef and mix in lightly. Slice one wheel of Finn Bread horizontally. Place each round half on a large piece of foil. Divide meat loaf mixture and pile onto bread rounds. Wrap tightly. Bake in a preheated 350° oven 25 to 30 minutes. Remove from oven. Open top of foil to expose meat. Place under a broiler a couple of minutes to brown. To serve, cut into wedges.

NOTE: The beef loaf may also be baked as a meat loaf; pack mixture into a loaf pan and bake in a preheated 400° oven 30 minutes.

DR. and MRS. JOHN E. WICKMAN
Abilene, Kansas

Dr. Wickman is the director of the Dwight D. Eisenhower Library.

Eggplant-Meatball Casserole

1 medium eggplant, peeled
1 can (about 16 oz.) peeled tomatoes, broken into pieces
4 oz. noodles, cooked and drained
¼ cup chopped parsley
¾ cup seasoned bread crumbs
1 lb. ground round
½ cup chopped onion
Salt and pepper
Oil

SERVES 4–6

Cut eggplant into 1-inch cubes. Cook in boiling salted water until tender; drain. Place in a lightly oiled 1½-quart casserole and mix with undrained tomatoes and cooked noodles. Sprinkle with parsley and ¼ cup of the crumbs.

Mix meat with remaining bread crumbs, the onion, salt and pepper. Shape into balls and brown in oil. Place meatballs on top of mixture in casserole. Cover and bake in a preheated 350° oven 30 minutes.

MRS. JAMES L. BUCKLEY, SR.
Portland, Oregon

Eggplant à la Grecque

1 large eggplant, peeled
1 tbsp. oregano
1 tsp. mixed herbs (fresh, if possible)
1 cup tomato paste
1 can (28 oz.) plum tomatoes, drained (reserve liquid)
1 lb. ground beef
2 tbsp. olive oil
Salt and pepper
6 slices provolone or mozzarella cheese

SERVES 6

Cut eggplant into 1-inch slices, either crosswise or lengthwise, depending on size and shape of baking dish to be used. Soak in salted water at least 1 hour (place a weighted plate or lid on top to hold under water).

Crush herbs in a mortar and combine with tomato paste and liquid from canned tomatoes. Simmer, uncovered, 15 minutes. Meanwhile, drain eggplant and cook gently in unsalted water until just tender, about 5 minutes. Drain.

In a skillet, lightly sauté meat in olive oil. Add the tomato sauce to meat and mix. Season with salt and pepper to taste. Rub a baking dish (about 13x9 inches) with additional olive oil and arrange eggplant slices in the dish. Surround with tomatoes. Spoon meat sauce over eggplant. Pour remaining sauce over and around tomatoes. Top each stack with a slice of cheese. Heat in a preheated 325° oven until cheese melts.

MRS. GEORGE S. BAKER, JR.
Bel Air, California

Bean Sprout-Beef Casserole

- 1½ to 2 lb. lean ground beef
- 12 to 16 oz. fresh bean sprouts, rinsed and drained
- 1 cup chopped celery
- 1 cup chopped green pepper
- 1 cup chopped green onions (include some tops)
- 2 cups thawed frozen peas
- Salt
- 1 can (10¾ oz.) condensed cream of mushroom soup
- 1 to 2 tbsp. water
- 1 cup crumbled potato chips

SERVES 6–8

Sauté beef until cooked through, then drain. Sauté bean sprouts in a small amount of the beef drippings until slightly soft.

Arrange half the beef in a lightly oiled 1½-quart casserole. Add celery, green pepper, onions, peas and bean sprouts in layers over beef, sprinkling each layer with salt. Top with remaining beef.

Mix soup and water and pour over meat. Top with crumbled potato chips. Bake, uncovered, in a preheated 350° oven 30 minutes.

This casserole may be assembled ahead of time and refrigerated overnight. Add potato chips just before baking.

MRS. JAMES R. WINSTON
Newport Beach, California

Cashew-Beef Casserole

- 1 lb. ground beef (round or chuck)
- 1 cup chopped onion
- 1 cup diced celery
- 2 tbsp. butter
- 8 oz. noodles, cooked *al dente* and drained
- 1 can (10¾ oz.) condensed cream of mushroom soup
- ½ cup milk
- 1 tsp. salt
- 1 tsp. pepper
- ½ tsp. rosemary
- 1 cup chopped salted cashews

SERVES 6–8

Brown beef, onion and celery in butter. Drain mixture, then alternate layers of meat mixture with noodles in a lightly oiled 1½-quart casserole. Mix soup, milk and seasonings and pour over casserole. Sprinkle with nuts. Cover and bake in a preheated 325° oven 1 hour. Uncover and bake 5 minutes longer to brown.

MRS. EWING KAUFFMAN
Kansas City, Missouri

Onion-Beef-Macaroni Casserole

1½ lb. ground beef
1 envelope dry onion soup mix
1 tbsp. flour
1 can (8 oz.) tomato sauce
2 cups water
1 cup macaroni, cooked and drained
¼ cup grated cheddar cheese

SERVES 6

Brown meat in a large skillet. Drain excess fat. Stir in soup mix, flour, tomato sauce and water. Cover and simmer 5 minutes. Stir in cooked macaroni.

Turn into a lightly oiled 1½-quart casserole and sprinkle with cheese. Bake, uncovered, in a preheated 400° oven 15 minutes.

DR. and MRS. NORMAN VINCENT PEALE
New York, New York

Western Casserole

1 lb. lean ground beef
2 tbsp. oil
½ cup chopped onion
¼ cup chopped green pepper
1 cup brown rice
2½ cups canned tomatoes
1 cup ripe olives, cut into large pieces
1 cup water
2 tsp. salt
2 to 3 tsp. chili powder
¼ tsp. pepper
½ tsp. Worcestershire sauce

SERVES 4–6

Brown beef in oil in a large skillet. Remove beef with a slotted spoon and set aside. To the same pan add onion, green pepper and rice. Cook, stirring, over high heat until mixture is lightly browned. Stir in tomatoes, olives, water, the meat and seasonings.

Bring to a boil, then pour into a lightly buttered 2-quart casserole. Cover and bake in a preheated 325° oven 45 to 60 minutes.

BARBARA WALTERS
New York, New York

Chili

- 1 can (6 oz.) tomato paste
- 4 cloves garlic (or more, if desired)
- 2 cans (20 oz. each) tomatoes
- 2 cans (20 oz. each) kidney beans, drained
- 1 lb. very lean ground chuck
- 1½ tsp. cocoa
- 2 tbsp. chili powder (or more, if desired)
- 1 tbsp. oregano
- Salt (about 1 tsp.)
- 1 tsp. cumin

SERVES 6

Rub a little oil or fat in a large skillet. Add tomato paste and crush half the garlic in it. Add undrained tomatoes and kidney beans and stir well. Cover tightly and simmer 30 minutes.

Flatten meat into a pancake shape and brown slowly in another skillet. Crush remaining garlic. Turn meat and sprinkle with the garlic, cocoa and seasonings. Make irregular cuts through meat to let seasonings go through. When other side has browned, add to tomato mixture. (Meat chunks may be left as large as you like.) Cover and simmer no longer than 1 hour (it is important to keep pan tightly covered throughout). Remove from heat. Allow to cool, then reheat 1 hour before serving. (Chili may be frozen until needed, then reheated.)

MR. and MRS. HERBERT BROWNELL, JR.
New York, New York

Pedernales River Chili

- 4 lb. chili meat*
- 1 large onion, chopped
- 2 cloves garlic, minced
- 1 tsp. oregano
- 1 tsp. cumin
- 6 tsp. chili powder (or more)
- 1½ cups canned whole tomatoes
- 2 to 6 generous dashes hot pepper sauce
- Salt
- 2 cups hot water

SERVES 10–12

Place meat, onion and garlic in a large heavy skillet or Dutch oven. Cook until meat is light-colored. Add remaining ingredients. Bring to a boil, lower heat and simmer, uncovered, about 1 hour. Skim fat during cooking.

Serve Texas-style, with a side dish of chili beans.

* Chili meat is coarsely ground round steak or well-trimmed chuck. If specially ground, ask your meatman to use a ¾-inch plate for a coarse grind.

MRS. LYNDON B. JOHNSON
Stonewall, Texas

Tamale Pie

4 large onions, chopped
¾ cup oil
3 cloves garlic, finely chopped
2 lb. ground beef
2½ cups canned cream-style corn
2½ cups canned tomato purée
1 can (about 8 oz.) tomato sauce
2 tbsp. Worcestershire sauce
2 tbsp. steak sauce (A-1)
2 tbsp. chili powder
Salt and pepper

TOPPING
1 cup cornmeal
1 cup water
1 can (4½ oz.) chopped ripe olives, drained
3 eggs, beaten

SERVES 6

Sauté onions in oil. Add garlic, then meat. Cook, stirring, until meat is brown and broken up. Add corn, tomato purée, tomato sauce and seasonings, mixing well. Pour into a baking dish, 15x10x2 inches.

To make the topping, mix cornmeal and water into a paste. Add olives and fold in eggs. Spoon on top of meat mixture. Bake, uncovered, in a preheated 350° oven 1 hour.

MRS. GEORGE RANDOLPH HEARST, SR.
Palm Springs, California

Tamale Casserole

3 large tamales, cut into bite-size pieces
1 cup canned solid-pack tomatoes, well drained
1 can (8 oz.) whole-kernel corn
2 cans (6 oz. each) sliced ripe olives, drained
1 bunch green onions, chopped
1 small bag corn chips, crumbled
1½ lb. ground beef, browned and crumbled, or 2 cups cut-up cooked chicken (in bite-size pieces)
½ cup chili sauce
1 can (6 oz.) Bloody Mary mix (Snappy Tom)
Grated cheddar or Monterey jack cheese

SERVES 6–8

Mix all ingredients except grated cheese. Turn into a lightly oiled 2-quart casserole and cover top with grated cheese. Bake in a preheated 350° oven 1 hour.

Casserole may be assembled ahead of time (do not add grated cheese) and stored in refrigerator until ready to bake. Add cheese just before placing in oven.

MRS. JOHN A. HARRIS
Palm Desert, California

Veal Piccata

1½ lb. boneless veal, thinly sliced
Salt and freshly ground black pepper
Flour
6 tbsp. butter
2 tbsp. light salad oil
¼ cup dry white wine
¼ cup lemon juice
Lemon wedges
Fresh parsley

SERVES 4

"This recipe should really be prepared in a chafing dish. But it can be prepared successfully on the stove—if you use very gentle heat."

Cut veal slices into pieces about 2x3 inches. Sprinkle with salt and pepper. Place veal between two sheets of waxed paper and, with the side of mallet, pound very thin (⅛ inch). Dust lightly with flour.

Over direct heat in the blazer pan of a chafing dish, heat about 3 tablespoons of the butter and 1 tablespoon of the oil. Add scallops, a few at a time, and cook gently until light brown on each side. (Don't try to hurry this; it will take about 5 minutes per side.) Add more butter and oil as needed.

When all veal is cooked, pour off fat and return veal to pan. Sprinkle with wine and lemon juice. Stir and scrape brown glaze from bottom of pan. Set blazer pan over pan of hot water and heat gently 3 to 5 minutes. Remove veal to a serving platter and add pan juices. Garnish with lemon wedges and parsley sprigs and serve with fettucine.

MRS. WILFORD GONYEA
Eugene, Oregon

Oven Veal Scaloppine

2 lb. boneless veal, thinly sliced
Flour
Olive oil
½ cup butter, melted
¾ cup sauterne
2 dried red chiles
2 medium cloves garlic
½ cup chopped parsley
Juice of 1 lemon

SERVES 6

Have butcher pound veal until very thin. Cut into pieces, 3x3 inches. Dust with flour and brown quickly in oil.

Place veal in a casserole and add butter, sauterne, chiles, garlic, parsley and lemon juice. Bake, uncovered, in a preheated 350° oven 45 minutes. Remove chiles.

MRS. MICHAEL W. McCARTHY
Manhasset, New York

Stuffed Veal Rolls

2 tbsp. butter or margarine
1/4 cup chopped onion
1/4 lb. fresh mushrooms, chopped
1 package (10 oz.) frozen chopped spinach, thawed and well drained
1/4 cup grated Parmesan cheese
1/2 tsp. grated lemon rind
1/2 tsp. basil
1/4 tsp. Tabasco sauce
1/2 tsp. salt
8 thin slices boneless veal (about 1 lb.)
1 cup chicken broth

SERVES 4

Melt butter in a large skillet. Add onion and mushrooms and sauté until tender. Add spinach, cheese, lemon rind, basil, Tabasco sauce and salt. Cover and simmer 5 minutes.

Place 2 tablespoons of the spinach mixture on the center of each veal slice. Roll up and secure with wooden toothpicks. Place veal rolls in the skillet and add broth. Cover and simmer 20 minutes or until veal is tender. Remove toothpicks before serving.

MARGUERITE K. MURPHY
Rancho Mirage, California

My Own Veal Casserole

2 tbsp. vegetable oil
2 lb. veal cutlets, 1 inch thick
1 red onion, sliced
6 large mushrooms, sliced
1 can (11 oz.) condensed golden onion soup
1 can vegetable cocktail juice (V-8)
1 can (16 oz.) peeled whole tomatoes, drained and cut into quarters (reserve juice)
Pinch of oregano
Pinch of rosemary
1/2 tsp. celery salt
1/2 tsp. salt
1/2 tsp. pepper
Seasoned bread stuffing
Grated Parmesan cheese

SERVES 4

Cover the bottom of a 2½-quart casserole with the oil. Arrange cutlets in casserole. Add onion and mushrooms. Mix soup and vegetable juice and pour over veal. Add tomatoes and their liquid. Add oregano, rosemary, celery salt, salt and pepper.

Cover and bake in a preheated 325° oven 1 hour 55 minutes. Remove cover. Top casserole with the stuffing and sprinkle well with cheese. Bake, uncovered, 5 minutes longer. Serve with additional grated cheese and French bread.

This dish can be prepared ahead of time; cover and keep warm.

MRS. JOSEPH CAMPBELL
Washington, D.C.

Supreme Veal Casserole

2½ lb. boneless veal steak, ½ inch thick
½ cup flour
2 tsp. paprika
2 tsp. salt
¼ tsp. pepper
5 tbsp. butter
1 clove garlic, minced
½ cup water
2 cups sour cream
2 cans (6 oz. each) water chestnuts, sliced
½ cup dry sherry
1 tsp. lemon juice
1 tsp. basil
1 tsp. MSG
½ tsp. rosemary
8 dried apricot halves, minced
2 tbsp. cornstarch
¼ cup water

SERVES 6–8

Pound veal until thin. Cut into strips, 1x2 inches. Mix flour, paprika, salt and pepper and dredge meat with mixture.

Heat butter in a skillet and sauté garlic just until it sizzles. Add meat and brown, being careful not to burn garlic. Remove meat to a casserole.

Add ½ cup water to skillet and stir well to loosen any brown particles. Lower heat and add sour cream, water chestnuts, sherry, lemon juice, basil, MSG and rosemary. Reserve some of the apricots and add remainder to skillet. Mix cornstarch with ¼ cup water and stir in. Pour mixture over meat. Top with reserved apricots. Cover and bake in a preheated 350° oven 40 minutes. Serve with rice or buttered noodles.

MRS. WEBSTER PULLEN
Omaha, Nebraska

Veal Stew with Red Wine

1½ lb. boneless veal or beef
6 slices bacon, cut in half
Flour
2 tbsp. bacon fat or oil
12 small onions
1½ cups beef broth
½ cup dry red wine

SERVES 6

Cut meat into 12 chunks. Wrap each piece with a half-slice of bacon. Dredge lightly with flour.

Heat fat in a heavy skillet. Add meat and onions and brown on all sides. Remove from pan and pour off all but 1 tablespoon fat. Stir in 1 tablespoon flour and blend until smooth. Add broth and wine. Return meat and onions to skillet. Cover and simmer 1½ to 2 hours, until meat is very tender. Season to taste.

MRS. RONALD REAGAN
Sacramento, California

From the Buffet—Help-yourself service: Sweet-and-Sour Carrots (page 153), Hot Curried Fruit (page 198), Mexican Rice with Sour Cream (page 143), Leg of Lamb Italian (page 77), Zucchini Florentine (page 161).

Soup's On—Sit back and relax while it simmers. Enjoy the hearty combination of chicken and ham in an authentic Creole Gumbo (page 40). Complete the meal plan with fluffy white rice and a crisp green salad.

Loin of Pork in Red Wine

1 pork loin (3 to 4 lb.)
Salt and pepper
Sage
Nutmeg
Oil
1/4 cup chopped onions
1/4 cup chopped parsley
1 bay leaf
1 cup dry red wine
1 cup canned beef broth
Whole onions
New potatoes (unpeeled)

SERVES 6

Rub pork with salt, pepper, sage and nutmeg. Brown in a little oil on top of the stove. Transfer to a rack in a roasting pan and add chopped onions, parsley, bay leaf and wine. Roast in a preheated 350° oven 2 hours. Arrange whole onions and new potatoes in a lightly oiled baking pan and place in the oven. Roast meat and vegetables 40 minutes longer. Add broth to pan containing meat. Arrange the partially cooked vegetables around the meat and roast 20 minutes longer.

MRS. ELLSWORTH VINES
La Quinta, California

Stuffed Pork Chops

1 cup day-old bread
(torn into pieces)
1/4 cup chopped celery
1/4 cup chopped onion
2 to 3 tbsp. chopped parsley
1/4 tsp. salt
1/8 tsp. pepper
Milk
6 rib pork chops, cut
at least 3/4 inch thick
2 tbsp. oil

SERVES 4–6

Make a dressing by combining bread, celery, onion, parsley, salt and pepper. Add just enough milk to moisten.

Trim excess fat from chops. Cut a pocket in the side of each chop and fill with some of the dressing. Sew up the pockets with coarse thread or fasten with toothpicks.

Brown chops in hot oil in a skillet. Remove to a baking pan. Pour 1/4 cup milk over meat. Cover and bake in a preheated 350° oven 1 hour. Juices can be thickened with a little flour.

MR. and MRS. BOB ROSBURG
Chesterfield, Missouri

Bob Rosburg was the winner of the 1972 Bob Hope Desert Classic.

Lemon Pork Chops

6 pork chops
2 tbsp. flour
1 tsp. salt
1/2 tsp. dry mustard
1/4 tsp. allspice
1/4 cup apple jelly
1 lemon, sliced

SERVES 4–6

Trim chops (save fat and use to brown chops). Mix flour, salt, mustard and allspice. Dredge chops with flour mixture, shaking off excess. Brown in hot fat; drain off excess. Top with apple jelly and lemon slices. Cover and simmer 40 minutes, basting frequently.

MRS. DWIGHT BABCOCK
Hot Springs, Arkansas

Pork Chops with Barbecue Sauce

1/2 cup minced onion
1 tbsp. margarine
1/2 cup water
1/2 cup chili sauce
2 tbsp. vinegar
1 tbsp. Worcestershire sauce
Juice of 1 lemon
2 tbsp. brown sugar
2 tbsp. prepared mustard
Hot pepper sauce
Salt and pepper
6 thick pork chops

SERVES 6

Sauté onion in margarine. Add remaining ingredients except pork chops and simmer 15 minutes. Adjust seasoning to taste.

Place chops on a rack in a roasting pan. Pour sauce over meat and bake, uncovered, in a preheated 350° oven 1 hour.

MR. and MRS. DOUG SANDERS
Houston, Texas
Doug Sanders was the winner of the 1966 Bob Hope Desert Classic.

Sweet-and-Sour Pork

1½ lb. lean pork shoulder
Peanut oil
½ cup water
2½ cups canned pineapple chunks, drained (reserve syrup)
¼ cup brown sugar
2 tbsp. cornstarch
¼ cup vinegar
2 to 3 tbsp. soy sauce
½ tsp. salt
1 small green pepper, cut into strips
¼ cup thinly sliced onion
Hot cooked rice

SERVES 6

Cut pork into thin strips, 2x½ inch. Brown in a small amount of oil. Add water. Cover and simmer (do not boil) until tender, about 1 hour.

In a bowl, combine reserved pineapple syrup, the brown sugar, cornstarch, vinegar, soy sauce and salt. Add to pork; cook, stirring, until gravy thickens. Add pineapple, green pepper and onion. Cover and cook 10 to 15 minutes. Serve over hot rice.

JEAN M. BENSON
Palm Desert, California

Lion's Head

2 lb. Chinese cabbage, washed and drained
2 tbsp. oil
1 tsp. salt
2 cups chicken broth or water
1¼ lb. pork tenderloin, coarsely ground
¼ lb. pure pork fat, coarsely ground
3 green onions, chopped (include tops)
½ cup chopped water chestnuts
⅔ cup soy sauce
2 tbsp. sherry
1 tsp. sugar
1 tsp. minced fresh gingerroot
1 tbsp. cornstarch
1 egg white

SERVES 4

Separate cabbage leaves and cut into strips 4 inches long. Heat oil in a skillet and stir-fry cabbage 3 minutes. Add salt. Place all but 1 cup of the cabbage in a deep flameproof earthenware pot with a lid. Add broth, cover and bring to a boil.

Mix pork, pork fat, green onions, water chestnuts, half the soy sauce, the sherry, sugar, gingerroot and cornstarch. Beat egg white until foamy and stir into meat mixture. Shape lightly into 4 meatballs. Pat the balls with a little soy sauce and gently place on top of cabbage. Add remaining soy sauce to the pot. Place the reserved 1 cup cabbage on top. Cover and cook over low heat 1½ hours.

To serve, push the cabbage to the side to reveal the "lion's head" (meatballs being the head, the cabbage the mane). Serve directly from the pot.

MRS. WILLIAM R. YANCEY
Indian Wells, California

Brownye's Baked Spareribs

4 cups water
2 cups catsup
½ cup Worcestershire sauce
⅓ cup vinegar
4 tbsp. lemon juice
½ cup brown sugar
4 cloves garlic, chopped
2 tsp. chili powder
½ tsp. Tabasco sauce
2 tsp. salt
½ tsp. pepper
7 to 9 lb. pork or beef ribs*
Thin lemon slices
1 large onion, chopped

SERVES 6–8

Make a sauce by combining all ingredients except the meat, lemon slices and onion. Simmer, uncovered, until slightly thickened, about 45 minutes.

Cut spareribs into serving pieces or, if preferred, leave them in whole slabs until ready to serve. Place meaty side up in a shallow baking pan or roaster. Sprinkle lightly with salt and pepper. Place 1 lemon slice on each serving piece, or several slices on each large slab of ribs. Bake, uncovered, in a preheated 450° oven about 45 minutes, turning occasionally so that all sides brown.

Reduce heat to 350° and remove lemon slices. Sprinkle meat with chopped onion and bake 10 minutes longer. If there is a large amount of fat in the pan, pour off at least half or draw off all with a baster.

Pour the barbecue sauce over ribs and, basting and turning often, bake 1½ hours longer or until ribs are well done. (Do not cover at any time.) If sauce becomes too thick, add a little hot water. The ribs should be nicely glazed when done.

* If desired, a shoulder clod roast could be combined with a smaller number of ribs.

FRANK M. MacFALL
La Quinta, California

Meat Loaf Combination

2 lb. boneless ham
1 lb. boneless pork
1 lb. boneless veal
1 cup milk
1 cup bread crumbs
3 eggs, slightly beaten
Salt and pepper
1 cup tomato sauce
Dash of marjoram (optional)

MUSTARD SAUCE #1
2 jars (8 oz. each) currant jelly
1 jar (6 oz.) prepared yellow mustard (French's)

MUSTARD SAUCE #2
2 tbsp. prepared mustard
½ cup vinegar
3 egg yolks
½ cup sugar
½ cup butter
½ cup tomato juice

SERVES 10

Have butcher grind meats together twice. Add milk, bread crumbs, eggs, salt, pepper, 1 tablespoon of the tomato sauce and the marjoram. Shape into a loaf and place in a lightly oiled baking dish. Bake in a preheated 375° oven 1½ hours, basting with remaining tomato sauce. Serve with one of the mustard sauces.

To make Mustard Sauce #1, heat all ingredients in the top of a double boiler over hot water. Good hot or cold.

To make Mustard Sauce #2, combine ingredients and cook in the top of a double boiler over hot water until thick. If too thin, thicken with cornstarch.

MRS. ROBERT CUSHMAN
Palm Springs, California

Ham Loaf

2 lb. picnic ham
2 lb. pork shoulder
1⅓ cups bread crumbs
1½ cups milk
3 eggs
Pepper
¾ cup vinegar
½ cup water
¼ cup catsup
3½ cups brown sugar
1½ tsp. prepared mustard

SERVES ABOUT 10

Have butcher grind ham and pork together. Mix bread crumbs, milk, eggs and pepper with ground meat. Shape into a loaf and place in a baking dish. Place in a cold oven and set temperature at 350°. Bake 1 hour.

While loaf bakes, make a glaze by mixing vinegar, water, catsup, sugar and mustard.

After 1 hour, pour fat from baking dish. Spread glaze on loaf and bake 1 hour longer.

MRS. WILLIAM H. HAMMER
Los Angeles, California

Fiesta Ham

2 cups soft bread crumbs
½ cup raisins
½ cup chopped unsalted peanuts
¼ cup butter
2 tbsp. dark corn syrup
1½ tsp. dry mustard
2 center-cut ham slices (½ inch thick)
Whole cloves
Thin orange slices

SERVES 4–5

Lightly mix bread crumbs, raisins, peanuts, butter, corn syrup and mustard. Place a slice of ham in a lightly oiled shallow baking dish and cover with dressing. Top with remaining ham slice and secure with toothpicks.

Pierce ham fat with a few cloves and place orange slices on top. Bake, uncovered, in a preheated 300° oven 1 hour.

MRS. MAURIE LUXFORD
North Hollywood, California

Italian Sausage with Green Peppers and Onions

12 sweet Italian sausages
2 cups water
6 large green peppers, cut into 1-inch strips
5 large onions, sliced
⅓ cup olive oil
Salt

SERVES 6–8

Pierce sausages with a fork. Place on the bottom of a broiler pan (do not use a rack). Add water. Bake in a preheated 350° oven, turning once, until water evaporates and sausages are lightly browned. While sausage bakes, sauté vegetables *separately* in oil until tender but not brown. Salt both vegetables lightly.

Remove pan of sausages from oven and drain off fat. (Leave sausages in pan.) Reduce heat to 325°. Cut sausages in half. Add peppers and onions to the broiler pan and simmer on top of stove a few minutes to absorb flavors in pan. Transfer all to a casserole or baking dish. Cover and bake about 30 minutes (or, if preferred, cover and simmer on top of stove). Serve with hot Italian rolls. (Dunking them in the casserole juices is recommended.)

This dish can be made several hours or even a day ahead and reheated. The flavor is even better.

MRS. WILLIAM BENDIX
Palm Springs, California

Rack of Lamb Henri

1 rack of lamb, Frenched, with all fat removed
1 clove garlic, peeled
3 pats butter (about 1 tbsp. each)
Salt and pepper
1 onion, cut into quarters
2 cloves garlic, unpeeled
1 tbsp. butter
½ cup dry sherry

SERVES 3

"This method of treating lamb was told to me years ago by Escoffier's nephew, Henri Charpentier—Master Chef and acknowledged creator of the Suzette Sauce for crêpes."

Rub bony side of rack with peeled garlic. Place the pats of butter lengthwise down the center of a large shallow baking pan. Place the lamb meat side down on butter. Sprinkle with salt and pepper. Arrange an onion quarter in each corner of pan. Dip unpeeled garlic cloves in water and place in the pan.

Roast lamb in a preheated 450° oven 15 minutes. Turn meat over, sprinkle with salt and pepper and roast 15 minutes longer. Remove lamb to a warm platter. Discard onions and garlic cloves. Add 1 tablespoon butter and the sherry to the pan juices. Bring to a boil, stir and pour over lamb.

MRS. WILLIAM O. FLEETWOOD
Indian Wells, California

Stuffed Leg of Lamb

1 onion, sliced
¼ lb. fresh mushrooms, sliced
Butter
1 package (12 oz.) frozen spinach soufflé, thawed (Stouffer's)
4 oz. seasoned bread stuffing
2 tbsp. butter, melted
3 tbsp. lemon juice
1 leg of lamb, boned (with large cavity)
Salt and pepper
Dry white wine or dry vermouth

SERVES 6

In a skillet, sauté onion and mushrooms in butter. Add uncooked spinach soufflé. Mix bread stuffing with melted butter; add lemon juice and add to ingredients in skillet, mixing thoroughly. Fill cavity of lamb with this mixture; close with skewers. Season meat with salt and pepper.

Roast in a medium oven (325° to 350°) about 2½ hours (adjust time according to size of leg), basting occasionally with wine.

MRS. HAROLD L. BEHLKE
La Quinta, California

Gigot d'Agneau aux Flageolets
LEG OF LAMB WITH DRIED BEANS

FLAGEOLETS
¼ lb. salt pork
2 cups dried flageolets*
1 medium onion, chopped
2 cloves garlic, minced
4 tbsp. tomato paste
Freshly ground black pepper
1 tbsp. Spice Islands bouquet garni (or a combination of thyme, tarragon, basil and rosemary)
½ cup minced parsley
1½ tsp. salt

LEG OF LAMB
1 leg of lamb (6 to 7 lb.)
1 tbsp. oil
2 or 3 cloves garlic, mashed
1 tbsp. Spice Islands bouquet garni (see above)
Coarse salt (½ tsp. per lb. of meat)
6 or 7 black peppercorns, cracked
1½ cups basting liquid (dry red wine, broth or coffee)

SERVES 8

The beans should be cooked well ahead, even the day before (they improve with age).

Remove rind from pork. Slice both pork and rind in narrow strips and brown in a top-of-stove beanpot or Dutch oven. Add beans, onion, garlic, tomato paste and pepper. Add enough water to extend 1 inch above beans. Bring to a boil slowly, then lower heat and cook gently, partially covered, to avoid splitting skins. Add boiling water as needed. (All beans have different cooking times, so follow package directions.) Add bouquet garni and parsley for the last hour of cooking. When tender (do not overcook), add salt and adjust all seasonings.

Make slits in top and underside of lamb. Mix oil, garlic, bouquet garni, salt and pepper. Rub lamb well with mixture, forcing deep into slits and around bone. Insert a meat thermometer in lamb and place on rack in a preheated 450° oven. Sear until well browned. Reduce heat and roast lamb in preferred manner (slow or fast method), basting occasionally. When thermometer registers 120° (for rosy-rare) or 130° (for pink-rare), remove from oven and place on a deep serving platter. (The lamb should be crisp outside, pink and juicy inside.) Let stand in a warm place 20 minutes before carving. Meanwhile, reheat flageolets.

At serving time, surround lamb with the reheated beans, mixing in all the meat juices (fat removed). As the meat is carved, additional juices will blend with the beans.

* Flageolets—the tiny, flutelike greenish beans, either fresh or dried—are the traditional French accompaniment to a leg of lamb. The dried are available in specialty stores in the United States; if unavailable, however, dried beans such as navy, great northern or baby limas make very suitable substitutes.

MRS. HARRISON ROBERTS
Indian Wells, California

Leg of Lamb Italian

1 leg of lamb
4 oz. pepperoni, skinned and chopped
¼ cup grated Parmesan cheese
1 egg
1 tsp. crushed basil
1 tsp. crushed rosemary
1 tsp. crushed oregano
1 clove garlic, slivered
Salt (½ tsp. per lb. of meat)
1 tsp. cracked Italian red pepper
Freshly ground black pepper
1 cup red wine

SERVES 6

With apple corer, puncture fat side of lamb in four or five places, leaving holes 1 inch deep. Remove meat from holes and place in a blender. Add pepperoni, cheese, egg and some of the herbs. Blend lightly and stuff mixture into holes. Make small slits in the fat. Insert slivers of garlic in slits and around bones. Rub well with salt, red and black peppers and remaining herbs.

Insert meat thermometer in lamb (do not touch bone). Sear lamb in a preheated 450° oven until well browned. Reduce heat and roast lamb in preferred manner (slow or fast method) to desired doneness, basting with wine. For "pink" lamb, remove from oven when thermometer registers 120° to 130°. Let stand 20 minutes in a warm place (room temperature) before carving.

MRS. ROGER ASHTON
Evergreen, Colorado

Lamb Shanks Mozait

4 lamb shanks
1 clove garlic, split in half
¼ cup flour
1 tsp. mint flakes
2 tsp. salt
¼ tsp. pepper
¼ cup salad oil
2 cups hot water
1 cup white wine
Curry powder or other seasonings (optional)

SERVES 4

Trim lamb shanks of excess fat and rub well with half the garlic. Combine flour, mint, salt and pepper. Roll shanks in flour mixture, coating well. Reserve remaining flour.

Heat oil in a heavy kettle and brown shanks well on all sides. Remove to a large casserole and add hot water, wine and remaining garlic. Cover and bake in a preheated 350° oven 2 hours or until tender. Remove shanks to platter.

To make gravy, skim excess fat from liquid in casserole. To thicken, mix a smooth paste of 1½ tablespoons of the reserved flour mixture and 3 tablespoons water for each cup liquid in pan. Stir paste into liquid to thicken. Curry powder or other seasonings may be added to the gravy.

MRS. JOHN PETERS
Indio, California

Lamb Shanks Desert Squire

Slivered garlic cloves
8 small lamb shanks
Crushed rosemary
Salt and pepper
Oil
2 cans (10¾ oz. each) condensed chicken broth
Bouquet garni (celery, parsley, rosemary, thyme and oregano tied in cheesecloth)
½ tsp. *glace de viande* or meat extract
4 to 6 potatoes, peeled and quartered
Lemon juice

SERVES 4

Insert slivers of garlic in lamb shanks. Rub with crushed rosemary, salt and pepper. Heat a small amount of oil in a Dutch oven and brown meat well. When lamb is brown, drain off excess fat. Add chicken broth and bouquet garni. Remove from heat, cover and bake in a preheated 350° oven 1 hour.

Remove from oven and skim off fat. Stir *glace de viande* into broth. Arrange potatoes around meat. Adjust seasonings. Return to oven and bake, uncovered, 1 hour longer. Turn potatoes occasionally.

Place lamb shanks on a large heated platter and surround with potatoes. Add a little lemon juice to the broth and serve on the side.

MRS. ORRIN HOMME
Rancho Mirage, California

Shish Kebab with Rice Pilaf

1 leg of lamb (5 to 6 lb.)
½ lb. onions, sliced
⅓ cup sherry
2 tbsp. oil
1 tsp. oregano
1 tbsp. salt
½ tsp. pepper

RICE PILAF
½ cup butter
3 cups rice
6 cups chicken, lamb or beef broth or hot water
Salt and pepper

SERVES 8–10

Remove fat and gristle from lamb. Bone the meat and cut into 1-inch cubes. Mix with sherry, oil and seasonings. Let mixture stand in refrigerator at least a few hours, preferably overnight.

To cook meat, place marinated cubes on skewers and broil over a charcoal fire or under a broiler to desired doneness.

To make Rice Pilaf, melt butter in a Dutch oven until it begins to bubble. Add rice and sauté well. Add broth, salt and pepper. Mix well with a fork. Cover and bake in a preheated 400° oven 30 minutes. Remove from oven, mix well with a fork and bake 15 minutes longer.

GEORGE MARDIKIAN
San Francisco, California

Andalusian Lamb

- 2 lb. boned leg of lamb
- 1/3 cup flour
- 2 tbsp. oil (for browning)
- 1 medium onion, chopped
- 3 cups hot water
- 1 bay leaf
- 3 1/2 tsp. salt
- 1/2 tsp. black peppercorns, cracked
- 1/2 cup chopped green pepper
- 1/2 cup rice
- 1 can (16 oz.) tomatoes
- 1 cup thawed frozen peas
- 1 egg
- 1 tsp. olive oil
- 1/2 tsp. cider vinegar

SERVES 6

Wipe lamb and cut it into 1 1/2-inch pieces. Dredge with flour, shaking off excess. Brown lamb in oil in a large skillet. Add onion and cook until wilted. Stir in water, bay leaf, salt and peppercorns. Cover and simmer about 1 1/2 hours or until lamb is almost tender. Add green pepper and rice and simmer 20 minutes. Add tomatoes and peas and simmer 10 minutes longer.

At end of cooking time, beat the egg and mix with olive oil and vinegar. Add to the stew, stirring until thickened (do not boil).

MRS. LOUIS J. CROSS
Chicago, Illinois

Lamb Stew with Savory Dumplings

- 1 1/2 lb. cubed lamb shoulder
- Butter or oil
- 1 cup sliced onions
- 1 cup diced carrots
- 1/2 cup diced green pepper
- 1/2 cup diced celery
- 3 cups beef broth
- 2 tbsp. flour
- 2 tsp. salt
- 1/4 tsp. pepper

SAVORY DUMPLINGS

- 1 cup biscuit mix
- 6 tbsp. milk
- 2 tbsp. chopped parsley
- 1 tsp. prepared horseradish
- 1/4 tsp. oregano
- 1/8 tsp. rosemary

SERVES 4

In a Dutch oven, brown lamb on all sides in a little butter. Add vegetables, broth, flour, salt and pepper; mix well. Cover and simmer, stirring occasionally, over low heat 1 hour.

To make dumplings, combine all ingredients and mix well. Drop by tablespoonfuls onto stew. Cover and simmer over low heat 20 minutes longer.

MRS. DEL WEBB
Scottsdale, Arizona

Moussaka

1 medium eggplant (about 1¼ lb.)
Flour
6 tbsp. butter or margarine
½ cup chopped onion
1 lb. ground lean lamb or beef
¼ cup finely chopped parsley
1 tsp. nutmeg
½ tsp. paprika
¼ tsp. pepper
Salt
1 can (8 oz.) tomato sauce or paste
½ cup dry white wine
1 medium tomato, thinly sliced
1 egg, beaten
½ cup grated mozzarella cheese

SERVES 4

Cut eggplant (peeled or unpeeled, as you wish) into slices ½ inch thick. Soak slices in salted cold water 30 minutes. Pat dry. Dredge with flour, brushing off excess. Sauté on both sides in a little of the butter until brown, adding more butter as needed. Drain on paper towels and set aside.

In a large skillet, sauté onion until tender. Add meat and sauté until no longer red. Blend in parsley, nutmeg, paprika and pepper. Add salt, tomato sauce and wine and simmer a few minutes.

Arrange a layer of eggplant slices in the bottom of a lightly buttered 2-quart casserole or shallow baking dish. Pour half the meat mixture over eggplant. Cover with half the remaining eggplant slices. Pour on remaining meat mixture. Top with remaining eggplant and the tomato slices, overlapping alternately.

Beat egg with 1 tablespoon flour until smooth. Stir in cheese. Add ½ teaspoon salt. Pour over casserole. Bake, uncovered, in a preheated 375° oven 30 minutes or until top is toasty-brown.

MRS. WILLIAM N. BIRCH
Thousand Palms, California

Lamb Kidney Sauté

4 lamb kidneys
2 tbsp. butter
2 slices bacon, finely chopped
1 tbsp. paprika
1 tsp. flour
⅔ cup red wine
½ cup water
Pinch of salt

SERVES 2

Remove membrane and fat from kidneys, then dice. Melt butter in a skillet. Add bacon and paprika and sauté briefly. Stir in kidneys, turning continuously. Cook thoroughly. Add flour and brown. Add wine, water and salt and boil until liquid is reduced to a thick sauce.

Serve at once with eggs fried slowly in butter.

ROBERT L. SCHULZ, Brigadier General, U.S.A. (Ret.)
Alexandria, Virginia

POULTRY & GAME

From Folksy to Frankly Fabulous

Viva! Vive! Or just plain hurray! All for
the many tempting ways there are to serve chicken.
Team it with dumplings for a good old-fashioned supper.
Flame it with brandy, lace it with lemon,
gild it with grapes and vermouth when you want to splurge.
Delicious treatments for turkey, game hens and ducklings are here, too.
And for sportsmen—or for those who share in the bounty—
be sure to check our field specials!

Chicken Three-in-One

BASIC RECIPE
3½ lb. chicken breasts and thighs
2 cups clear chicken broth
1 cup dry French vermouth
¼ tsp. tarragon or Italian seasoning
Salt and pepper
3 medium celery stalks, sliced
2 carrots, sliced
2 onions, sliced
Chopped parsley

CHICKEN IN ASPIC
2½ cups strained defatted broth (from Basic Recipe)
1 tbsp. unflavored gelatin
Cooked chicken, skinned and sliced (from Basic Recipe)
2 tbsp. chopped parsley

CASSEROLE OF CHICKEN IN WINE SAUCE
Broth (from Basic Recipe)
5 tbsp. butter
3 tbsp. flour
½ cup light cream
Cooked chicken (from Basic Recipe)
Cooked vegetables (from Basic Recipe)
3 tbsp. grated Swiss cheese

SERVES 4–6

"Why 'Three-in-One'? The first recipe, a delicately flavored chicken stew, is also the foundation for two other very different dishes."

BASIC RECIPE (CHICKEN STEW)
Combine chicken, broth and vermouth in a heatproof casserole. Bring to a simmer and add seasonings. Cover and simmer 20 minutes. Add vegetables and cook until they are crisp-tender, about 15 minutes. Remove chicken to a serving platter and sprinkle with parsley. Surround with the vegetables and, if desired, rice, potatoes or peas. The broth may be thickened for a sauce.

CHICKEN IN ASPIC
Clarify broth. Heat 2 cups of the broth (if cold). Soften gelatin in remaining ½ cup broth. Add hot broth and stir until dissolved. Cool.

Arrange chicken slices on a platter or in individual molds. Pour gelatin mixture over chicken and sprinkle with parsley. Chill until set. Unmold (if in molds) and serve with a green salad, French bread and white wine.

CASSEROLE OF CHICKEN IN WINE SAUCE
Reduce broth to 2 cups. Make a roux of 4 tablespoons of the butter and the flour. Stir into broth and cook, stirring, until sauce thickens. Slowly add cream. Taste and correct seasoning.

Put a little sauce into a buttered baking dish. Arrange chicken pieces on bottom, followed by vegetables. Top with sauce and sprinkle with cheese. Dot with remaining tablespoon butter. Heat, uncovered, in a preheated 375° oven until top is brown. Serve at once. Accompany with rice or noodles, peas or asparagus, green salad and white wine.

The casserole may be assembled ahead of time and refrigerated. Heat in a preheated 375° oven about 30 minutes.

MRS. JOHN CLOCK
Long Beach, California

Bean Pot Chicken

2 medium broiler-fryer chickens, cut into serving pieces
½ cup butter
Salt and pepper
Paprika
6 medium onions, peeled
Heavy cream

SERVES 6

Put chicken pieces in a bean pot along with butter, salt, pepper and paprika. Place whole onions on top. Add just enough water to cover contents. Cover pot and bake in a preheated 325° to 350° oven 3 hours.

Pour off juices into a saucepan. Reduce liquid slightly over moderate heat. Stirring constantly, gradually add enough heavy cream to thicken sauce to desired consistency. Taste for seasoning. Strain over chicken in the pot.

Serve right from the bean pot; accompany with rice.

MRS. WILLIAM S. PALEY
New York, New York

Chicken and Dumplings

1 stewing chicken (4 to 5 lb.), cut into serving pieces
Boiling water
1 stalk celery
1 sprig parsley
1 tbsp. chicken stock base
Salt and pepper

DUMPLINGS
1 cup flour
1½ tsp. baking powder
1½ tsp. salt
1 egg, beaten
⅓ cup milk
2 tbsp. cool melted chicken fat or salad oil

SERVES 6

Place chicken in a kettle and cover with boiling water. Add celery, parsley, chicken stock base, salt and pepper. Cover and cook until almost tender, 1 to 2 hours (depending on size of chicken).

While chicken cooks, make dumplings. Sift together flour, baking powder and salt. Combine egg, milk and melted fat. Add all at once to dry ingredients. Stir quickly, until ingredients form a soft dough.

About 15 minutes before chicken has finished cooking, drop dough by teaspoonfuls onto chicken. (There should be about 3 cups liquid in the kettle; add boiling water if necessary.) Cover tightly and steam 15 minutes. Serve immediately.

MRS. ROBERT A. HAMILTON
Los Angeles, California

Poulet Vallée d'Auge

4 whole chicken breasts (with skin), split and boned
½ cup Calvados or applejack
1 tbsp. minced fresh or 1 tsp. dried tarragon
Grating of nutmeg
Salt and white pepper
3 tbsp. clarified butter
½ cup chicken broth or cider
½ cup light cream
2 egg yolks
Whole fresh tarragon leaves (optional)

SAUTEED APPLES
3 tbsp. clarified butter
8 medium Golden Delicious or tart green apples, pared, cored and cut into eighths
2 tbsp. minced shallots or chives
1 tbsp. minced fresh or 1 tsp. dried tarragon
Grating of nutmeg
Salt and white pepper

SERVES 4

This is a classic dish from Normandy's Auge Valley—chicken flamed with Calvados (apple brandy) and served with sautéed apples. For variety, pheasant, partridge, goose—or even sweetbreads—may be substituted for the chicken.

Rub chicken with some of the Calvados and a mixture of tarragon, nutmeg, salt and white pepper. Shape into tidy ovals, tucking ragged edges under and securing with toothpicks. Set aside.

Gently heat two skillets, each containing 3 tablespoons clarified butter. Place chicken pieces in one skillet and sauté over low heat, turning often (do not brown).

When chicken has cooked about 10 minutes, warm the remaining Calvados, pour over chicken and ignite. Shake pan gently until flame dies, then add broth. Cover and continue to cook over low heat 30 minutes or until done.

While chicken cooks, combine apples, shallots and seasonings in the other skillet. Mix well and sauté until apples are tender and lightly browned, about 30 minutes. When both apples and chicken are done, taste for seasoning and adjust. Spread apples on a heated serving platter. Remove toothpicks from chicken and arrange on the apples. Keep warm while preparing sauce.

Combine juices from both pans in one skillet. Blend cream and egg yolks; stir into juices. Cook over low heat (do not boil), stirring constantly until slightly thickened. (The sauce should be thin.) Taste for seasoning. Strain into a warm sauceboat. Spoon a small amount over chicken. Garnish with tarragon leaves and serve immediately.

If you are the kind of cook who likes to "wing it," create your own specialty: combine whole or cut-up chicken with apples, cream and your favorite herbs. Don't forget to lace generously with Calvados or applejack.

MRS. HARRISON ROBERTS
Indian Wells, California

Chicken Thighs aux Deux Moutardes

¼ cup butter or margarine
8 chicken thighs
4 shallots, minced
⅓ cup Calvados, applejack or chicken broth
2 tsp. Dijon mustard
2 tsp. dry mustard (Colman's)
2 cups heavy cream
⅛ tsp. mace
Salt and pepper
Chopped parsley

SERVES 4

Melt butter in a skillet. Add chicken and sauté gently, turning once, until golden brown, about 8 minutes. Add shallots and Calvados. Reduce heat, cover and simmer 15 minutes.

Remove chicken to a warm casserole. Stir the mustards into cream, pour into the skillet and boil vigorously 5 minutes. Season with mace, salt and pepper and pour over chicken. Sprinkle with chopped parsley before serving.

This dish may be prepared ahead and reheated gently.

MRS. WILLIAM O. FLEETWOOD
Indian Wells, California

Venus Chicken

½ cup flour
¾ tsp. salt
½ tsp. pepper
1 tsp. paprika
6 whole chicken breasts, split
2 tbsp. butter
2 tbsp. cooking oil
2 tbsp. finely chopped shallots
½ cup sliced mushrooms
¼ cup brandy
¼ cup dry vermouth
½ cup chicken broth
½ to 1 cup seedless grapes
½ cup slivered almonds, cashews or walnuts

SERVES 6

Mix flour, salt, pepper and paprika. Lightly dust chicken with mixture.

Heat butter and oil in a skillet. When bubbling, add chicken, shallots and mushrooms. Sauté over medium heat, turning chicken to brown evenly. When browned, add brandy. Wait a moment for brandy to warm, then ignite. When flame dies, add vermouth, broth and grapes. Cover and simmer 15 minutes. Stir in nuts just before serving.

MRS. J. GILTNER IGLEHEART, JR.
La Jolla, California

Lemon Chicken

- 3 whole chicken breasts, split, skinned and boned
- Salt and pepper
- ½ cup butter
- ¼ cup dry vermouth or dry sherry
- 3 tbsp. lemon juice
- 2 tbsp. grated lemon rind
- 1½ cups chicken broth
- 1½ tbsp. flour
- ⅓ cup water or chicken broth
- Grated Parmesan cheese
- 6 thin pats of butter
- Sautéed mushrooms and/or cooked artichoke hearts (optional)

SERVES 3

Sprinkle chicken breasts with salt and pepper. Melt butter in a skillet and brown chicken on all sides. Sauté 10 minutes or more, until cooked through. Remove chicken to ovenproof serving platter.

Add vermouth, lemon juice and rind to skillet. Stir and scrape pan drippings, then add broth. Blend flour and water and stir into broth. Stir constantly until slightly thickened. Pour over chicken. Sprinkle generously with cheese. Place a pat of butter on top of each piece of chicken. Heat and brown under broiler, adding sautéed mushrooms and/or cooked artichoke hearts, if desired.

MRS. JOHN BYRNE
Omaha, Nebraska

Chicken Augusta

- 2 cups heavy cream
- 3 slices bread, trimmed and cubed
- 1 lb. finely ground beef tenderloin
- 1 egg
- 3 whole chicken breasts, skinned, boned and finely ground
- Salt and pepper
- Butter or margarine
- 2 cups chicken broth
- 1 lb. fresh mushrooms, sautéed in butter
- Finely chopped parsley

SERVES 8–10

Pour cream over bread (use a large bowl). Add beef and egg; mix well. Add chicken, salt and pepper and mix thoroughly. Chill 2 hours, then shape mixture into 8 to 10 logs. Chill 3 hours longer.

Heat butter in a skillet and sauté logs on all sides until golden brown. Remove to a hot serving dish. Stir broth into skillet and simmer a few minutes. Pour over logs. Garnish with mushrooms and sprinkle with parsley. Serve immediately.

MRS. POLLARD SIMONS
Dallas, Texas

Spanish Chicken 

8 tbsp. butter
3 lb. chicken pieces
1 large green pepper, chopped
1 large onion, chopped
1 can (about 15 oz.) whole tomatoes
1 can (10½ oz.) tomato purée
1½ cups chicken broth
2 tbsp. sugar
Oregano
Thyme
Cumin
Salt and pepper
½ lb. small mushrooms
2 cups cooked small peas

SERVES 4

Heat 4 to 6 tablespoons butter in a large skillet, preferably one with an enameled or non-stick surface. Add chicken and brown well. Add green pepper and onion; sauté, then add tomatoes, tomato purée, broth and sugar. Stir in seasonings. Cover and simmer until chicken is tender, about 30 to 40 minutes.

While chicken cooks, sauté mushrooms in 2 tablespoons butter. Before serving, stir mushrooms and peas into chicken and heat through.

AMBASSADOR and MRS. WALTER H. ANNENBERG
London, England

Chicken Paprika

2 tbsp. shortening
1 large onion, chopped
1 green pepper, chopped
1 tbsp. paprika
1 broiler-fryer chicken, cut into serving pieces
1 tomato, peeled and sliced
1 tbsp. salt
About 4 cups water
2 tbsp. flour
½ cup water
½ cup sour cream

SERVES 4

Melt shortening in a stewing pot. When hot, brown onion and green pepper. Remove pot from heat and stir in paprika (it burns easily). Return to medium heat. Add chicken, tomato, salt and enough water to not quite cover chicken (about 4 cups). Cover and simmer 1 hour.

Blend flour and ½ cup water. Stir into liquid in pot and bring to a slow boil. Reduce heat and stir in sour cream; heat (do not boil). Serve over dumplings, mostaccioli noodles or rice, or in soup plates, accompanied by sourdough bread.

This dish can be prepared the day before and reheated.

ELIZABETH L. WARREN
Rancho Mirage, California

Country Captain

1 tender stewing chicken (3½ to 4 lb.), cut into serving pieces and skinned
Flour
Salt and pepper
Shortening
2 onions, finely chopped
2 green peppers, finely chopped
1 small clove garlic, minced
About ½ lb. fresh mushrooms (canned may be used)
1 tsp. salt
½ tsp. white pepper
2 tsp. curry powder
2 cans (16 oz. each) tomatoes
½ tsp. chopped parsley
½ tsp. powdered thyme
¼ lb. blanched almonds
Hot cooked rice
3 tbsp. currants
Parsley

SERVES 6

"The origin of Country Captain has never really been ascertained. Some say that it came to Georgia long ago, from India via England. It is known that a famous Georgia hostess thought enough of this dish to serve it to President Franklin D. Roosevelt and some of his distinguished guests at Warm Springs.

"A favorite anecdote concerns General George Patton. He was en route through Georgia and could spend only a few hours in Columbus, and so he wired: 'If you can't give me a party and have Country Captain, put some in a bucket and bring it to the train.' "

Roll chicken in a mixture of flour, salt and pepper. Heat shortening in a skillet and sauté chicken until golden. Remove to a covered roasting pan and keep warm in oven (this is the secret of its success).

Put onion, green pepper, garlic and mushrooms into drippings in skillet and cook very slowly, stirring constantly. Season with salt, white pepper and curry powder. Stir in tomatoes, chopped parsley and thyme. Heat and pour over chicken. (If sauce does not completely cover chicken, deglaze skillet with a little water and pour over chicken.) Cover roasting pan tightly, place in a preheated moderate oven (325° to 350°) and bake until chicken is tender, at least 45 minutes. While chicken bakes, toast almonds to a golden brown.

To serve, place chicken in the center of a large platter and surround with rice. Drop currants into sauce in roasting pan, stir and pour over rice. Scatter almonds over top of rice and garnish with parsley.

MRS. JOHN S. D. EISENHOWER
Phoenixville, Pennsylvania

Orange Chicken

½ cup butter
2 broiler-fryer chickens, cut into serving pieces
4 tsp. salt
½ tsp. pepper
2 tsp. paprika
3 large onions, sliced
1 can (6 oz.) frozen orange juice concentrate
½ cup honey
¼ cup lemon juice
2 tsp. ginger
1 tsp. nutmeg
1 cup sliced ripe olives
1 cup seedless orange sections

SERVES 8

Heat butter in a heavy skillet and brown chicken. Sprinkle with salt, pepper and paprika. Transfer chicken to a heavy casserole and keep warm. Separate onions into rings and sauté in the same skillet until tender. Spread over chicken.

Combine orange juice, honey, lemon juice, ginger and nutmeg. Pour into the skillet and bring to a boil, stirring constantly. Pour over chicken. Stir in olives. Cover and bake in a preheated 350° oven 1 hour. Add orange sections and heat through.

MRS. J. H. SHANKLAND
Indian Wells, California

Chicken à la Maryland

1 broiler-fryer chicken, cut into serving pieces
Salt and pepper
Flour
1 egg, slightly beaten
Bread crumbs
⅓ cup butter, melted

WHITE SAUCE
2 tbsp. butter
2 tbsp. flour
1 cup hot milk or light cream
½ tsp. salt
⅛ tsp. white pepper

SERVES 4

Season chicken with salt and pepper. Dip first in flour, then egg; roll in crumbs to coat. Place in a well-greased broiler pan and bake, uncovered, in a preheated 480° oven 20 minutes. Reduce temperature to 275° and bake until tender, about 15 minutes, basting every 5 minutes with melted butter.

While chicken bakes, make White Sauce. Melt butter in a heavy saucepan. Remove from heat and blend in flour. Return to heat and cook, stirring, until roux bubbles. Pour in ⅔ cup of the milk all at once, stirring constantly. Gradually add remaining milk. Boil, stirring constantly, until mixture thickens. Remove from heat and stir in salt and white pepper.

Arrange baked chicken on a serving platter. Cover with White Sauce and serve immediately.

MOLLIE PARNIS
New York, New York

Crunchy Baked Chicken

- 1 chicken (3 lb.), cut into serving pieces, or 3 lb. split chicken breasts
- 1 egg, slightly beaten
- 2 tbsp. milk
- 1 cup instant mashed potato flakes
- ½ cup grated Parmesan cheese
- ¼ cup butter or margarine
- ½ tsp. salt
- ⅛ tsp. pepper

SERVES 4–6

Dry chicken well. Blend egg and milk. Mix potato flakes and cheese. Dip chicken first in milk mixture, then roll in potato-flake mixture, coating thoroughly. (Reserve remaining potato-flake mixture, if any.)

Melt butter in a baking dish. Arrange chicken, skin side down, in the dish. Sprinkle with some of the salt and pepper. Bake, uncovered, in a preheated 400° oven 30 minutes. Turn chicken; sprinkle with salt, pepper and any remaining potato-flake mixture. Bake 30 minutes longer or until fork-tender.

This dish can be frozen, then thawed and reheated.

MRS. RALPH G. WAHLMARK
Palm Springs, California

Raisin Teriyaki Chicken

- 1 chicken (2½ to 3 lb.), cut into serving pieces
- ½ cup chopped raisins
- ½ cup soy sauce
- ½ cup dry sherry
- 1 clove garlic, crushed
- 1 tsp. brown sugar
- ½ tsp. ginger

SERVES 4

Arrange chicken in a shallow baking dish, large enough to hold chicken in one layer. Mix remaining ingredients and pour over chicken. Marinate 2 to 3 hours at room temperature. Cover and bake in the sauce in a preheated 350° oven 1 hour.

MRS. WALTER L. MINTZ
Indian Wells, California

Chicken Diable

- 1/4 cup butter
- 1/2 cup honey
- 1/4 cup prepared mustard
- 1 tsp. curry powder
- 1 tsp. salt
- 1 broiler-fryer chicken (about 3 lb.), cut into serving pieces

SERVES 4

Melt butter in a shallow baking pan and stir in honey, mustard, curry powder and salt. Roll chicken in this mixture to coat all sides.

Arrange chicken, skin side up, in a single layer in the pan. Bake, uncovered, in a preheated 350° oven 1 hour or until tender.

MRS. CARLETON LAUGHLIN
Palm Desert, California

Cheese Chicken Rolls

- 4 whole chicken breasts, split, skinned and boned
- Salt
- 2 oz. Swiss cheese, cut into 2x1/2x1/2-inch strips
- 4 tbsp. crumbled blue cheese
- 1 cup very fine dry bread crumbs
- 1 tbsp. butter or margarine, melted
- 1/2 cup flour
- 2 eggs, beaten

SERVES 4–6

Pound chicken breasts to 1/4-inch thickness and lay flat on waxed paper. Sprinkle with a little salt. Place a strip of Swiss cheese across small end of chicken breast and sprinkle with blue cheese. Roll up lengthwise, tucking in sides; fasten with a toothpick, if necessary. Toss bread crumbs with melted butter. Coat each chicken roll with flour. Dip in eggs, then roll in bread crumbs. Arrange in a lightly greased shallow baking pan and bake, uncovered, in a preheated 325° oven 40 to 45 minutes or until chicken is done.

Breaded chicken rolls may be covered and kept in the refrigerator until ready to bake.

Served with fresh fruit, these are delicious for a light lunch. Good also chilled and cut into 1/4-inch rounds and served as cocktail snacks.

MRS. WILFORD KEMP
Sebastopol, California

King Ranch Casserole

1 large broiler-fryer chicken
12 corn tortillas
1 large onion, chopped
1 large green pepper, chopped
1 can (10¾ oz.) condensed cream of chicken soup
1 can (10¾ oz.) condensed cream of mushroom soup
1 can (10 oz.) tomatoes/green chiles,* crushed in blender
1 tbsp. chili powder
Garlic salt (optional)
½ lb. cheddar cheese, grated

SERVES 6

Wrap chicken in heavy-duty foil and place in a shallow baking pan. Bake in a preheated moderate oven (325° to 350°) 1½ hours. Remove chicken from oven and increase temperature to 375°. Reserve pan juices. Bone chicken and cut into bite-size pieces.

Soften tortillas in the hot pan juices and arrange in a baking pan, about 13x9x2 inches. Cover with chicken and sprinkle with onion and green pepper. Blend soups, tomatoes and seasonings; pour mixture over tortillas. Sprinkle cheese on top and bake 30 minutes.

*Ortega's "Acapulco Hots" and Ro-Tel's "tomatoes and green chiles" are marketed in some states. If these or other brands are unavailable, a combination of tomatoes and green chile sauce could be substituted.

MRS. MICHEL T. HALBOUTY
Houston, Texas

Chicken Leeann

4 chicken legs with thighs attached, skinned
2 whole chicken breasts, split and skinned
Butter or margarine
1 can (about 16 oz.) whole baby carrots, drained
1 can (about 16 oz.) small whole new potatoes, drained
1 can (10¾ oz.) condensed cream of mushroom soup
½ cup dry sherry
Salt and pepper
24 fresh mushroom caps
1 package (10 oz.) frozen green peas, thawed

SERVES 8

Brown chicken lightly in butter. Transfer to a large greased casserole. Add carrots and potatoes. Blend soup, sherry, salt and pepper; pour over ingredients in casserole. Cover and bake in a preheated 350° oven 1 hour.

Remove from oven and arrange mushroom caps and peas on top. Cover and bake 25 minutes longer.

MRS. ROBERT S. HOWARD
Palm Springs, California

Chicken Enchiladas in Green Sauce

- 3 whole chicken breasts
- 6 large husked fresh or canned tomatillos*
- 2 medium avocados, peeled and diced
- 2 jalapeño peppers, diced
- 1/4 onion, chopped
- 1/4 cup water
- 3 cloves garlic
- 1/2 tbsp. salt
- 1/8 tbsp. pepper
- 4 cups sour cream
- 1/3 cup cooking oil
- 12 corn tortillas
- 5 slices process American cheese

SERVES 6

Cook chicken in salted water. When tender, remove (reserve 1/3 cup of the broth). Bone and shred chicken.

In a blender, combine tomatillos, avocados, peppers, onion, water, garlic, salt and pepper. Blend until smooth. Turn mixture into a saucepan. Add sour cream and the reserved broth. Blend and heat gently (*do not boil*).

Heat oil in a skillet and soften tortillas, one at a time.

Place some chicken in each tortilla. Roll up, securing with toothpicks if necessary. Arrange in one layer in a greased shallow baking dish. Cover with the warm sauce and top with cheese slices. Place in a preheated 400° oven. Immediately reduce temperature to 300° and bake until cheese is melted and crusty, about 15 minutes.

*Also called husk tomatoes, ground cherries or jamber-berries. If unavailable, small green tomatoes may be substituted.

MRS. JOHN POPKESS
La Quinta, California

Sandpiper Chicken

- 1 broiler-fryer chicken (2 1/2 to 3 lb.), cut into serving pieces
- 1/2 cup prepared mustard
- 1/4 cup honey
- 3 tbsp. butter or margarine
- 2 tbsp. soy sauce
- 1 tbsp. lemon juice
- 1/2 tsp. salt

SERVES 4

Arrange chicken skin side up in a foil-lined shallow baking pan, large enough to hold chicken in one layer. Combine remaining ingredients in a saucepan and heat. Pour hot sauce over chicken (reserve some for basting). Cover pan and bake in a preheated 350° oven 45 minutes. Remove cover and bake 45 minutes longer, basting chicken occasionally.

MRS. PAUL BEKINS
Sioux City, Iowa

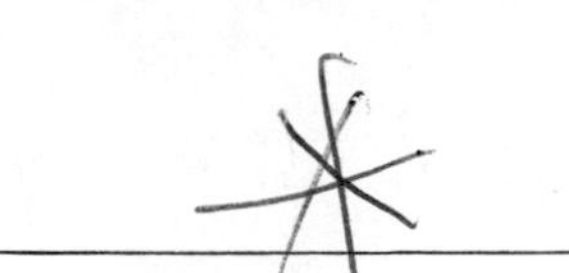

Brunch too

Casserole of Baked Chicken

2 whole chicken breasts
1 can (10¾ oz.) condensed cream of chicken soup
1 cup sliced celery
1 cup button mushrooms
3 hard-boiled eggs, chopped
¾ cup mayonnaise
½ cup chopped almonds
1 tbsp. minced onion
1 tbsp. lemon juice
1 tsp. salt
½ tsp. freshly ground black pepper
2 cups finely crushed potato chips

SERVES 6–8

"Many dishes appeal to me, but I think this one is my favorite.

"I like to serve a small Caesar salad as a first course; and wild rice, fresh, firm asparagus spears and a small glass of sherry with the casserole. While white wine would normally be served, the sherry is best, even if unconventional. (I do have the best housekeeper-cook in the country!)"

Poach chicken until tender. Bone and cut meat into bite-size pieces. Combine with remaining ingredients except potato chips and mix well. Pour into a greased baking dish or casserole. Top with potato chips. Bake in a preheated 375° oven 20 to 25 minutes.

MILTON S. EISENHOWER
Baltimore, Maryland

Nice too

Chicken Casserole Royale

1½ cups cubed cooked chicken
1 cup cooked rice
¼ cup slivered almonds
1 can (10¾ oz.) condensed cream of mushroom soup
1 small onion, diced
1 cup mayonnaise
1 tbsp. lemon juice
¾ cup diced celery
¼ cup sauterne
½ tsp. dry mustard
1 tbsp. Worcestershire sauce
½ tbsp. prepared horseradish
½ can (4-oz. size) water chestnuts, sliced
2 hard-boiled eggs, diced
Finely crushed potato chips

SERVES 4

Combine all ingredients except potato chips. Mix and place in a buttered casserole. Refrigerate overnight.

Remove casserole from refrigerator 1 hour before baking. Sprinkle top lightly with potato chips. Bake, uncovered, in a preheated 375° oven 30 minutes.

MRS. HAROLD HAMILTON
Palm Springs, California

Chicken Tortilla Casserole

- 5 whole chicken breasts
- 1 can (10¾ oz.) condensed cream of chicken soup
- 1 can (10¾ oz.) condensed cream of mushroom soup
- 1 cup sour cream
- 1 can (6 oz.) pitted ripe olives, drained
- 1 can (4 oz.) whole green chiles, seeded and chopped
- 1 onion, chopped
- 6 corn tortillas, cut into ½-inch strips
- 10 oz. sharp cheddar cheese, shredded

SERVES 8–10

Poach chicken until tender. Cool, then bone and cut meat into bite-size pieces.

Blend soups and sour cream. Mix with olives, chiles and onion. Spread a small amount of sauce on bottom of a 2½-quart casserole. Arrange a layer of tortilla strips, followed by layers of chicken, sauce and cheese. Repeat as necessary. Top with cheese. Cover casserole with foil and bake in a preheated 350° oven 45 minutes, or until bubbly.

The casserole may be assembled the day before and refrigerated until ready to bake.

MRS. GORDON ORPUT
Portland, Oregon

Chicken Soufflé

- 2½ cups diced cooked chicken
- 1 cup finely sliced celery
- 1 small onion, minced
- ¾ cup mayonnaise
- Salt and pepper
- 8 slices white sandwich bread, trimmed and cubed
- 5 eggs
- 3 cups milk
- 1 can (10¾ oz.) condensed cream of mushroom soup
- 1 cup grated sharp cheddar cheese

SERVES 6–8

Generously butter a rectangular baking dish, 11½x7½x2 inches (it is important that dish be this size).

Mix chicken, celery, onion, mayonnaise, salt and pepper. Put half the bread in the baking dish. Cover with chicken mixture and add remaining bread. Beat eggs and milk together, then pour gently over ingredients in dish. Cover and refrigerate overnight.

Remove from refrigerator 1½ hours before baking. Place in a preheated 325° oven and bake, uncovered, 15 minutes. Mix soup and cheese. Remove baking dish from oven and spoon soup mixture on top. Return to oven and bake 1 hour longer. Serve immediately.

MRS. CHUCK ASTON
Palm Desert, California

Creamed Chicken Livers in Wine

3 to 4 tbsp. butter
1½ lb. chicken livers
1 large onion, thinly sliced
¼ cup port
¾ cup heavy cream
Salt and pepper

SERVES 4

Heat butter in a large skillet. Add chicken livers and onion and sauté gently until onion is soft and livers turn brown but are pink inside. Add wine and stir over low heat, scraping pan thoroughly to incorporate all particles into sauce. Add cream and heat (do not let it boil). Season to taste. Serve with rice.

MRS. FERNANDO DE ECHAVARRIA
New York, New York

Barbara Ann de Echavarria is Mamie Eisenhower's granddaughter.

Wild Rice–Turkey Casserole

1½ cups uncooked wild rice
4 cups water
1 tsp. salt
1 lb. bulk pork sausage
1 can (3 oz.) whole mushrooms (undrained)
2 cans (10¾ oz. each) condensed cream of mushroom soup
1 tsp. Worcestershire sauce
12 slices cooked turkey or chicken
1½ cups bread crumbs
¼ cup butter, melted

SERVES 8

Wash rice (following package directions) several hours before casserole is to be served. Bring water to a boil and add salt. Gradually add rice. Cover and simmer 30 to 40 minutes; drain.

Cook sausage over medium heat, stirring to break into bits. When brown, drain and combine with mushrooms, soup and Worcestershire sauce. Lightly stir sausage mixture into drained cooked rice. Spoon half the mixture into a baking dish, 12x8x2 inches. Add turkey slices, then spoon in remaining rice mixture.

Mix bread crumbs with butter and sprinkle over top. Bake in a preheated 375° oven about 45 minutes.

The dish may be prepared ahead (do not sprinkle with crumbs). Cover and keep in refrigerator until 1 hour before serving. Add crumbs at that time, then bake.

MRS. PHILIP KNOX
Woodinville, Washington

Turkey Tetrazzini

- 1/4 cup butter
- 3/4 lb. mushrooms, sliced
- 1/2 small green pepper, slivered
- 3 tbsp. flour
- 2 tsp. salt
- 1/4 tsp. pepper
- 2 1/2 cups light cream
- 4 cups diced cooked turkey
- 2 tbsp. sherry
- 2 pimientos, chopped
- 2 egg yolks, beaten
- 1 package (6 oz.) fine spaghetti, cooked
- Grated Parmesan cheese

SERVES 6

Heat butter and sauté mushrooms and green pepper 5 minutes. Stir in flour, salt and pepper. Add cream and cook over low heat until sauce has thickened. Add turkey, sherry and pimientos. When warm, remove from heat. Combine turkey mixture with egg yolks and mix well.

Place spaghetti in a well-buttered shallow baking dish. Pour turkey mixture over spaghetti and sprinkle with cheese. Bake in a preheated 300° oven 45 minutes. Just before serving, brown under broiler.

MRS. JOHN MARTINO
Palm Desert, California

Cornish Hens à la Carnwarth

- 1/2 cup butter
- 2 cups quartered or sliced mushrooms
- 1/4 cup flour
- 2 cups warm chicken broth
- Salt and pepper
- Cayenne pepper
- 2 packages (8 oz. each) cream cheese, softened
- 1 cup medium dry sherry
- 4 cups cooked noodles
- 8 cups cubed cooked Rock Cornish game hens or chicken
- 1 small jar pimientos, diced
- 12 pitted ripe olives, cut in half
- 3/4 cup slivered almonds

SERVES ABOUT 10

Melt half the butter in a saucepan. Add mushrooms and cook 5 minutes, tossing constantly. Remove from pan and set aside. Add remaining butter to the pan; when melted, stir in flour to make a roux. Remove from heat and, using a whisk, beat in warmed broth. Bring to a boil, stirring constantly. Reduce heat and simmer over low heat 5 minutes, stirring occasionally. Add seasonings. Beat in cream cheese, a little at a time, until thoroughly blended. Stir in sherry.

Mix one-third of the sauce with the noodles and place in a large buttered casserole. Arrange meat on noodles. Combine pimientos, olives and 1/2 cup of the almonds; sprinkle over meat. Pour remaining sauce over all. Sprinkle with remaining almonds. Place in a preheated 350° oven and heat thoroughly, 20 to 30 minutes.

MRS. EDWARD MARSHALL BOEHM
Trenton, New Jersey

Duck à l'Orange

FOR EACH DUCKLING:
2 cups parboiled rice (wild rice or mixture of wild and white)
About ½ cup chopped onion
About ½ cup diced dried apricots
Dry vermouth or white wine
Salt
1½ cups orange juice
2 seedless oranges, peeled and broken into segments

Combine rice, onion and apricots. Add enough dry vermouth to moisten, then mix.

Salt cavity of duck and stuff with rice mixture. Place stuffed duck, breast side up, on a rack in an uncovered roaster. Roast in a preheated 325° oven 45 minutes per pound for a 3- to 4¼-pound duck; roast 40 minutes per pound for a 4¼- to 5-pound duck.

Baste duck every 10 minutes with freshly squeezed orange juice (at least 1½ cups per duck). Thirty minutes before duck is done, drain off fat from pan. Ten minutes before duck is done, add orange segments.

MARY LIVINGSTONE and JACK BENNY
Beverly Hills, California

Wild Duck

1 medium wild duck
½ tsp. poultry seasoning
½ tsp. MSG
½ tsp. basil
⅛ tsp. garlic powder
½ onion
Rind of ½ lemon
½ cup lemon juice
½ cup soy sauce
½ cup dry sherry
Additional MSG
Celery salt
Pepper
Paprika

SERVES 1 OR MORE

Prepare duck for cooking (be sure to remove oil sac under tail). Combine poultry seasoning, ½ teaspoon MSG, the basil and garlic powder; use to dust cavity of duck. Put onion and lemon rind in cavity and skewer openings. Blend lemon juice, soy sauce and sherry for a marinade. Put duck and marinade in a large plastic bag and marinate at least 4 hours.

Just before roasting, remove duck from marinade and sprinkle with MSG, celery salt, pepper and a heavy layer of paprika. (The paprika makes the skin crisp.) Fill cavity with marinade and place duck on a rack in a roasting pan. Roast in a very hot oven (about 475°) 25 to 30 minutes for medium rare.

MRS. JAMES D. GARIBALDI
Palm Springs, California

Roast Wild Duck

1 wild duck (2 to 3 lb.)
1 tbsp. salt
1 tsp. pepper
1 medium onion
1 stalk celery
½ cup red wine
Cornstarch

SERVES 2

Prepare duck for cooking. Put salt, pepper, onion and celery in cavity. Skewer openings. Place breast down in roasting pan (do not cover). Brown in a preheated 450° oven 45 minutes. Add enough water to cover the duck halfway. Add wine and cover pan. Reduce temperature to 350° and roast 3 hours, adding water as necessary to maintain the same level in pan.

To make gravy, remove duck and thicken liquid with cornstarch.

MRS. ROBERT RAIBLE
Gilbert, Louisiana

Ontario Northland Railway Roast Wild Goose

1 wild goose
8 qt. skim milk
1 tbsp. salt
1 tsp. baking soda

DRESSING
8 to 10 slices dry bread
3 slices bacon, diced and fried
3 stalks celery, diced
1 small apple, diced
¼ green pepper, diced
¼ onion, diced
½ cup butter, melted
¼ tsp. mace

SERVES 5 (ABOUT 1 SERVING PER POUND)

Prepare goose for cooking (be sure to remove oil sac under tail). Soak goose overnight at room temperature in a mixture of milk, salt and soda.

To make dressing, mix remaining ingredients and let stand 1 hour. Lightly stuff goose and skewer openings. Place in a roasting pan; cover and roast in a preheated 250° oven 4 hours. Raise temperature to 350°. Remove cover and roast 30 minutes longer or until brown.

Serve with spiced peaches or pears.

SGT. JOHN MOANEY
Gettysburg, Pennsylvania

NOTE: Sgt. Moaney first became associated with General Eisenhower on September 1, 1942, and thereafter accompanied him throughout the European theater during World War II, then to Columbia University and the White House. Sgt. and Mrs. Moaney were always with General and Mrs. Eisenhower at their Palm Desert home in the winter months, and they are still employed by Mrs. Eisenhower on the farm in Gettysburg. Mrs. Moaney has been with the family for 26 years.

General Eisenhower's Quail Hash

Quail
Onion
Salt and pepper
Good chicken broth
Flour

1 QUAIL PER SERVING

Prepare quail for cooking (use whatever number of quail seems sufficient for the company). Put quail into a large saucepan and generously cover with water. Add onion and salt. Poach slowly 10 to 15 minutes or until meat can be removed easily from bones. Remove quail from saucepan and dice meat. Season with salt and pepper.

Meanwhile, make a gravy with chicken broth and flour. Pour over diced quail. Reheat, if necessary, before serving.

MAMIE DOUD EISENHOWER
Gettysburg, Pennsylvania

General Joyce's Quail

4 quail*
Light cream
Flour
Salt and pepper
Butter
1 cup beef broth
2 tbsp. Worcestershire sauce
2 tbsp. lemon juice
Onion salt
1 cup sour cream

SERVES 4

Prepare quail for cooking. Dip quail in cream, then roll in a mixture of flour, salt and pepper. Heat butter in a pan with a tight cover and lightly brown quail on all sides. Mix broth, Worcestershire sauce, lemon juice and a little onion salt. Pour over birds. Cover tightly and simmer very slowly 1 hour or until tender.

Remove birds to a hot serving platter. Add sour cream to sauce in pan and blend well, stirring until hot (do not boil). Pour sauce over birds and serve with wild or white rice.

* You may substitute 1 pheasant for the 4 quail in this recipe; cut into pieces as you would a frying chicken.

MRS. KENYON JOYCE
San Francisco, California

FISH & SEAFOOD

A Catch of Prizes

Coddled in cream and wine, baked with bacon, simmered with
peppers, oregano and other good things Italian—
here's sumptuous fare indeed for devotees of fish and seafood.
Fresh from the wharf or via the fish market,
these gifts of sea and stream show that you
put extra care into planning the meal.
Proffer a chilled fish mousse at lunch, oyster stew
for a midnight supper, the regal lobster anytime—see how friends
and family welcome the refreshing change.

Paupiettes de Sole Dugléré

ROLLED FILLETS OF SOLE WITH TOMATOES

Salt and pepper
18 to 20 shallots or green onions, finely chopped
8 fresh or thawed frozen sole fillets (about 2 lb.)
Freshly ground white pepper
4 large ripe tomatoes, peeled, seeded and chopped
1 cup minced parsley
1½ cups dry white wine
1 cup water
4 tbsp. flour
½ cup butter or margarine, melted
1 cup light cream
3 egg yolks, beaten
2 tbsp. cognac

SERVES 8

Butter the bottom of a heavy, shallow, flameproof baking dish, about 14x10 inches. Sprinkle with salt and pepper, and scatter some shallots over the bottom. Set aside.

If fillets are not halved, cut in half, following the backbone "seam." Pull fillets apart and remove the string. To make each *paupiette,* roll each strip of sole lengthwise, starting at the small end, into a tight cylinder. Fasten with toothpicks. Stand each *paupiette* upright in the baking dish. Scatter remaining shallots over fish. Sprinkle with salt and white pepper. Add tomatoes and half the parsley. Mix wine and water and add to dish. Butter a piece of waxed paper and lay over the top of the baking dish, buttered side down.

Place over high heat and bring to a boil, then place in a preheated 400° oven. Leave in oven 10 to 12 minutes, or just long enough to flake the sole. Remove from oven and discard toothpicks. Remove *paupiettes* to a serving platter. Cover them with additional waxed paper and keep warm.

Pour broth from baking dish into a saucepan. Bring to a rolling boil and reduce by one-third. Blend flour with half the butter and add to broth bit by bit, whipping constantly with a wire whisk. Cook about 10 minutes, until slightly thickened. Add ¾ cup of the cream and bring to a boil. Combine egg yolks and remaining cream. Add to the hot broth, whipping constantly. Add cognac. Beat in remaining butter. Pour sauce over fish and sprinkle with remaining parsley.

MRS. W. CALDER McCALL
Portland, Oregon

Poached Sole in Wine

2 lb. fresh sole
1 cup dry white wine
1½ tbsp. lemon juice
Salt
6 to 8 fresh mushrooms, sliced, or 1 can (4 oz.) sliced mushrooms, drained
Butter
2 egg yolks, slightly beaten
1 cup warm light cream
1 tbsp. chopped parsley
¼ to ½ cup slivered blanched almonds, browned in butter

SERVES 4

Poach fish in a mixture of wine, lemon juice and salt 8 to 10 minutes. While fish cooks, sauté mushrooms in a little butter and set aside. Remove sole to a covered dish and keep warm. Simmer the poaching liquid 10 minutes longer. Combine egg yolks and cream in a bowl and slowly pour the hot poaching liquid into them, beating constantly. Stir in sautéed mushrooms and parsley. Pour sauce over sole, garnish with almonds and serve on hot plates.

Any mild white fish can be used in this recipe; Mahi Mahi (dolphin) is especially good.

MRS. LAMBERT L. NAGLER
Eugene, Oregon

Fillets of Sole with Bananas

4 large sole fillets
Flour
Salt and pepper
Paprika
¼ cup butter
½ cup dry sherry or dry white wine
2 tbsp. lemon juice
2 tbsp. brown sugar
½ tsp. ginger
2 bananas, quartered lengthwise
Toasted slivered almonds

SERVES 4

Dust fillets with a mixture of flour, salt, pepper and paprika. Melt butter in a large skillet. Brown fillets 2 to 3 minutes on each side, until golden and flaky. Remove to a heated platter. Drain skillet of all but 2 to 3 tablespoons butter. Add sherry, lemon juice, brown sugar, ginger and bananas. Simmer 2 minutes. Arrange bananas around fish. Pour sauce over all and sprinkle with almonds.

VELMA DAWSON
Palm Springs, California

Sole-Shrimp Casserole

2 lb. fresh or thawed frozen sole fillets
2 cans (10¾ oz. each) condensed cream of shrimp soup
2 tbsp. sherry
1 cup bread crumbs
¼ cup grated Parmesan cheese
1 tsp. seasoned salt

SERVES 6

Place half the sole in a buttered baking dish. Mix soup and sherry. Cover sole with half the soup mixture. Top with remaining fish and soup mixture. Sprinkle with crumbs, cheese and seasoned salt. Bake, uncovered, in a preheated 375° oven 1 hour.

JOHN ROSENKRANS
Seneca Falls, New York

Mr. Rosenkrans is the president of Eisenhower College.

Flounder en Papillote

1 onion, finely chopped
½ cup butter
3 to 4 tbsp. flour
1½ cups milk, scalded
¼ tsp. nutmeg
1 tbsp. Worcestershire sauce
Salt and pepper
2 eggs, beaten
1 oz. white wine or dry sherry
½ lb. cooked shrimp, chopped
½ lb. cooked crabmeat, flaked
Melted butter
4 whole flounder fillets, cut in half

SERVES 4

Sauté onion in butter until soft. Slowly blend in flour and cook until dry. Add milk, nutmeg, Worcestershire sauce, salt and pepper. Cook, stirring, over low heat until blended. Add eggs and cook slowly, stirring, until thickened. Remove from heat and add wine, shrimp and crabmeat. Adjust seasoning.

Cut four 10-inch squares of parchment paper or foil and brush with melted butter. Spoon 2 tablespoons sauce on one square. Top with one flounder fillet half. Add more sauce, another fillet and more sauce. Repeat layers on remaining squares, dividing the sauce and fillets evenly. Bring two opposite sides of the square together and fold up; then seal ends. Place on a baking sheet. If using parchment paper (not foil), brush paper again with melted butter. Bake in a preheated 350° oven 35 minutes. Serve directly from the bags: simply open and fold back edges.

MRS. WILLIAM R. YANCEY
Indian Wells, California

Fish Mousse with Horseradish Sauce

4 cups water
2 tbsp. white wine vinegar
2 tsp. salt
Black peppercorns
2 onions, chopped
2 carrots, chopped
2 stalks celery, finely chopped
1 lb. halibut fillets
1 lb. shrimp, shelled and deveined
2 tbsp. unflavored gelatin
¾ cup mayonnaise
1 cup whipping cream
Large whole shrimp for garnishing (optional)

HORSERADISH SAUCE
1 cup whipped cream
1 tbsp. prepared horseradish
1 tbsp. chili sauce
1 tbsp. mayonnaise

SERVES 6–8

Combine water, vinegar, salt and peppercorns and bring to a boil. Add vegetables and cook. When almost done, add fish and shrimp. Reduce heat and poach about 10 minutes, until fish breaks at the touch of a fork. Cool, then strain liquid. Flake fish. Chop shrimp if large. Set seafood aside.

Heat half the strained stock. Soften gelatin in remaining stock; when dissolved, combine stocks and chill. When the aspic has thickened slightly, add mayonnaise and beat until frothy. Add fish and shrimp. Whip cream and fold in. Adjust seasoning. Pour into a well-greased 6- to 8-cup ring mold or 6 to 8 individual molds. Chill.

Serve with Horseradish Sauce. Use as a first course for dinner, or as a luncheon main dish. If desired, garnish mousse with large whole shrimp.

To make the Horseradish Sauce, mix ingredients and chill until ready to serve.

MRS. A. R. SIMON
Palm Springs, California

Halibut in White Wine Sauce

- 1 thick halibut steak (about 1½ lb.), seasoned
- 2 slices lemon
- 2 slices onion
- 2 cloves
- 4 tbsp. butter
- 4 tbsp. flour
- 1 tsp. salt
- ¼ tsp. pepper
- ¾ cup white wine
- 1 tsp. Worcestershire sauce
- 12 small cooked shrimp or 1 can (3 oz.) sliced mushrooms, drained
- Chopped parsley
- Mashed potatoes

SERVES 2–3

Place seasoned halibut in a casserole. Add lemon, onion, cloves and enough water to barely cover fish (about 2 cups). Cook, uncovered, in a preheated 425° oven 20 minutes. Remove fish. Reduce oven temperature to moderate (350° to 375°). Strain fish stock, reserving 1½ cups.

Melt butter in a saucepan. Add flour, salt and pepper and mix well. Add the reserved stock, the wine and Worcestershire sauce. Bring to a boil, stirring constantly.

Break fish into small pieces and place in a buttered shallow baking dish. Add shrimp and parsley. Pour sauce over. Decorate with mashed potatoes and bake, uncovered, 30 minutes.

MRS. ROBERT CROOKER
Palm Desert, California

Curried Salmon Steaks

- ¾ cup finely chopped onions
- 8 tbsp. butter
- 6 salmon steaks
- Flour
- Salt and pepper
- Curry powder
- 1 cup sour cream

SERVES 6

In a large skillet, sauté onions in 4 tablespoons of the butter until transparent. Remove onions and set aside. Melt remaining butter in the skillet. Sprinkle salmon steaks with flour, salt, pepper and a generous amount of curry powder (use less if you prefer a milder flavor). Sauté steaks, turning once, until they break at the touch of a fork. Remove to a warm serving platter.

Return onions to skillet. Add 1 tablespoon curry powder and mix well. Gradually stir in sour cream. Heat sauce but do not allow to boil. Pour sauce over steaks and serve immediately.

MRS. ALBERT J. LILYGREN
Kirkland, Washington

Albacore Creolla

1 albacore (8 to 10 lb.)
2 cups dry white wine
4 tbsp. olive oil
2 tbsp. halved mushrooms
2 tbsp. finely chopped onions
2 tbsp. chopped ripe olives
1 tbsp. chopped green pepper
1 tbsp. Worcestershire sauce
Juice of 1 lime or ½ lemon
2 tsp. oregano, thyme or basil
3 dashes Tabasco sauce
Garlic salt
Freshly ground black pepper
Chopped parsley
4 bay leaves
1 cup mayonnaise

SERVES 10–12

"When your husband lands an atunito *(in other words, an albacore), you can surprise him with this delicious, albeit perhaps a bit 'drunken,' fish."*

Skin fish and prepare for cooking. Place on a rack in a large roasting pan with a tight-fitting lid. Add wine, cover tightly and steam on top of stove or in a preheated 450° oven 15 minutes *after* wine starts bubbling.

While fish steams, combine all remaining ingredients except bay leaves and mayonnaise. After fish has steamed 15 minutes, remove cover and spread mixture over fish. Arrange bay leaves on the fish, cover and bake in a preheated 450° oven 1 hour. Baste every 10 minutes (let your guests take turns; they'll enjoy it).

When fish is done, remove carefully to a serving platter. Discard bay leaves. Add mayonnaise to juices in roaster. Blend well and serve over fish.

NOTE: For a 20-pound fish, use 3 cups wine and increase other ingredients accordingly; bake 1½ hours.

BILLIE DOVE MILLER
Palm Springs, California

Fish Cakes

1 lb. salt cod
4 cups hot mashed potatoes
2 eggs
¼ cup heavy cream
1 tbsp. butter
Dash of pepper
Oil for deep-frying

SERVES 6

Soak codfish in cold water 8 hours or overnight, changing the water occasionally; drain. Add fresh water to cover, bring to a boil and simmer, covered, 15 minutes. Drain and shred fish and mix with mashed potatoes. Then add eggs, cream, butter and pepper; mix well. Drop by spoonfuls into hot oil (380°) and fry 2 to 5 minutes. Drain on paper towels. Serve immediately.

MRS. JOHN H. WHITNEY
New York, New York

Baked Fish Dinner

1 whole fish (3 to 4 lb.)—bass, trout, etc.
Salt
1 carrot
1 medium onion, grated
1 cup sour cream
1 cup rice
1 package (10 oz.) frozen green peas

SERVES 4–6

Thoroughly scale and clean fish. Remove head and fins with kitchen shears. Salt fish lightly inside and out. Place the carrot in the cavity and pin the opening with a skewer so that the fish will hold its shape. Place in a buttered shallow baking dish. Combine onion and sour cream and spread generously (about 1/4 inch thick) all over fish. Bake, uncovered, in a preheated 375° oven 12 minutes to the pound (do not overcook).

While fish is baking, cook rice until dry and fluffy. Cook peas according to the package directions. When the fish is done, remove to a platter and arrange the peas and rice at one end of the dish. Serve at once.

JACQUELINE COCHRAN ODLUM
Indio, California

Byers Peak Ranch Trout

1 small whole trout (not more than 10 in. long), cleaned
2 slices bacon
2 to 3 tbsp. condensed cream of mushroom soup

SERVES 1

"This was one of General Eisenhower's favorite dishes when he stayed at my ranch. It is indeed delicious."

Dip trout in hot water 1 minute. With a dull knife, cut off the two sides, making fillets. On a large piece of foil, place 1 slice of bacon and top with 1 fillet. Spread on the mushroom soup. Put on the remaining fillet and another slice of bacon. Fold up the foil and seal edges. Put the package on a charcoal fire and roast about 4 minutes, turning once.

AKSEL NIELSEN
Denver, Colorado

Prawn Madras Curry

1 tbsp. coriander
1 tsp. turmeric
½ tsp. dry mustard
½ tsp. ginger
½ tsp. cumin
½ tsp. coarse red chile pepper
Lemon juice, tamarind juice or vinegar
2 cloves garlic, minced
1 small onion, chopped
Ghee or butter
12 to 18 shelled cooked prawns or large shrimp
1 tbsp. thick coconut milk*
Grated coconut

SERVES 4–6

Blend the first 6 ingredients with just enough lemon juice to make a paste. Let this curry paste set to develop all the flavors while you prepare the prawn mixture. (The composition of the paste may be varied to taste by using minced fresh chiles instead of dried, or by using a flavored vinegar.)

Sauté garlic and onion 3 minutes in a little *ghee* (preferably) or butter. Add the curry paste and simmer gently over low heat 4 to 5 minutes. Add prawns and coconut milk. Continue to cook, stirring lightly, just until seafood is warmed through and liquid is absorbed. Sprinkle with grated coconut and serve with rice.

*COCONUT MILK
If fresh coconuts are handy, the milk can be made as follows. Crack open the coconut and remove the dark outer skin. Cut the white meat into small pieces. Put in a blender with a little water and whirl until finely chopped (you can also grate the meat by hand). One good-sized coconut yields about 3 cups grated meat. Wrap 3 cups of the chopped or grated coconut in cheesecloth and place in a strainer over a large, deep bowl. Pour 1 quart hot water over the wrapped coconut. Let drain 10 minutes; then, into another bowl, squeeze out milk through the cheesecloth.

If available, frozen fresh grated coconut or frozen coconut milk may be used.

Canned coconut contains sugar, so if used in place of fresh, the sweetness must be taken into account lest it change the flavor of the dish. To make an acceptable milk from canned coconut, combine 2 cans coconut with 1½ cups whole milk. Gradually bring to a boil, then remove from heat and let stand until cool. Strain through at least two layers of cheesecloth, squeezing out the liquid.

MRS. GERALD R. FORD
Washington, D.C.

Barbecued Shrimp Scampi Style

- 2 lb. jumbo shrimp (allow 4 or 5 per person)
- 2 to 4 cloves garlic, minced
- 1 tbsp. salt
- ¼ cup minced parsley
- 1 cup high-quality Italian olive oil
- 1 to 2 tbsp. lemon juice

SERVES 4

Using scissors, cut shrimp shells up the back and remove vein (do not remove shells). Place in a shallow glass dish. Crush garlic into salt and parsley. Combine with olive oil and lemon juice and pour over shrimp. Marinate in refrigerator 2 hours.

To cook, place shrimp in a hinged grill and barbecue over a low fire 4 or 5 minutes, turning once. Serve in their shells with Fettucine Alfredo and grilled herbed tomatoes or eggplant.

Variation: For an alternate marinade, combine ⅓ cup each of soy sauce, dry sherry and peanut oil. Stir in grated fresh ginger and minced garlic (optional) to taste. Serve with fried rice.

WILLIAM O. FLEETWOOD
Indian Wells, California

Shrimp de Jonghe

- 1 clove garlic
- ¾ cup butter, at room temperature
- 1 tbsp. chopped onions
- 1 tbsp. chopped parsley
- ¼ cup dry sherry
- Paprika
- Salt
- 24 large shrimp, cooked, shelled and deveined
- 1 cup dry bread crumbs

SERVES 4–6

Crush garlic to a pulp in butter. Heat until melted, then remove from heat. Add onions, parsley, sherry, paprika and a little salt. Toss shrimp in this mixture to coat well. Arrange in 4 to 6 buttered individual shells or ramekins or in a buttered shallow casserole. Sprinkle crumbs on top. Bake, uncovered, in a preheated 350° oven 20 minutes or until heated through.

MRS. CHARLES R. HOPSON
Cathedral City, California

Shrimp Amandine

- 3/4 cup rice
- 2 lb. shrimp, shelled and deveined
- 1/4 cup chopped green pepper
- 1/4 cup chopped onion
- 2 tbsp. butter or margarine
- 1 can (10 3/4 oz.) condensed cream of tomato soup
- 1 cup light cream
- 1/2 cup dry sherry
- 1/2 cup sliced blanched almonds
- 1 tsp. salt
- 1/8 tsp. pepper
- 1/8 tsp. mace
- Paprika
- Melon balls (optional)
- Watercress (optional)

SERVES 6–8

Cook rice as directed on package. Simmer shrimp, covered, in salted boiling water 5 minutes; drain. Reserve a few whole shrimp for garnish; split remaining shrimp in half (down their backs).

Sauté green pepper and onion in hot butter 5 minutes. Combine with soup, cream, sherry, half the almonds, the salt, pepper, mace, shrimp and rice. Mix and place in a buttered 1 1/2-quart casserole. Top with remaining almonds and sprinkle with paprika. Bake, uncovered, in a preheated 350° oven 30 minutes. Top with reserved whole shrimp and bake 10 minutes longer. If desired, garnish individual servings with melon balls and watercress.

This dish may be prepared a day ahead; do not combine shrimp or rice with other ingredients until ready to bake.

MRS. JACK L. HARGAN
Cathedral City, California

Gumbo Delight

- 4 cups fresh black-eyed peas
- 4 to 6 thin slices pork fat
- Salt and pepper
- 2 tbsp. butter
- 2 tbsp. bacon drippings
- 2 medium onions, finely chopped
- 1 lb. fresh okra, thinly sliced
- 2 1/2 cups canned tomatoes, chopped
- 2 1/2 cups canned cream-style corn
- 2 1/2 lb. fresh shrimp, cooked, shelled and deveined
- Shrimp for garnishing (optional)

SERVES 8–12

Bring 2 quarts water to a boil. Add peas and salt pork. Cook, covered, over low heat until tender, about 1 hour. Skim if necessary. During cooking, taste liquid for salt; add if needed. When peas are done, drain in colander. Discard salt pork and set peas aside.

While peas are cooking, heat butter and bacon drippings. Sauté onions and okra until onions are golden brown. Add tomatoes and simmer 5 minutes. Add corn and cooked peas. Season to taste. Return to a simmer, add shrimp and cook just long enough to heat through. Garnish with additional shrimp, if desired.

MRS. POLLARD SIMONS
Dallas, Texas

Lobster Cardinal

Water (enough to cover)
6 lobsters (1½ lb. each)
12 tbsp. butter or margarine
4 tbsp. flour
1½ tsp. salt
2 tbsp. dry white wine
4 tbsp. chopped canned mushrooms
Grated Parmesan cheese

SERVES 6

Bring water to a rapid boil in a very large kettle and drop in lobsters. When water returns to a boil, cook lobsters 15 minutes. Remove from water and cool. Boil the water rapidly until reduced to 2 cups; set aside. Place each lobster on its back and, with a sharp knife, cut through the soft underside the entire length of the body. Remove and discard the stomach portion, which is under the head. Remove meat from claws and body and cut into 1-inch pieces. Place body shells in a shallow baking pan.

Melt 4 tablespoons of the butter in a saucepan. Add flour and salt and blend. Gradually add the 2 cups liquid, stirring constantly until smooth and thickened. Cook 15 minutes, stirring frequently. Add wine and mushrooms, then remaining butter, a little at a time.

Spread a little sauce in the bottom of each shell. Add lobster meat. Top with remaining sauce and sprinkle with cheese. Place pan 3 to 4 inches from heat in a preheated broiler. Broil about 5 minutes, until mixture is hot and lightly browned.

JACQUELINE KENNEDY ONASSIS
New York, New York

Lobster Stew

2 chicken lobsters (¾ to 1¼ lb. each)
½ cup butter
4 cups light cream
Salt and freshly ground black pepper

SERVES 4

Boil lobsters 10 to 15 minutes. Immediately remove meat from shells and cut into fairly large pieces.

Melt butter in a saucepan. Add lobster meat and cook, stirring, over low heat 8 minutes. Remove from heat and cool slightly. Very slowly add cream, stirring constantly. Add salt and pepper.

Let stew stand in refrigerator 24 hours before serving. Reheat over low heat, stirring constantly (do not boil).

This recipe may be modified for more or fewer people: Allow ½ chicken lobster per person and proportionately increase or decrease other ingredients.

AMBASSADOR and MRS. C. DOUGLAS DILLON
New York, New York

Lobster Tails Fra Diavolo

12 littleneck clams
2 lobster tails (12 oz. each), shelled
¼ cup olive oil
2 cloves garlic
3 oz. white wine
2 lb. tomatoes, peeled and chopped (or crushed in blender)
½ tsp. salt
½ tsp. oregano
¼ tsp. crushed dried red pepper
Chopped parsley

SERVES 4

Scrub clams under cold water. Cut lobster meat into medallions 2 inches thick.

Heat oil in a deep skillet. Add garlic and lobster medallions to pan and cook gently until garlic browns, turning lobster once. Discard garlic. Add wine and simmer 2 minutes. Add tomatoes, salt, oregano and red pepper. Cover and cook over medium heat 15 to 20 minutes. Add clams. Cover and cook until clams open, about 7 to 10 minutes longer. Sprinkle with parsley.

Serve with linguini on the side, using any extra sauce on the pasta.

MRS. WILLIAM SORRENTINO
Palm Springs, California

Lobster Quiche

- 4 oz. Swiss cheese, shredded
- 4 oz. Gruyère cheese, shredded
- 1 tbsp. flour
- 3 eggs
- 1 cup light cream
- ½ tsp. prepared mustard
- ¼ tsp. salt
- Pepper
- ¼ tsp. Worcestershire sauce
- Tabasco sauce
- 1 unbaked pie shell
- 1 can (about 7 oz.) lobster or crabmeat, drained and flaked

SERVES 6

Mix cheeses and flour; set aside. Beat eggs; blend in cream, mustard, salt, pepper, Worcestershire sauce and Tabasco sauce. Put about three-fourths of the cheese mixture in the pie shell. Add a layer of the lobster, followed by remaining cheese mixture. Pour egg mixture over all and bake, uncovered, in a preheated 400° oven 30 minutes or until custard is set.

MRS. J. EARLE BROWN
Fort Worth, Texas

Coquilles St. Jacques

- 1 lb. fresh mushrooms, sliced
- 5 tbsp. butter
- 1 lb. scallops
- ¾ cup dry vermouth
- ¼ cup water
- 1 bay leaf
- ½ tsp. salt
- 3 tbsp. flour
- 1 cup light cream
- Buttered bread crumbs

SERVES 6

Sauté mushrooms rapidly in 2 tablespoons of the butter and set aside. Combine scallops, vermouth, water, bay leaf and salt in a saucepan and bring to a boil. Reduce heat, cover and simmer 5 minutes. Drain scallops, reserving 1 cup of the broth. Discard bay leaf. Cut scallops into quarters.

Make a white sauce of the remaining 3 tablespoons butter, the flour, reserved broth and cream. Add mushrooms and scallops and spoon into 6 scallop shells. Top with bread crumbs and bake, uncovered, in a preheated 400° oven 10 minutes.

ADMIRAL and MRS. ARTHUR RADFORD
Washington, D.C.

Deviled Crab

½ cup minced onion
¼ cup minced celery
¼ cup minced green pepper
1 clove garlic, minced
1 tbsp. chopped parsley
8 tbsp. butter
2 cups soft bread crumbs
½ cup heavy cream
2 eggs, beaten
1 hard-boiled egg, minced
1 tbsp. white wine vinegar
1 tsp. Worcestershire sauce
1 tsp. salt
¼ tsp. thyme
Tabasco sauce
1 lb. lump crabmeat

SERVES 6

Sauté onion, celery, green pepper, garlic and parsley in 6 tablespoons of the butter for 10 minutes. Cool. Combine 1 cup of the bread crumbs, the cream, beaten eggs, hard-boiled egg, vinegar, Worcestershire sauce, salt, thyme, and a few drops of Tabasco sauce (or more, to taste) with sautéed vegetables. Add crabmeat and toss lightly to mix. Spoon into 12 scallop shells or 6 lightly buttered individual baking dishes.

Melt the remaining 2 tablespoons butter and toss with remaining 1 cup bread crumbs. Top crab mixture with the buttered crumbs. Place shells in a shallow baking pan, with ¼ inch water in pan. Bake in a preheated 450° oven 10 minutes or until browned.

This recipe may also be used for a casserole.

MRS. ROBERT HAYNIE
Hillsborough, California

Deviled Crab Winner

1 can (10¾ oz.) condensed cream of mushroom soup
2 cans (about 6½ oz. each) crabmeat, drained
4 hard-boiled eggs, chopped
1 cup cracker crumbs
1 tbsp. Worcestershire sauce
1 tbsp. chopped parsley
2 tbsp. butter, melted
2½ tsp. prepared mustard
Salt
Cayenne pepper
Paprika
Grated cheddar cheese
Tartar sauce

SERVES 8

Combine soup, crabmeat, eggs, crumbs, Worcestershire sauce, parsley, half the butter and 1½ teaspoons of the mustard. Add seasonings to taste and mix. Fill 8 individual shells. Sprinkle with cheese. Mix remaining butter and mustard and dot cheese with mixture. Bake in a preheated 350° oven about 30 minutes. Serve with tartar sauce.

MRS. DEAN W. MILLER
Palm Desert, California

Crab Mayonnaise Casserole

- 2 cups mayonnaise
- 2 cups half-and-half
- 8 slices sandwich bread, trimmed and cubed
- 3 lb. crabmeat
- 12 hard-boiled eggs, quartered
- 1 can (4 oz.) sliced mushrooms, drained
- 1 can (5 oz.) water chestnuts, drained and sliced
- 2 tbsp. minced onion
- 2 tbsp. chopped green pepper
- 1 jar (2 oz.) pimientos, drained and diced
- ¼ cup dry sherry
- Crushed corn chips

SERVES 10

Blend mayonnaise and half-and-half in a bowl. Add remaining ingredients except corn chips; mix gently. Turn into a 3-quart casserole. Cover and refrigerate overnight.

Before baking, bring casserole to room temperature. Top with crushed corn chips. Bake, uncovered, in a preheated 325° oven 1 hour. Serve with rice.

JULIE NIXON EISENHOWER
Washington, D.C.

Crab Casserole Céleste

- 8 slices bread, trimmed
- 2 cups crabmeat
- ½ cup mayonnaise
- 1 onion, minced
- 1 green pepper, minced
- 1 cup minced celery
- 4 eggs
- 3 cups milk
- 1 can (10¾ oz.) condensed cream of mushroom soup
- Grated cheese

SERVES 6

Butter a large casserole and arrange half the bread in the bottom. Mix crabmeat, mayonnaise and vegetables. Turn into the casserole and cover with remaining bread. Beat eggs slightly, mix with milk and pour over all. Refrigerate, covered, until ready to bake. (The casserole really should be mixed the night before, though early in the morning will do.)

Bake, uncovered, in a preheated 325° oven 15 minutes. Remove and cover with undiluted soup. Sprinkle top with cheese and bake 1 hour longer.

MRS. JOHN J. CONWAY
Sutter, Alaska

For the Outdoor Gourmet—As an appetizer or main course, try Barbecued Shrimp Scampi Style (page 110).

A Patio Supper—For good times with good friends and hearty appetites: San Francisco Cioppino (page 121).

Cold Crab Soufflé

- 1 lb. crabmeat
- 1 tbsp. unflavored gelatin
- ½ cup cold water
- 1 cup milk
- 4 eggs, separated
- 2 tbsp. flour
- 1 tbsp. minced onion
- 1½ tsp. lemon juice
- 1 tsp. grated lemon rind
- ½ tsp. Worcestershire sauce
- 1 tsp. salt
- ⅛ tsp. pepper
- ⅛ tsp. dry mustard
- ½ cup sour cream
- Crabmeat for garnish
- Lemon slices

SERVES 8

Remove cartilage from crabmeat and place crab in refrigerator to chill.

Meanwhile, soften gelatin in cold water in the top of a double boiler. Add milk, egg yolks, flour, onion, lemon juice, lemon rind, Worcestershire sauce, salt, pepper and mustard. Blend well. Place over boiling water and cook, stirring constantly, until sauce is thickened. Remove from heat and cool. Chill, stirring now and then, until mixture mounds on a spoon.

Flake chilled crabmeat and combine with half the sour cream (reserve remainder in refrigerator). Beat egg whites until stiff but not dry; fold into chilled gelatin mixture. Gently blend in crabmeat mixture.

Grease a 1-quart soufflé dish. Fold a long strip of waxed paper lengthwise; fasten around dish to extend 2 to 3 inches above the top. Spoon mixture into dish and chill until firm. (A lightly oiled 1½-quart mold may also be used.)

Serve surrounded by chunks of additional crabmeat, lemon slices and remaining sour cream.

MRS. RALPH WAYCOTT
Oceanside, California

Crab Soufflé

1/4 cup butter
3 tbsp. flour
1 cup milk
4 egg yolks, beaten
1/4 cup grated cheddar cheese
1 tsp. salt
Dash of nutmeg
Dash of cayenne pepper
5 egg whites
1/4 tsp. cream of tartar
1 cup flaked fresh crabmeat

SERVES 4

Make a roux with the butter and flour. Add milk and cook, stirring, until thickened. Pour a little of the hot sauce over egg yolks, beating as you pour. Continue to pour sauce over the yolks, beating until well blended. Pour mixture back into saucepan and cook, stirring, over moderate heat until thickened. Stir in cheese, salt, nutmeg and cayenne pepper. Remove from heat and allow to cool slightly.

Beat egg whites with cream of tartar until stiff. Stir crabmeat into sauce. Add about a fourth of the beaten egg whites and beat vigorously. Fold in remaining egg whites.

Add a collar of waxed paper around a greased 1-quart soufflé dish. Pour in mixture. Place in a pan of hot water and bake in a preheated 300° oven about 1 hour.

MRS. JOSEPH HALL
San Marino, California

Deviled Oysters

1 qt. oysters, shucked
1 cup cracker crumbs
2 tbsp. finely chopped parsley
2 tbsp. Worcestershire sauce
2 tbsp. catsup
4 dashes Tabasco sauce
1 tbsp. lemon juice
Salt and pepper
1/2 cup finely chopped celery
1/4 cup minced onion
2 tbsp. olive oil
Fine dry bread crumbs
Butter

SERVES 6

Simmer oysters in their own liquor until the edges curl. Remove from pan with a skimmer or slotted spoon and set aside. Stir cracker crumbs, parsley, Worcestershire sauce, catsup, Tabasco sauce, lemon juice, salt and pepper into oyster liquor.

Sauté celery and onion in the oil, then add to cracker crumb mixture. Fold in oysters and turn into a buttered casserole. Sprinkle with bread crumbs and dot with butter. Bake, uncovered, in a preheated 425° oven about 15 minutes or until oysters are very hot.

MRS. DALE FISCHER
Eugene, Oregon

In Individual Dishes

Baked Seafood Casserole

1 lb. crabmeat
1 lb. cooked shrimp
1 cup mayonnaise
½ cup finely chopped celery
½ cup chopped green pepper
¼ cup minced onion
1 tsp. Worcestershire sauce
½ tsp. salt
2 cups crushed potato chips

SERVES 6 GENEROUSLY

Mix all ingredients except potato chips and turn into a casserole. Top with potato chips. Bake, uncovered, in a preheated 400° oven 20 minutes.

Corn chips or buttered bread crumbs may be substituted for the potato chips.

MAMIE DOUD EISENHOWER
Gettysburg, Pennsylvania

San Francisco Cioppino

½ cup olive oil
1 large onion, minced
½ cup minced celery
½ cup minced green pepper
1 to 3 cloves garlic, minced
2½ cups canned Italian plum tomatoes
1 can (8 oz.) tomato sauce
¼ cup minced parsley
1 tsp. basil
1 tsp. oregano
1 tsp. crushed rosemary
6 black peppercorns, cracked
Salt
Pinch of saffron
1 bottle (8 oz.) clam juice (or 1 cup fish stock, if available)
2 cups dry white wine
1 to 2 lb. fresh or quick-frozen halibut, cod, sea bass or striped bass, cut into 2-inch squares
1 lb. shelled raw shrimp, deveined
1 lb. scrubbed mussels and/or clams in shells
1 to 3 crabs in shells, bodies split and cleaned, claws cracked

SERVES 8

"San Franciscans are justly proud of all the dishes in their fine cuisine, but real 'soul,' to them, is a foggy night, the Wharf, the sourest of sourdough bread, a carafe of California wine and Cioppin' ('Chi-pin'). This flavorsome fish stew was contributed to our western shores by Italian fishermen. As does any good fish stew, it simply makes the most of the best seafood available, and enhances it with a sauce fragrant with garlic and well spiced with Italian seasonings."

Heat oil in a large saucepan and sauté onion, celery, green pepper and garlic 10 minutes. Add tomatoes, tomato sauce, parsley and seasonings. Cover and simmer 1 hour, adding clam juice if mixture becomes too thick. Add wine and cook 10 minutes longer. Adjust seasonings.

Arrange seafood in layers in a deep kettle. Pour boiling sauce over seafood, cover and simmer 20 minutes.

To serve, heap into soup plates and pour sauce over all.

MRS. HARRISON ROBERTS
Indian Wells, California

Neptune's Delight

1 cup dry white wine
1 small onion, thinly sliced
1 tbsp. minced parsley
1 tsp. salt
1 lb. fresh or thawed frozen sea scallops
1 can (3 oz.) broiled sliced mushrooms
4 tbsp. butter
2 tsp. lemon juice
4 tbsp. flour
1 cup light cream
1/3 cup grated Gruyère or good Swiss cheese
Pinch of pepper
1 can (7 oz.) Alaska king crabmeat, drained and flaked
1 can (5 1/2 oz.) shrimp, drained
1 cup buttered soft bread crumbs

SERVES 6–8

Combine wine, onion, parsley and salt in a saucepan; bring to a boil. Reduce heat, add scallops and simmer 5 minutes. Add mushrooms and their liquid, 2 tablespoons of the butter and the lemon juice. Simmer until butter melts. Drain scallops and mushrooms, reserving liquid. Cut scallops in half. Measure liquid and add enough water to make 2 cups.

In another saucepan, melt remaining butter and blend in flour. Add the 2 cups cooking liquid and the cream. Cook and stir over low heat until thickened and smooth. Add cheese and pepper; stir until cheese melts. Stir in scallops, mushrooms, crabmeat and shrimp. Heat to serving temperature. Turn into a buttered shallow 2-quart casserole and sprinkle with crumbs. Brown under broiler.

This dish may be prepared ahead of time and stored in the refrigerator (do not add bread crumbs or biscuits until ready to heat). Bring to room temperature before heating in oven.

Variation: Omit bread crumbs. Arrange tiny, bite-size unbaked biscuits around edge of casserole. Do not broil, but place in a preheated 375° oven just long enough to bake biscuits.

MRS. WILLIAM JUVONEN
Indian Wells, California

EGGS & CHEESE

Light, Lively, Utterly Delicious

Variety is the nice of life here! Eggs and cheese are
the basic ingredients, but how differently
they present themselves. Some brunch it, some lunch it.
Some stand up as superb hors d'oeuvres.
Think of these when you need a hot item to boost the buffet
or to star at your next midnight supper.
And be sure to note the Mexican specialties—
they offer plenty of protein . . . and lots of Latin charm.

Cheese Eggs Melchior

Butter
2 eggs
3 tbsp. heavy cream
Salt and pepper
Grated Gruyère cheese

SERVES 1

When tenor Lauritz Melchior was a guest at the Boeseke ranch, he enjoyed preparing breakfast for everyone. This is one of his simple but elegant treatments for eggs.

Melt a little butter in an individual baking dish. Break 2 eggs into the dish and top with 1 tablespoon of the cream; season with salt and pepper. Cover with grated cheese and remaining cream. Place dish in a pan of hot water. Broil until eggs turn golden brown. Insert tip of silver knife in whites to test for doneness (eggs should be on the soft side).

MRS. ELMER BOESEKE, JR.
Lander, Wyoming

Super-Deluxe Omelet

Butter
2 heaping tsp. flour
1½ cups hot light cream or rich milk
¼ tsp. salt
4 tbsp. grated Parmesan cheese
1 large can tuna, drained and flaked
4 tbsp. butter, clarified
Juice of 1 lemon
Grated rind of ½ lemon
10 eggs
Salt and pepper
Dash of cold water
2 tbsp. chopped chives

SERVES 6

Melt 2 heaping teaspoons butter in the top of a double boiler. Blend in flour and cook 2 minutes. Add cream and cook, stirring, until thick. Remove from heat. Add salt, cheese and tuna. Mix well. Cover and place over hot water to keep hot.

Combine clarified butter, lemon juice and rind. Heat and keep warm.

Break eggs into a bowl. Add salt, pepper and cold water and beat with a fork. Heat a little butter in a large omelet pan. When hot, add eggs all at once. Cook over low heat until eggs are set. With a fork, lift omelet so that uncooked eggs will run under and cook.

When eggs are slightly thickened, spread tuna mixture over half the omelet. Raise heat to brown bottom of omelet slightly. Fold plain half of omelet over tuna. Remove omelet, upside down, to a warm serving platter. Pour butter sauce over omelet and sprinkle with chives.

MRS. WILLIAM DEMAREST
Palm Springs, California

Spinach Frittata

3 tbsp. olive oil
½ cup thinly sliced onions
10 eggs
1 cup finely chopped uncooked spinach
⅓ cup grated Parmesan cheese
1 tbsp. chopped parsley
1 small clove garlic, pressed
1 tsp. salt
¼ tsp. pepper

SERVES 6

Heat oil in a heavy, ovenproof 10-inch skillet. Add onions and sauté until tender and golden, about 5 minutes. Combine remaining ingredients in a large bowl and beat with wire whisk or fork until well blended. Turn mixture into skillet on top of onions (do not stir together). Cook over low heat about 3 minutes, lifting from bottom with a spatula as eggs set.

Bake, uncovered, in a preheated 350° oven 10 minutes or until top sets. Remove from oven. With spatula, loosen bottom and side and slide onto a serving platter. Cut into wedges.

MRS. JOSEPH RAPKIN
Milwaukee, Wisconsin

German Pancake Omelet

3 eggs
½ cup light cream
¼ tsp. salt
2 tbsp. butter
2 tbsp. vegetable oil
½ cup butter, melted (keep warm)
Sugar and cinnamon, blended
1 jar (6½ oz.) applesauce, heated

SERVES 1–2

Beat together eggs, cream and salt. Heat a 10-inch ovenproof skillet (preferably iron) until very hot. Add 2 tablespoons butter and the oil. Tilt pan to coat all surfaces, including sides. Pour in eggs and tilt pan until eggs cover bottom and sides. Cook 3 minutes over medium heat, then put immediately into a preheated 400° oven. Bake until pancake puffs very high and is lightly browned, about 5 minutes.

Remove from oven and transfer pancake to a warm plate. Pour some of the melted butter over pancake, then sprinkle with sugar-cinnamon mixture. Spoon on applesauce and roll up. Pour on remaining butter and sprinkle with additional sugar-cinnamon mixture. Serve immediately.

MRS. ALAN LADD
Palm Springs, California

Quiche Lorraine

1 9-inch frozen pie shell
½ cup chopped onions
6 slices bacon, crisply fried and crumbled (reserve fat)
½ lb. (scant) Swiss cheese, shredded
1½ cups light cream
3 eggs, beaten
½ cup diced cooked ham
¾ tsp. salt
Pepper
Cayenne pepper

SERVES 4–6

Bake pie shell in a preheated 400° oven 10 minutes. Remove and set aside. Reduce oven temperature to 375°.

Sauté onions in reserved bacon fat, then drain. Mix well with remaining ingredients and pour into pie shell. Bake 10 minutes. Reduce oven to 325° and bake until quiche is browned and puffed, 30 to 40 minutes. Place on a hot platter. Let stand a few minutes before slicing.

MRS. PHILIP WEST
Palm Desert, California

Quiche Lorraine Monaco

4 slices bacon, fried and crumbled (reserve fat)
1 cup diced cooked ham
1 cup cubed natural Swiss cheese
1 cup light cream
3 eggs, lightly beaten
1 tbsp. butter, diced
½ cup flour
½ tsp. nutmeg
¼ tsp. salt
⅛ tsp. pepper
1 small bottle cap club soda

SERVES 6

Coat a large pie plate with a little of the reserved bacon fat (discard remainder).

Combine all ingredients and mix well. Pour into pie plate. Let set at room temperature 6 hours.

Bake in a preheated 500° oven 15 minutes. Reduce temperature to 350° and bake 10 minutes longer, or until top is golden brown.

Cut into small pieces or cubes, this quiche makes a delicious hors d'oeuvre. (Serves 14 to 18.)

MRS. WILLIAM CASTLEMAN, JR.
Monte Carlo, Monaco

Corn Quiche

- Pastry for 9-inch pie crust
- 1 can (12 oz.) whole-kernel or Mexican-style corn, drained
- 1/4 cup grated Swiss or cheddar cheese
- 5 eggs
- 1 1/2 cups light cream
- 1 small onion, minced
- 1 tsp. seasoned salt
- 1/8 tsp. pepper
- 4 to 6 slices bacon, crisply fried and crumbled

SERVES 6

Line a 9-inch pie pan with pastry and bake in a preheated 400° oven 10 minutes. Remove from oven.

Mix corn and cheese and pour into baked pastry shell. Beat eggs with cream, onion, seasonings and half the bacon. Pour over corn mixture. Sprinkle remaining bacon on top. Bake in a 400° oven 25 minutes. Reduce temperature to 350° and bake 20 minutes longer.

This quiche freezes well.

MRS. ALEXANDER H. BRADSHAW
London, England
Susan Bradshaw is Mamie Eisenhower's granddaughter.

Cheese Soufflé

- 1/4 cup butter
- 1/4 cup flour
- 1 1/2 cups milk
- 2 cups shredded sharp cheese
- 1/2 tsp. salt
- Dash of cayenne pepper
- Dash of freshly ground black pepper
- Worcestershire sauce
- 4 eggs, separated

SERVES 4

"Ray and I are very fond of this never-fail cheese soufflé. We often serve it for Sunday luncheon or supper with broiled ham, sliced tomatoes or green salad and a fruit dessert. It's a most reliable recipe: measure precisely, time accurately — and eat the results promptly!"

Melt butter in the top of a double boiler over boiling water. Blend in flour thoroughly. While roux cooks, scald milk in a separate pan (don't let it boil). Add scalded milk all at once to the roux, stirring constantly until smooth and very thick. Remove top of double boiler and let cool several minutes. Add cheese and stir until melted. Stir in seasonings, then egg yolks, one at a time. Taste for seasoning and adjust. (Mixture can be set aside at this point.)

One hour before soufflé is to be served, beat egg whites until stiff but not dry. Fold carefully into cheese mixture and pour into a 2-quart soufflé dish. Bake in a preheated 375° oven 45 minutes. Serve at once.

MR. and MRS. RAY BOLGER
Beverly Hills, California

Cheese and Mushroom Soufflé

Softened butter
3 tbsp. butter
1/4 lb. fresh mushrooms, washed, peeled and chopped or 1 can (3 oz.), drained and chopped
4 tbsp. flour
1 cup milk
1/2 lb. sharp cheddar cheese, grated
4 egg yolks, beaten
1 tsp. dry mustard
1 tsp. salt
1/4 tsp. pepper
4 egg whites, stiffly beaten
1/4 cup chopped salted almonds

SERVES 4

Using softened butter, butter bottom only of a soufflé dish or deep 2-quart casserole. Set aside.

Melt butter in a saucepan. Add mushrooms and cook slowly 5 minutes. Blend in flour. Add milk and stir constantly until mixture thickens. When it reaches a boil, remove from heat. Add cheese and stir until melted. Stir in egg yolks and seasonings, blending thoroughly. Fold in egg whites.

Pour mixture into soufflé dish and sprinkle with almonds. Bake in a preheated 350° oven 1 hour or until well puffed and firm to the touch. Serve immediately.

MRS. MARSH JOHNSON
Reno, Nevada

Almond Rarebit

1/2 cup cornstarch
4 cups evaporated milk
4 tsp. Worcestershire sauce
12 drops Tabasco sauce
4 tsp. dry mustard
Salt
2 lb. American cheese, diced
Toasted bread or English muffins
Slivered almonds

SERVES 6

Mix cornstarch with 1/2 cup of the milk until smooth. Add remaining milk and stir well. Blend Worcestershire and Tabasco sauces, mustard and salt into a smooth paste. Mix well with cheese. Stir in cornstarch mixture. Heat in top of a large double boiler over hot water until cheese melts and mixture is smooth. Stir frequently. Pour over toast and sprinkle with almonds.

This rarebit will not string. Leftover rarebit may be stored in a tightly covered jar in refrigerator up to 2 weeks; use as a vegetable sauce or a dip.

MRS. C. CURTIS TOWLE
Rancho Mirage, California

Cheese Pudding

- 3/4 lb. sharp cheddar cheese, cubed
- 6 slices white bread, buttered and cubed
- 4 eggs, beaten
- 2 cups milk
- 1/4 tsp. dry mustard
- 1/2 tsp. salt

SERVES 6

Mix cheese and bread and place in an ungreased casserole, about 13x9x3½ inches. Mix remaining ingredients and pour over bread mixture. Chill overnight, or a minimum of 4 hours. Bring to room temperature before baking.

Place casserole in a pan of warm water and bake in a preheated 350° oven 45 to 60 minutes, or until a knife inserted in center comes out clean. Leave in oven a few minutes after turning off heat.

MRS. RALPH B. BEAL
Indian Wells, California

Swiss Gruyère Fondue

- 2 thin loaves sourdough French or Italian bread
- 1/2 lb. *imported* Emmenthal (Swiss) cheese
- 1/2 lb. Gruyère cheese
- 2½ tbsp. flour
- 1 clove garlic, split
- 2 cups dry white wine (Rhine or Chablis)
- 1 tsp. fresh lemon juice
- 3 tbsp. Kirsch
- Nutmeg or paprika

SERVES 6

Cut bread into 1-inch cubes (do not remove crust). Dice or shred cheeses and dredge with flour.

Rub a fondue pan with garlic. Pour in wine and heat until bubbles begin to rise from bottom. *Do not cover or let boil.* Reduce heat to very low. Add lemon juice, then cheese by handfuls, stirring constantly with a wooden spoon. When cheese begins to melt, gently stir in Kirsch and season with nutmeg. Stir until smooth.

To serve, let everyone spear bread cubes with fondue forks and dunk them in the cheese.

MRS. FRANK KOENEN
North Hollywood, California

Cheese-Spinach Crêpes

CREPE BATTER
1 cup milk
4 eggs
2 tbsp. salad oil
3/4 cup flour
1 tsp. sugar
1/2 tsp. salt

CHEESE SAUCE
1/3 cup butter
1/3 cup flour
1 tsp. salt
1/8 tsp. pepper
3/4 tsp. dry mustard
2 1/2 cups milk, scalded
1 1/2 cups grated sharp cheddar cheese

SPINACH SAUCE
2 packages (10 oz. each) frozen chopped spinach
2 tbsp. butter
1 cup Cheese Sauce (above)

MUSHROOM SAUCE
1 lb. fresh mushrooms, sliced
4 tbsp. butter
1 cup Cheese Sauce (above)

SERVES 8

Combine ingredients for Crêpe Batter. Beat with rotary beater until blended. Cover and refrigerate several hours.

About an hour before serving time, make sauces (keep warm until ready to use with crêpes). To make Cheese Sauce, melt butter in a medium saucepan. Remove from heat and add flour, salt, pepper and mustard. Stir until smooth. Add milk slowly, stirring constantly. Return to medium heat and bring to a boil, stirring constantly. Reduce heat and simmer 1 minute. Add cheese and stir over low heat until cheese melts. (Makes 3 cups.)

To make Spinach Sauce, cook spinach according to package instructions and drain very well, squeezing out all water. Sauté in butter. Stir in 1 cup Cheese Sauce.

To make Mushroom Sauce, sauté mushrooms in butter. Remove a few from the pan and reserve for garnishing. Add 1 cup Cheese Sauce to the mushrooms in pan.

To cook crêpes, lightly butter an 8-inch crêpe pan or heavy skillet. Heat over medium heat until butter is bubbly. Pour about 1/4 cup batter into pan. Quickly rotate pan to spread batter. Cook until crêpe is lightly browned; turn and brown other side. Repeat until all batter has been used. (Makes 10 to 12 crêpes.)

Place a crêpe on a buttered heatproof platter. Spoon on some of the Mushroom Sauce. Add another crêpe and top with Spinach Sauce. Repeat sequence until you have a torte-like structure, topping with a crêpe. Place in a preheated 350° oven and heat 20 to 30 minutes. Remove and pour on some heated Cheese Sauce. Garnish with reserved mushrooms. To serve, cut into wedges. Pass the remaining Cheese Sauce.

The crêpes may be cooked a day or even a week ahead. Store in freezer after 2 days; to freeze, place each crêpe between waxed paper and wrap in foil.

MRS. ROBERT H. PHINNY
Fremont, Michigan

Quick Chile Casserole

- 2 cans (7 oz. each) green chiles, seeded
- 2 cans (14½ oz. each) solid-pack plum tomatoes, drained
- 1 lb. Monterey jack cheese, grated
- Salt and pepper
- 6 eggs, beaten
- 1 cup sour cream
- Chopped green onions (optional)

SERVES 6

Mix chiles, tomatoes, cheese, salt and pepper and place in an ungreased large, round, shallow casserole. Fold eggs into sour cream and pour on top of chile mixture. Bake in a preheated 350° oven 30 minutes or until puffy and golden brown. Sprinkle chopped green onions on top. Cut into wedges to serve.

MRS. WALTER MARKS
Palm Springs, California

Margaret Martinez's Enchiladas

- 2 tbsp. shortening
- 2 tbsp. flour
- 1 can (28 oz.) Mexican-style red chile sauce
- 2⅓ cups water
- 1 tbsp. crushed oregano
- 1 tbsp. vinegar
- 2 tbsp. bottled Italian salad dressing
- 1 large or 2 medium dill pickles, finely chopped
- 2 lb. Tillamook or sharp cheddar cheese, shredded
- 1 can (6 oz.) pitted ripe olives, drained and sliced
- 2 medium onions, finely chopped
- 12 corn tortillas

SERVES 6

Melt shortening in a large skillet or saucepan. Stir in flour and cook a few minutes. Stir in chile sauce, water, oregano, vinegar, salad dressing and pickles. Simmer, uncovered, at least 10 minutes.

Spread a little of this sauce on bottom of a baking dish, about 13x9x3½ inches. Measure 1 cup cheese and set aside. Mix remaining cheese, the olives and onions. Sprinkle a little cheese mixture in the baking dish. Dip tortillas in the warm sauce to soften. Put about 2 tablespoons cheese mixture on each tortilla. Roll up tortillas and place in baking dish, seam sides down. Cover with remaining sauce and any remaining cheese mixture. Sprinkle with reserved cheese. Place in a preheated 325° oven and bake about 30 minutes.

MRS. EUGENE HOUSTON
Palm Desert, California

Cheese Enchiladas

1 can (28 oz.) Mexican-style red chile sauce
28 oz. water (use chile sauce can)
½ tsp. minced garlic
1 tsp. salt
⅓ cup flour
½ cup water
1 lb. longhorn or mild cheddar cheese, shredded
½ lb. Monterey jack cheese, shredded
½ tsp. salt
¾ cup finely chopped white onions
12 corn tortillas
¼ cup cooking oil
12 large ripe olives, cut in half

SERVES 6

In a large kettle combine chile sauce, water, garlic and 1 teaspoon salt. Bring to a boil, reduce heat and simmer, covered, 45 minutes, stirring frequently. Make a paste of flour and ½ cup water and blend into sauce, stirring to prevent lumps. Simmer 10 minutes, then set aside to cool.

Combine cheeses and ½ teaspoon salt. Toss lightly to mix, taking care not to mash. Set aside. Place chopped onions in a sieve. Pour 1 cup boiling water over onions and drain.

Fry tortillas in hot oil until heated but not crisp. Drain on paper towels. Dip each warm tortilla in warm (not hot) chile sauce. Place on a plate and fill with ½ cup mixed cheeses, 1 teaspoon onion and 2 olive halves. Roll up tortillas and place loosely side by side, seam sides down, in a baking dish about 13x9x3½ inches. Cover thoroughly with remaining chile sauce. Bake in a preheated 350° oven 45 minutes or until cheese bubbles. Serve immediately.

MRS. HAROLD C. CROSS
Carlsbad, California

Tacos de Jocoqui

6 corn tortillas
Butter or oil for frying
½ lb. Monterey cream cheese or Monterey jack cheese, cubed
3 green chiles, cut in half and seeded
1½ cups tomato purée
Salt and pepper
2 cups sour cream

SERVES 6

To soften tortillas, fry in hot butter 1 second on each side. Place on each tortilla a few cubes of cheese, half a chile and 2 to 3 tablespoons tomato purée. Sprinkle with salt and pepper. Roll and place seam sides down in an ungreased shallow baking dish, about 12x7½ inches. Cover with sour cream and bake in a preheated 350° oven 30 minutes.

MRS. N. JOE JARED
Palm Desert, California

PASTA, RICE & GRAINS

Menu-Makers of Distinction

Here's your way to break the meat-and-potatoes routine.
Do something deliciously different—
as a main dish or a savory serve-on-the-side!
Any one of these recipes could be the collector's item
you've been searching for, the dish that's destined
to be your own specialty of the house.
Are you the continental type? Pick a pasta.
Or dramatize the roast with an unusual rich dish!
Discover what variety like this can do
for your reputation as a cook!

Macaroni and Cheese

8 oz. long macaroni
½ cup butter
3 tbsp. flour
2 cups half-and-half or milk
1 tsp. Worcestershire sauce
½ tsp. salt
¾ lb. sharp cheddar cheese, grated
Ritz crackers, finely crushed
Butter

SERVES 6

Break macaroni into thirds and cook in rapidly boiling salted water 15 to 20 minutes. Drain and rinse well.

Melt ½ cup butter in a saucepan over low heat. Blend in flour. Slowly stir in half-and-half; add Worcestershire sauce and salt. Heat and stir until thickened slightly, like a cream sauce; then add cheese. Stir until cheese melts and sauce is smooth. Fold into macaroni. Pour into a buttered 2-quart casserole and top with a thin layer of cracker crumbs. Dot with butter. Bake, uncovered, in a preheated 325° oven 25 minutes.

MRS. LELAND BAKER
Indian Wells, California

Conchiglie

16 oz. large macaroni shells
2 lb. ricotta cheese
¼ lb. mozzarella cheese, finely diced
⅓ cup grated Parmesan cheese
3 eggs, lightly beaten
¼ cup bread crumbs
2 tbsp. finely chopped parsley
¼ tsp. salt
4 cups sauce for pasta (tomato, tomato-mushroom, meat, meatless or any good spaghetti sauce)

SERVES 12 (AS MAIN DISH)

Cook shells in 6 quarts boiling salted water about 15 minutes. Stir occasionally but carefully, as the shells must not be broken. Remove from heat but do not drain. Add enough cold water so that the shells can be handled comfortably. (Leave in water until ready to fill, one by one.)

Prepare the filling by thoroughly mixing cheeses, eggs, bread crumbs, parsley and salt. Pour a thin layer of the sauce of your choice on the bottom of a baking dish. Hold a shell in the hollow of your hand and spoon in some filling. Close shell. Without crowding, arrange filled shells in the baking dish. Pour a small amount of sauce over and around shells. Cover with foil and bake in a preheated 350° oven 30 minutes. Before serving, add more sauce (heated) around shells and sprinkle with additional grated Parmesan cheese. Pass any remaining sauce.

This dish can be frozen (unbaked) for use at another time.

MRS. WILLIAM DEMAREST
Palm Springs, California

Change-of-Pace Pasta—Conchiglie (left), giant macaroni shells, are stuffed with cheese and richly sauced.

An Easygoing Dinner—Start off with Spinach Salad (page 165) as the prelude to Orange Chicken (page 89).

Clam Linguine

16 oz. linguine
1/3 cup olive oil
1/4 cup butter
3 cloves garlic, minced
1/2 tsp. salt
1 tsp. freshly ground black pepper
1/2 tsp. basil
1/2 tsp. oregano
2 cans (7 1/2 oz. each) minced clams, drained (reserve liquid)
3 tbsp. chopped parsley
1/2 cup grated Parmesan cheese (optional)

SERVES 4–6

Cook linguine according to the package directions. Drain well.

Meanwhile, heat oil and butter in a porcelain or enameled iron saucepan. Add garlic and sauté gently 2 minutes (do not brown). Add salt, pepper, basil, oregano and reserved clam liquid. Simmer 2 to 3 minutes. Add clams to the sauce and heat well. Add parsley. Pour clam sauce over hot well-drained pasta and mix gently. If desired, sprinkle with Parmesan cheese.

MRS. HUBERT WOLFE
Salt Lake City, Utah

Spinach Noodle Casserole

1 package (8 oz.) spinach noodles
Olive oil
1 carton (16 oz.) sour cream (2 cups)
Garlic
Salt and pepper
1 package (10 oz.) frozen spinach
1 small onion, finely chopped
1/2 cup (or more) grated good Swiss cheese
1/4 cup grated Parmesan cheese
1/2 cup mayonnaise
1 egg, beaten
Salt and pepper
Beau Monde seasoning
Bread crumbs
Additional Parmesan cheese
Butter

SERVES 6–8

Cook noodles as directed on the package; drain well. Add a touch of olive oil and stir. Then add sour cream and seasonings to taste. Mix gently and set aside.

Meanwhile, barely cook spinach and drain well. Combine drained spinach, onion, cheeses, mayonnaise and egg. Add salt, pepper and Beau Monde to taste.

In a well-buttered casserole, mix the noodle mixture with the spinach mixture. Cover with bread crumbs and sprinkle with additional Parmesan cheese. Dot top with butter. Bake in a preheated 350° oven about 30 minutes.

Especially good with veal.

GENERAL and MRS. WILLIAM WESTMORELAND
Charleston, South Carolina

Spaghetti Fiorello

- ½ cup sweet butter
- 1½ oz. smoked bacon, cut in strips
- 1½ oz. prosciutto, cut in strips
- 1½ oz. cooked smoked tongue, cut in strips
- 1 tbsp. A-1 sauce
- ¼ tsp. cayenne pepper
- ½ cup heavy cream
- 12 oz. spaghetti, cooked *al dente* and drained
- 2 oz. Parmesan cheese, grated (about ½ cup)

SERVES 4

Melt butter in a large saucepan. Add bacon, prosciutto and tongue and sauté 4 to 5 minutes, until browned. Add A-1 sauce, cayenne pepper and half the cream. Cook 2 minutes, stirring. Add the hot, freshly-cooked spaghetti and remaining cream. Heat and toss gently. Remove from heat, sprinkle with Parmesan cheese and serve on hot plates.

MRS. JOSEPH LINSK
Palm Springs, California

Spaghetti Giovanni

- ¼ cup butter or margarine
- ½ lb. fresh mushrooms, sliced
- 1 large onion, minced
- 1 green pepper, minced
- ¾ lb. crabmeat, flaked
- 1 cup sour cream
- 1½ cups grated cheddar cheese
- ½ tsp. salt
- ¼ tsp. pepper
- 9 oz. spaghetti

SERVES 4

Melt butter in a saucepan. Sauté mushrooms, onion and green pepper 10 minutes. Add crabmeat, sour cream, 1 cup of the grated cheese, the salt and pepper. Cook, stirring, over very low heat until cheese melts.

Meanwhile, cook spaghetti according to the package directions (do not overcook). Rinse with cold water and drain. Mix sauce with spaghetti and turn into a buttered 2-quart casserole. Sprinkle with remaining cheese and bake, uncovered, in a 325° oven until top is brown, about 20 minutes.

HELEN HUNTINGTON
Palm Desert, California

Baked Green Noodles

2 tbsp. olive oil
1/4 cup minced carrots
1 small onion, minced
1 stalk celery, minced
1/2 lb. ground beef or veal
1/2 tsp. salt
1/8 tsp. pepper
1 tbsp. tomato paste
1 1/2 tsp. flour
1 1/2 tsp. water
16 oz. green lasagne noodles
1/4 cup butter or margarine
3 tbsp. flour
1/2 tsp. salt
2 cups nonfat or low-fat milk
1 cup grated Parmesan cheese
Butter or margarine

SERVES 8

Heat oil in a skillet and sauté carrots, onion and celery. Add beef, 1/2 teaspoon salt and the pepper and cook until meat is browned. Stir in tomato paste. Dissolve 1 1/2 teaspoons flour in the water and stir into meat mixture. Cook slowly, until meat is cooked through and sauce has thickened.

While meat cooks, cook noodles according to the package directions, then drain.

Make a cream sauce by melting butter in a saucepan. Blend in 3 tablespoons flour and 1/2 teaspoon salt. Add milk, stirring constantly. Cook, stirring, until thick and smooth.

Butter a 2 1/2- or 3-quart shallow baking dish and line with a layer of noodles. Cover with a thin layer of meat sauce followed by a generous layer of cream sauce. Sprinkle on a layer of Parmesan cheese. Continue layers in this order, ending with a layer of cheese. Dot with butter. Bake 10 minutes, uncovered, in a preheated 450° oven. Reduce temperature to 300° and bake 35 minutes longer.

MRS. BENJAMIN FREEMAN
Palm Springs, California

Lasagne

1 lb. (5 links) sweet or hot Italian sausage, skinned and chopped
¾ lb. ground beef
½ cup finely chopped onion
2 cloves garlic, crushed
2 tbsp. sugar
1½ tsp. basil
½ tsp. fennel seed
1 tsp. Italian herb seasoning (optional)
Salt
¼ tsp. pepper
¼ cup chopped parsley
1 can (35 oz.) Italian-style plum tomatoes
2 cans (6 oz. each) tomato paste
1 to 2 small cans (8 oz. each) herb or onion tomato sauce
½ cup water
12 curly lasagne noodles
1 carton (15 to 16 oz.) ricotta or cottage cheese (about 2 cups)
1 egg
¾ lb. mozzarella cheese, thinly sliced
¾ cup grated Parmesan cheese

SERVES 6–8

In a 5-quart Dutch oven, sauté sausage, beef, onions and garlic over medium heat, stirring frequently, until well browned, about 20 minutes. Add sugar, basil, fennel seed, Italian herb seasoning, 1 tablespoon salt, the pepper and half the parsley. Mix well. Add tomatoes with their juice, tomato paste, tomato sauce and water. Mash tomatoes with a wooden spoon. Bring to a boil, reduce heat and simmer, covered, until thick, about 1½ hours. Stir occasionally.

To cook the noodles, bring 3 quarts water and 1 tablespoon salt to a boil in an 8-quart kettle. Add lasagne noodles, two or three at a time. Return to a boil and cook, uncovered, 10 minutes or until just tender. Stir occasionally. Drain and rinse with cold water. Drain on paper towels.

In a medium bowl, combine ricotta cheese with egg, remaining parsley and ½ teaspoon salt. Mix well.

Spoon 1½ cups meat sauce on the bottom of a baking dish, 13x9x2 inches. Arrange six noodles lengthwise in dish, overlapping to cover. Spread with half the ricotta cheese mixture. Top with a third of the mozzarella slices. Spoon 1½ cups meat sauce over mozzarella and sprinkle with ¼ cup of the Parmesan cheese. Add, in layers, remaining noodles, ricotta cheese mixture, half the remaining mozzarella and the remaining meat sauce. Top with remaining mozzarella. Sprinkle with remaining Parmesan cheese.

Cover with foil, molding it tightly around edge of dish. Bake in a preheated 375° oven 25 minutes. Remove foil and bake 25 minutes longer or until bubbly. Cool 15 minutes before serving.

MR. and MRS. HUBERT M. GREEN
Birmingham, Alabama

Hubie Green was the winner of the 1974 Bob Hope Desert Classic.

Cannelloni Napoletana

4 eggs
1¼ cups sifted flour
1 cup milk
1½ cups well-flavored tomato sauce
Melted butter (for griddle)
2 cups warm béchamel sauce
Salt and pepper
½ cup grated Parmesan cheese
½ lb. mozzarella cheese, diced
2 tbsp. butter, melted

SERVES 6–8

Beat eggs until light. Gradually beat in flour, then milk. Heat a griddle (preferably one with a nonstick surface) until very hot and brush with a little melted butter. Ladle on just enough batter to make thin 6- to 8-inch rounds. Brown quickly, turning once. There will be 14 to 16 "pancakes."

Spread about ½ cup of the tomato sauce on the bottom of an oblong baking dish. Generously season the warm béchamel sauce (which should not be too thick) with salt and pepper. Set aside 3 tablespoons of the Parmesan cheese and stir remainder into the béchamel sauce. Spread each pancake with the sauce; add a few pieces of mozzarella cheese and roll up. Arrange the pancake rolls, seam sides down, in the baking dish and top with remaining tomato sauce. Sprinkle with reserved Parmesan cheese and the melted butter.

Bake, uncovered, in a preheated 400° oven about 30 minutes. If desired, put under broiler for a few minutes to brown. Serve at once.

MRS. W. AVERELL HARRIMAN
Washington, D.C.

Rice and Spinach

- 2 onions, chopped
- 1 clove garlic, chopped
- ½ cup cooking oil
- 1 cup rice
- 1 cup boiling water
- Salt and pepper
- 3 bunches fresh spinach, washed well and cut into small pieces
- Juice of 1 lemon
- 1 tbsp. dried mint, crushed, or chopped fresh mint (optional)

SERVES 6

In a large skillet, brown onion and garlic lightly in oil. Add rice to the onion mixture and cook, stirring, 1 minute (to coat rice with oil). Add water, salt and pepper and simmer, covered, 15 minutes. Add spinach and lemon juice and toss with rice. Cook over medium heat 10 minutes longer or until rice is done.

Drain and mound on a serving platter. Garnish with mint, if desired.

MRS. JOHN PETERS
Indio, California

Browned Rice Pilaf

- ¼ cup butter
- 1 cup rice
- 2 medium onions, chopped
- 1 clove garlic, pressed (optional)
- ½ tsp. thyme
- ¼ tsp. rosemary
- 1 can (10½ oz.) condensed beef broth
- 1 can (10¾ oz.) condensed consommé
- ¼ cup chopped celery
- ¼ cup chopped green onions
- ¼ cup slivered almonds

SERVES 8

Melt butter in a large skillet. Add rice, onions, garlic, thyme and rosemary; stir over low heat until rice is brown. Put into a buttered casserole and, with a fork, stir in undiluted broth and undiluted consommé. Cover and bake in a preheated 350° oven 1¾ hours. Stir in celery, green onions and almonds and bake 15 minutes longer.

MRS. ALBERT J. LILYGREN
Kirkland, Washington

Mexican Rice with Sour Cream

1 cup rice
Salt and pepper
1 can (4 oz.) green chiles, drained and seeded
2 cups sour cream
¾ lb. Monterey jack cheese, grated
2 tbsp. butter

SERVES 4

Cook rice until just tender and season with salt and pepper. Cut chiles into small pieces. Put a layer of one-third of the rice in a buttered 2-quart casserole; add, in layers, half the chiles and a third each of the sour cream and cheese. Repeat layers of rice, chiles, sour cream and cheese; top with layers of remaining rice, sour cream and cheese (no chiles). Dot with butter. Bake, uncovered, in a preheated 350° oven 30 to 35 minutes.

MRS. LLOYD NIX
Rancho Santa Fe, California

Rice and Fruit Curry

1 can (about 15 oz.) mangoes*
1 cup diced fresh or canned pineapple
2 bananas, sliced
2 fresh peaches,* peeled and sliced
2 cups Sauternes (the sweet white Bordeaux)
1½ cups chicken broth
1 tbsp. arrowroot
3 tbsp. pistachio nuts
3 tbsp. seedless raisins, plumped in warm water and drained
1 to 2 tbsp. curry powder
Salt
4 cups hot cooked rice
Shredded coconut

SERVES 4–6

Drain canned fruit well. Pour Sauternes over all fruit and let stand 2 hours. Strain wine into a saucepan, reserving fruit. Add broth to the wine and simmer, uncovered, 15 minutes. Dissolve arrowroot in a little cold water; stir into wine mixture with nuts and raisins. Add curry powder and salt and simmer, stirring, 5 minutes longer or until thickened.

Heat serving plates and on each one put a mound of hot, fluffy rice. Arrange some of the reserved fruit on each mound and pour hot sauce over each serving. Serve shredded coconut on the side.

* Crenshaw melon or drained canned pears may be substituted for mangoes. Canned peaches may be substituted for fresh.

MRS. WILLIAM O. FLEETWOOD
Indian Wells, California

Singapore Fried Rice

Light oil (peanut, etc.)
¼ cup raisins
1 cup thinly sliced green onions
½ cup trimmed, cubed white bread
1 egg, slightly beaten
6 slices bacon, diced
10 green onions, chopped
1 clove garlic, minced or pressed
¼ lb. cooked ham, diced
4 cups cool cooked rice
½ green pepper, cut into 1-inch pieces
Soy sauce

SERVES 4–6

Pour oil into a skillet or wok to a depth of 1 inch and heat until hot. Add raisins and toss in oil until they puff up, about 1 minute. Remove with slotted spoon and drain on paper towels. Add the sliced green onions and cook, tossing, until brown and crisp. Remove and drain. Add bread cubes and toss quickly until lightly browned and crisp. Remove and drain on paper towels. Pour the beaten egg into the pan and fry like a pancake, turning once. Remove, drain on paper towels and cut into long, thin strips.

Remove pan from heat and wipe clean with paper towels. Return to heat and sauté bacon gently 2 to 3 minutes. Raise heat to high and add the chopped green onions, garlic and ham. Stir-fry constantly until bacon is cooked and other ingredients are lightly browned. Add rice and green pepper; stir and toss to mix well. Heat through, adding just enough soy sauce to color slightly.

Place fried rice on a hot serving platter. Sprinkle with the reserved raisins, green onions, bread cubes and egg strips.

MRS. TOM CHAMBERS
Singapore

Bulgur Pilaf

2 tbsp. cooking oil
¼ cup broken spaghetti (1- to 1½-inch pieces)
1 cup bulgur wheat
¼ cup instant minced onion
2 cups chicken consommé

SERVES 4

Place oil and spaghetti in the top of a double boiler. Place *directly* over heat and, stirring constantly to avoid burning, brown the spaghetti. When spaghetti has browned, place top of double boiler over boiling water. Add the bulgur wheat, stirring to coat the grains with oil. Add onion and consommé. Cover and cook, stirring several times with a fork, until all liquid has been absorbed.

MRS. MATTHEW CONLEY
Long Beach, California

Savory Wild Rice

1 package (about 8 oz.) wild rice
Chicken broth
1 lb. sliced bacon, cut into ½-inch strips
4 bunches green onions, chopped (include some tops)
1 lb. fresh mushrooms, sliced
1 green pepper, chopped
1 cup chopped celery leaves
Oregano

SERVES 4

Cook rice according to the package directions, substituting chicken broth for water.

Meanwhile, partially cook bacon in a heavy skillet over medium heat. Raise heat, add remaining ingredients and cook until vegetables are done. Drain off all but a third of the bacon fat. Combine bacon and vegetables with the hot cooked rice.

MRS. ROBERT HAYNIE
Hillsborough, California

Wild Rice Casserole

1 cup wild rice
1 can (10¾ oz.) condensed cream of chicken soup
⅓ cup water
1 can (about 4 oz.) sliced mushrooms
½ tsp. salt
¼ tsp. pepper
½ cup slivered salted almonds

SERVES 6

Cook rice according to the package directions. Drain in a wire sieve and rinse thoroughly with cold water.

Place cooked rice in a buttered 1½-quart casserole. Dilute soup with the ⅓ cup water and add to rice. Stir in mushrooms (with their liquid), salt and pepper. Cover and bake in a preheated slow oven (300° to 325°) 1 to 1½ hours. Before removing from oven, stir in almonds.

This dish may be prepared for the oven a day ahead, and then refrigerated, covered. Bring to room temperature before baking as directed above. Add almonds just before serving.

MRS. MAX THOMPSON
Palm Desert, California

Charleston Grits

- 1 cup quick-cooking hominy grits
- 4½ cups boiling water
- 2 eggs, beaten
- Milk (about ¾ cup)
- 8 oz. garlic cheese, diced
- 8 oz. sharp cheddar cheese, diced
- ½ cup butter, diced
- 6 drops Tabasco sauce
- 1 tsp. salt
- 1 cup bread crumbs or crushed cornflakes

SERVES 12

Cook grits, covered, in boiling water until all liquid is absorbed. Combine the beaten eggs with enough milk to measure 1 cup; beat together. Add egg mixture, cheeses, butter, Tabasco sauce and salt to cooked grits. Blend well and pour into a well-buttered casserole. Sprinkle with bread crumbs. Bake, uncovered, in a preheated 400° oven until brown, about 10 minutes.

MRS. J. GILTNER IGLEHEART, JR.
La Jolla, California

Hominy Grits Cheese Soufflé

- ¾ cup hominy grits
- 3 cups boiling water
- 1 cup diced cheddar cheese
- 7 tbsp. butter or margarine
- ½ tsp. salt
- 4 eggs, well beaten
- Grated Parmesan cheese
- Paprika

SERVES 8

Simmer grits, covered, in boiling water until all liquid is absorbed. Cool slightly. Stir in cheddar cheese, butter and salt. Add eggs and pour into a buttered casserole. Sprinkle with Parmesan cheese and paprika. Bake, uncovered, in a preheated 350° oven 1 hour.

This dish may be partially prepared several hours ahead of time (through the addition of cheese, butter and salt). Let sit, at room temperature, until 1 hour before serving, then add eggs and continue as directed above.

GWEN ELDRED
Cathedral City, California

VEGETABLES

How Does Your Garden Grow?

Artful artichoke to zesty zucchini! You can browse through this alphabet of varied vegetables and pick a winner every time. Best of all, this is a garden that knows no season. If you're a fanatic about "fresh," there are plenty here. But frozen, canned and dried varieties are also well represented. From leafy greens to basic beans, here are vegetables with verve—a treasury of favorites to spark the imagination and tempt the taste.

Artichokes Florentine

4 to 6 fresh artichokes
¼ cup salad oil
¾ cup white wine
2 cloves garlic, finely chopped
½ tsp. oregano
1 tsp. salt
Dash of pepper
½ cup tomato purée

SERVES 4–6

Wash artichokes and trim tops. Cut each into quarters and cut away the fuzzy choke. Cook in boiling salted water to cover 5 minutes. Drain.

Pour oil into a 3-quart flameproof casserole. Arrange artichokes in the oil. Add wine, garlic, oregano, salt and pepper. Place casserole over direct heat and bring wine to a boil. Cover and remove from heat. Place in a preheated 350° oven and bake 35 minutes. Remove cover and add tomato purée. Bake 10 minutes longer, basting artichokes occasionally.

MRS. DWIGHT BABCOCK
Hot Springs, Arkansas

Artichoke Hearts and Mushrooms en Brochette

2 packages (about 9 oz. each) frozen artichoke hearts
About 40 medium to large mushroom caps
¼ cup butter
Salt and pepper
Nutmeg
3 tbsp. olive oil
1 clove garlic, cut in half

SERVES 8

Cook artichokes according to package directions and drain. Peel mushroom caps.

Heat butter in a large skillet. When hot, sauté artichokes and mushrooms together 3 minutes, turning often. Remove carefully with a slotted spoon and thread alternately on eight skewers. Sprinkle with salt, pepper and nutmeg on all sides.

Add olive oil to skillet and heat. Sauté garlic 3 minutes, then discard. Roll brochettes in the oil and broil over hot coals or under broiler 5 minutes, turning frequently. Serve piping hot.

MRS. ROBERT S. CALLENDER
Indian Wells, California

Artichoke Bottoms Gratin

1 can (14 oz.) artichoke bottoms, drained
2 tbsp. butter
½ cup chopped fresh mushrooms
4 tbsp. grated Swiss cheese

SERVES 4

Sauté artichokes in butter. Arrange in a shallow baking dish and keep warm. Sauté mushrooms. Mound sautéed mushrooms evenly on each artichoke. Cover with cheese and broil until cheese melts.

MRS. MITCHELL J. SIMON
Rancho Mirage, California

Asparagus Tarragon

1½ lb. fresh asparagus spears
⅓ cup slivered almonds
6 tbsp. oil
¼ cup vinegar
1 tsp. sugar
1 tsp. tarragon, crumbled
¼ tsp. salt
⅛ tsp. pepper

SERVES 4

Break off woody ends of asparagus spears and discard. Steam asparagus, or drop into 2 to 3 inches of boiling salted water and gently cook, uncovered, until spears are crisp-tender. Drain and chill.

Sauté almonds in 2 tablespoons of the oil, stirring until golden brown. Remove to a paper towel to drain. To the hot oil in skillet add remaining oil, the vinegar, sugar, tarragon, salt and pepper. Heat 1 minute, then pour dressing over chilled asparagus, turning to coat thoroughly. Let cool before serving. Garnish with the almonds and, if you wish, spoon a little dressing across the spears.

MRS. NORBERT CHAPLICKI
Palm Springs, California

Baked Beans Wisconsin Style

- 3 cups cooked navy beans
- 1½ cups sour cream
- 1 cup tomato sauce
- ½ cup sautéed onions (chopped or sliced)
- 1 tbsp. sugar
- 1 tsp. salt
- ½ tsp. pepper
- 6 slices bacon, crisply fried
- ¾ cup grated process sharp cheese

SERVES 6

Mix beans, sour cream, tomato sauce, onions, sugar, salt and pepper. Turn into a baking dish. Bake, uncovered, in a preheated 350° oven 20 minutes.

Remove from oven. Top with bacon slices and sprinkle with cheese. Return to oven and bake 20 minutes longer. Serve from the baking dish.

GENERAL OMAR N. BRADLEY
Los Angeles, California

Lima Bean Casserole

- 8 slices bacon
- 2 onions, diced
- 4 cans (11 oz. each) lima beans, drained (reserve 1 cup liquid)
- 1 can (10¾ oz.) condensed tomato soup
- 1 green pepper, diced
- 2 cloves garlic, crushed
- ¼ cup brown sugar
- ⅓ cup wine vinegar
- 1½ tbsp. prepared mustard
- 2 tsp. Worcestershire sauce
- 2 tsp. chili powder

SERVES 8

Fry 4 slices of the bacon until crisp. Drain and crumble. Set aside. Pour off all but 3 tablespoons fat from the skillet. Sauté onions in the fat remaining in skillet.

Combine lima beans and the reserved bean liquid in a buttered 2-quart casserole. Add sautéed onions, cooked bacon and all remaining ingredients except uncooked bacon. Mix well. Top with reserved bacon slices. Bake, uncovered, in a preheated 325° oven 1 hour.

MRS. STANLEY SPENCER
Los Angeles, California

Green Beans Gourmet

- 2 packages (9 oz. each) frozen cut green beans
- 1 can (10¾ oz.) condensed cream of mushroom soup
- ½ jar (8-oz. size) Cheez-Whiz spread
- 1 can (4 oz.) sliced mushrooms
- 1 can (8 oz.) water chestnuts, drained and sliced
- 1 can (6¼ oz.) cashew nuts
- 1 jar (5 oz.) macadamia nuts
- 1 can (6 oz.) French-fried onion rings

SERVES 8–10

Cook beans according to package directions. Drain well and place in a buttered casserole. Immediately add soup, cheese spread, mushrooms (with their liquid), water chestnuts and nuts. Mix well. Cover with onion rings. Bake, uncovered, in a preheated moderate oven (325° to 350°) 30 minutes.

MRS. STEVEN J. REES
Fort Lee, Virginia

Mrs. Rees is Mamie Eisenhower's niece.

String Bean Casserole

- 2 packages (9 oz. each) frozen cut green beans
- 1 can (20 oz.) bean sprouts, washed, crisped in ice and drained
- 1 can (20 oz.) sliced broiled-in-butter mushrooms or 1 lb. fresh mushrooms, sautéed in butter
- 1 can (16 oz.) water chestnuts
- 1 can (10¾ oz.) condensed cream of mushroom soup
- Grated Herkimer cheese (a white New York cheddar)
- 1 can (3½ oz.) French-fried onion rings, slightly broken

SERVES 12

Cook and season beans according to package directions, then drain. Drain canned vegetables well. Slice water chestnuts. Layer half each of the green beans, bean sprouts, mushrooms, water chestnuts and soup in a buttered 2½- to 3-quart casserole; repeat layers. Top with cheese. Bake, uncovered, in a preheated 400° oven 20 minutes. Sprinkle onions on top and bake 10 minutes longer.

MRS. HARRY JOE BROWN
Palm Springs, California

Arizona Ranch-Style Frijoles

- 2 lb. dried pinto beans
- 2 tsp. salt
- 2 large onions, diced
- 4 cloves garlic, minced
- 1 can (28 oz.) tomatoes
- 1 can (7 oz.) green chiles, seeded and chopped
- 1 can (12 oz.) taco sauce
- 1 tsp. cumin
- ½ tsp. pepper

SERVES 10

Pick over beans, then soak in cold water overnight. Drain and rinse. Add enough water to cover by about 2 inches. Add salt and cook over moderate heat for about an hour, adding boiling water if needed. Add remaining ingredients. Reduce heat and cook, uncovered, 1 to 1½ hours or until beans are tender.

Variation: These frijoles may easily be converted into a delicious Chile Con Carne. Sauté 2 pounds chopped beef with 1 chopped onion in any kind of cooking fat. When brown, add to the beans after the first hour of cooking.

SENATOR and MRS. BARRY GOLDWATER
Scottsdale, Arizona

Cabbage Fry

- 2 large onions, sliced
- 2 tbsp. cooking oil
- 4 cups shredded cabbage
- 2 cups chopped celery
- 2 carrots, grated
- 1 green pepper, chopped
- 1 cup sliced fresh mushrooms
- 2 tbsp. sugar
- Salt and pepper
- 2 large tomatoes, chopped

SERVES 6

Brown onions in oil in a large skillet. Add cabbage, celery, carrots, green pepper and mushrooms. Season with sugar, salt and pepper; mix gently. Spoon tomatoes over top of mixture. Cover and cook over low heat 5 minutes.

MRS. WALTER SCOTT
Palm Desert, California

Sweet-and-Sour Carrots

1 bunch small carrots, scrubbed (don't peel)
1 clove garlic
2 tsp. cornstarch
2 tsp. sugar
2 tbsp. white vinegar
1 cup water
1 tbsp. peanut oil
2 thin slices fresh gingerroot
1 tsp. salt

SERVES 4

Slice carrots diagonally into 1-inch pieces. Pound garlic with flat side of a cleaver. Blend cornstarch and sugar with vinegar and 1/4 cup of the water.

Heat oil in a wok or heavy skillet over high heat. Add gingerroot and garlic. Cook, tossing, until they stop sizzling, then remove. Add carrots to the wok and stir-fry 2 minutes. Add salt and 1/2 cup of the water; cover and cook until tender, 3 to 4 minutes.

Reduce heat and add remaining 1/4 cup water. Make a well in center of carrots. Gradually stir cornstarch mixture into the well. When it begins to thicken, increase heat and stir carrots with the mixture until you have a translucent sauce. Serve hot.

MRS. GERALD R. FORD
Washington, D.C.

Far East Celery

4 cups sliced celery
1 can (5 oz.) water chestnuts, drained and sliced
1/4 cup sliced pimiento
1 can (10 3/4 oz.) condensed cream of chicken soup
1/2 cup buttered bread crumbs
1/4 cup toasted slivered almonds
2 tbsp. butter

SERVES 6

Cook celery in a small amount of water until crisp-tender, about 8 minutes. Drain and place in a lightly buttered 1-quart casserole. Stir in water chestnuts, pimiento and soup. Cover top with bread crumbs and almonds; dot with butter. Bake, uncovered, in a preheated 350° oven 35 minutes.

MRS. JOHN BRANDIS
Portland, Oregon

Corn Pudding

12 ears fresh corn (preferably white), grated
Butter
Brown sugar
Salt and pepper
Buttered bread crumbs
Paprika

SERVES 6

"Absolutely no milk, cream or eggs!"

Place a layer of corn in a lightly buttered 1½-quart shallow casserole. Dot with pieces of butter, then sprinkle with brown sugar, salt and pepper. Repeat layering process until all corn is used, ending with a top layer of butter and brown sugar.

Top with buttered bread crumbs and sprinkle with paprika. Bake, uncovered, in a preheated 250° oven 3 hours.

MOLLIE PORTER CULLUM
La Quinta, California

New England Corn Pudding

¼ cup butter
¼ cup sifted flour
2 cups milk, heated
3 cups drained whole-kernel corn (canned or frozen)
2 eggs, slightly beaten
1½ tbsp. sugar
2 tsp. salt
⅛ tsp. pepper

SERVES 8

Melt butter in a saucepan. Add flour and stir until smooth. Add milk gradually to flour mixture, stirring constantly until smooth. Simmer, stirring constantly, 2 to 4 minutes, until mixture thickens. Add corn and remaining ingredients; mix well.

Pour into a buttered 1½-quart casserole. Bake, uncovered, in a preheated 325° oven 1 hour, or until a silver knife inserted near center comes out clean. Place under broiler a few seconds to brown top.

VERNON STOUFFER
Scottsdale, Arizona

Stuffed Cucumbers

- 3 large cucumbers, peeled
- ¼ cup butter
- 2 tbsp. finely chopped onion
- ¼ cup fresh bread crumbs
- ½ cup minced cooked chicken
- 1 tbsp. toasted slivered almonds
- ¼ tsp. salt
- ⅛ tsp. freshly ground black pepper
- ¼ tsp. thyme
- Chicken broth

SERVES 4–6

Cut cucumbers crosswise into 2-inch pieces and scoop out seeds with an apple corer or knife. Place the cucumber tubes in boiling salted water. Simmer 3 minutes, then drain. Set aside.

Heat half the butter. Add onion and sauté until tender but not brown. Add bread crumbs, chicken, almonds, salt, pepper and thyme. Moisten with a little chicken broth. Stuff cucumber tubes with the chicken mixture and place on their sides in a lightly buttered shallow baking dish. Dot with remaining butter and add enough broth to reach halfway up the cucumber pieces. Bake, uncovered, in a preheated 325° oven until cucumbers are almost tender, about 20 minutes.

MRS. ROBERT G. BACKSTROM
Palm Springs, California

Eggplant Sandwiches

- 1 eggplant, peeled
- 1 egg, beaten
- Bread crumbs
- Salad oil
- Tomato slices
- Mayonnaise
- American cheese slices
- Bacon slices, crisply fried and drained

Cut eggplant into ½-inch slices. Dip into beaten egg, then into bread crumbs. Sauté in hot oil until golden brown on both sides, about 6 to 8 minutes. Drain and place on an ungreased baking sheet. On each slice of eggplant place 1 tomato slice, 1 teaspoon mayonnaise and 1 cheese slice. Heat under broiler until cheese starts to bubble, then add 1 slice crisp bacon. Run under broiler again for a few seconds. Serve hot.

The number of "sandwiches" will depend on the size of the eggplant.

MRS. JOHN BERRY
Dayton, Ohio

Eggplant Pizza Style

2 medium eggplant
1 egg, beaten
1/4 cup milk
Cornmeal
Olive oil
Salt and pepper
1 tsp. crushed oregano
2 tomatoes, sliced
1 onion, sliced
1 green pepper, sliced
2 cans (8 oz. each) pizza sauce
1/2 lb. Monterey jack cheese, sliced
Grated Parmesan cheese
Chopped parsley

SERVES 8

Cut unpeeled eggplant into 1/2-inch slices. Combine egg and milk. Dip eggplant slices first into egg mixture, then into cornmeal. Let dry on waxed paper a few minutes. Sauté in olive oil until lightly browned. Drain on paper towels.

Arrange eggplant in a large shallow baking dish, overlapping slices. Sprinkle with salt, pepper and oregano. Arrange tomato, onion and green pepper slices over eggplant. Salt lightly. Pour pizza sauce evenly over all. Top with a layer of cheese slices and sprinkle with Parmesan cheese and parsley. Cover with foil and bake in a preheated 350° oven 30 minutes. Remove foil and bake 15 minutes longer.

MRS. ROBERT P. BOOTH
Eugene, Oregon

Stuffed Mushrooms

1 lb. fresh mushrooms
4 slices bacon, diced
1 medium onion, minced
2 tbsp. minced green pepper
1 tsp. salt
Dash of paprika
1 tsp. butter
1 package (3 oz.) cream cheese, softened
1/2 cup buttered bread crumbs

SERVES 4–6

Clean mushrooms and remove stems. Sauté bacon, onion, green pepper, salt and paprika in butter. Whip cheese until smooth and stir in bacon mixture. Fill mushroom caps with this mixture and sprinkle with buttered bread crumbs.

Pour 1/4 cup hot water into a large baking pan, about 13x9 inches. Place mushroom caps in the pan and bake in a preheated 375° oven about 15 minutes.

Traditionally served with steak, these are also delicious as a cocktail party snack.

MRS. ROBERT STEFFEY
Palm Springs, California

French Onion Scallop

- 6 large onions, sliced
- 1/4 cup butter
- 1/4 cup flour
- 1/2 tsp. salt
- 1/4 tsp. pepper
- 2 cups milk
- 1 tsp. Worcestershire sauce
- 6 slices Swiss cheese, cut up
- 8 slices French bread, buttered and cut into large cubes

SERVES 6

Cook onion slices in boiling water 10 to 12 minutes, until just tender. Drain and arrange in a buttered shallow baking dish.

While onions cook, melt butter in a saucepan. Blend in flour, salt and pepper. Slowly stir in milk and Worcestershire sauce. Cook, stirring, until sauce thickens, then boil 1 minute. Reduce heat to low and stir in cheese. Remove from heat when cheese melts. Pour over onion in baking dish and stir to mix. Arrange bread cubes around edge.

Bake in a preheated 350° oven 30 minutes or until bread is golden brown.

MRS. EDWARD G. HUNT
Palm Springs, California

Deep-Fried Parsley

- 1 cup flour
- 1/4 tsp. salt
- 1 egg, slightly beaten
- 1 cup milk
- 1 tbsp. corn oil
- 4 small bunches parsley, rinsed well and dried
- Oil for deep-frying
- Lemon juice

SERVES 4–6

Sift flour with salt. Mix egg, milk and oil; add gradually to flour, beating with a rotary beater until smooth.

Trim parsley stems, leaving about 1-inch lengths for easy handling. Dip parsley into the batter and deep-fry in hot oil (375°), a few sprigs at a time, 2 to 5 minutes. Drain. When ready to serve, sprinkle with lemon juice.

MRS. ROBERT A. HAMILTON
Los Angeles, California

Mashed Potato and Cream Cheese Casserole

- 2 cups mashed cooked potatoes
- 1 package (8 oz.) cream cheese, softened
- 1 small onion, finely chopped
- 2 eggs
- 2 tbsp. flour
- Salt and pepper
- 1 can (3½ oz.) French-fried onion rings

SERVES 6–8

Put the potatoes in a large mixing bowl. Add cream cheese, onion, eggs and flour. Beat at medium speed until well blended. Increase speed to high and beat until light and fluffy. Season with salt and pepper.

Spoon into a greased 9-inch square baking dish. Cover top with onion rings. Bake, uncovered, in a preheated 300° oven 35 minutes.

If the dish is prepared ahead, do not add onion rings until ready to bake.

MRS. JOHN R. CLARK, JR.
Indian Wells, California

Sweet Potato Puffs

- 2 cups mashed cooked sweet potatoes
- 1 tsp. salt
- ¼ tsp. nutmeg
- ½ cup chopped walnuts
- 6 slices drained canned pineapple
- 3 tbsp. butter, melted
- 6 marshmallows
- 6 walnut halves

SERVES 6

Mix potatoes, salt and nutmeg. Form into six balls and roll in nuts. Place balls on pineapple slices and brush with melted butter. Place in a buttered shallow baking dish and bake in a preheated 350° oven 20 minutes.

Remove from oven and press a marshmallow into the top of each potato ball. Press a walnut half into each marshmallow. Return to oven and bake until marshmallows are melted and golden brown, about 5 minutes.

ELISABETH E. STEWART
Pasadena, California

Spinach Casserole

1 package (10 oz.) frozen chopped spinach, thawed
4 cups cottage cheese
8 oz. process American cheese food (Velveeta), grated
6 eggs, beaten
½ cup butter or margarine, melted
6 tbsp. flour

SERVES 10

Drain spinach well. Mix with remaining ingredients and turn into a lightly buttered glass baking dish. Bake, uncovered, in a preheated 350° oven 30 to 45 minutes. Do not let the top brown.

DON FAIRFIELD
Indian Wells, California

Baked Banana Squash

1 lb. banana squash, peeled
½ cup butter, melted
⅔ cup granulated sugar
⅓ cup brown sugar
¼ tsp. salt

SERVES 6

Cut squash crosswise into 1-inch pieces. Put a teaspoon of water in the bottom of a lightly buttered oblong baking dish; arrange squash in the dish. Pour butter over squash. Mix remaining ingredients and sprinkle on top. Bake, uncovered, in a preheated 400° oven 30 to 35 minutes.

SGT. JOHN MOANEY
Gettysburg, Pennsylvania

Tomato Pudding

2 cans (16 oz. each) solid-pack tomatoes, forced through a sieve
1 cup brown sugar
½ onion, chopped
8 cloves
8 peppercorns
1 bay leaf
6 to 8 slices white bread, toasted and cubed
⅓ cup butter, melted

SERVES 6

Combine all ingredients except bread and butter and bring to a boil. Place bread cubes in a buttered 1½-quart casserole. Pour melted butter over bread and toss with a fork. Strain tomato mixture and pour over bread cubes. Bake, uncovered, in a preheated 375° oven 45 minutes.

MRS. HAROLD FLORSHEIM
Highland Park, Illinois

Fluffy Turnips

6 medium turnips, peeled and cubed
2 eggs, separated
1 tsp. grated lemon rind
1 tsp. salt
1/8 tsp. basil
Dash of cayenne pepper
2 tbsp. brown sugar

SERVES 6

Cook turnips in water until tender, about 20 minutes. Drain and mash. Beat egg yolks and add to turnips along with lemon rind, salt, basil and cayenne pepper. Beat egg whites until stiff and fold gently into turnip mixture.

Pour into a lightly buttered 1½-quart casserole and sprinkle with brown sugar. Bake, uncovered, in a preheated 350° oven 20 minutes.

MAMIE DOUD EISENHOWER
Gettysburg, Pennsylvania

Zucchini-Cheese Casserole

12 zucchini (unpeeled), sliced crosswise
12 fresh medium tomatoes, peeled and sliced, or sliced canned whole tomatoes
1 large Bermuda onion, sliced
1½ cups cracker crumbs
1 cup grated sharp cheese
Salt and pepper
½ cup butter
1 tbsp. brown sugar

SERVES 8–10

Butter a 3-quart casserole and arrange single, alternating layers of zucchini, tomatoes and onion. Sprinkle each layer with cracker crumbs, cheese, salt and pepper; dot each layer with butter. Sprinkle brown sugar on each tomato layer. Top all with a layer of cheese. Bake in a preheated 300° oven 1 to 1½ hours.

This casserole can be cooked ahead and reheated just before serving (if refrigerated, bring to room temperature first).

MRS. EARL E. PINNELL
Palm Desert, California

¿Quién Sabe?

- 2 lb. zucchini (unpeeled), cut into 1/4-inch slices
- 1 large eggplant, peeled and cut into 1-inch cubes
- 1 package (8 oz.) cream cheese, diced or grated
- 1 package (3 oz.) cream cheese, diced or grated
- 1 egg, beaten
- 1 can (4 oz.) chopped green chiles
- Bread crumbs
- Butter

SERVES 8

Cook zucchini and eggplant in separate pans of salted water until slightly tender. Drain well and combine. Lightly mix cream cheese, egg and chiles; mix with vegetables (mixture will be soupy).

Pour into a lightly buttered 1½-quart casserole. Top with bread crumbs and dot with butter. Bake, uncovered, in a preheated 350° oven 30 minutes.

MRS. SCOTT TALIAFERRO
Abilene, Texas

Zucchini Florentine

- Flour
- Salt and pepper
- 6 zucchini (unpeeled), thinly sliced lengthwise
- 2 eggs, slightly beaten
- Combination of olive oil and peanut oil, or clarified butter
- 1/2 cup clarified butter
- 1 tbsp. lemon juice
- 3 tbsp. minced parsley

SERVES 6

Season flour with salt and pepper and dredge zucchini slices. Shake off excess and dip into beaten eggs.

Heat the oils and sauté zucchini, a few slices at a time. Drain immediately on paper towels and keep warm in a low oven.

Heat the clarified butter in a small skillet over medium heat until a light golden brown. Season with salt and pepper. Stir in lemon juice and parsley.

Arrange zucchini in fan-shaped wedges on a round platter. Drizzle with the brown butter and serve immediately.

MRS. LEIGH BATTSON
Los Angeles, California

Baked Zucchini Casserole

2 lb. zucchini (unpeeled), cut up
1/2 tsp. salt
2 medium onions, minced
1 clove garlic, minced
1 tbsp. butter
2 slices fresh bread, cubed
1 cup grated cheddar cheese (about 1/4 lb.)
4 eggs, well beaten
2 tbsp. minced parsley
2 tsp. Worcestershire sauce
1 tsp. salt
Dash of Tabasco

SERVES 6–8

Cook zucchini in a little water with 1/2 teaspoon salt until tender. Drain and mash.

Sauté onions and garlic in butter. Add to zucchini along with remaining ingredients. Mix well. Spoon into a well-buttered casserole. Set in a pan of hot water and bake, uncovered, in a preheated 350° oven 30 minutes or until firm.

MRS. WINSTON R. FULLER
San Marino, California

Mixed Vegetable Dish

6 turnips
6 new potatoes
6 carrots
4 parsnips
1 rutabaga
1 large onion
Butter
Salt and pepper

SERVES 8

Peel and cube vegetables. Combine in a large saucepan and cook in boiling water to cover until tender. Drain. Mash (like potatoes) and add butter. Season to taste.

Good with any meat or fowl.

ALICE FAYE HARRIS
Palm Springs, California

Papa-San's Vegetables

2 tbsp. corn oil
2 carrots, sliced
2 stalks celery, cut into 1-inch pieces
1 medium onion, sliced
1/2 green pepper, sliced
2 tbsp. soy sauce
2 tbsp. catsup
2 tbsp. water

SERVES 4

Heat oil in a skillet. Add vegetables and cook over medium heat, tossing to coat with oil, just until onion is crisp-tender, about 3 minutes. Add soy sauce, catsup and water. Cover and cook over low heat 10 minutes. Do not overcook.

MRS. RICHARD L. CRUTCHER
Palm Desert, California

SALADS & SALAD DRESSINGS

The Refresher Course

Salads come on crisp or creamy, delicately molded or spooned into a big, inviting help-yourself bowl. Some serve as first courses, some as main dishes, some as cool interludes between entrée and dessert. But always they please the palate and refresh the eye. You'll find a coast-to-coast selection of salads here— for any reason, for every season. And there's a special collection of couturier dressings, too.

✱ Dolores Hope's Antipasto Salad

Iceberg lettuce, very cold and dry
Salami, cut into slivers
Mozzarella cheese, diced
Marinated artichoke hearts, chilled and drained
Garbanzo beans, chilled and drained
Italian pickled peppers (mild peperoncini), chilled and drained
Celery hearts and tops, chopped
Pimientos, drained and cut into slivers
Ripe olives, chilled and drained
Anchovies, torn or cut into small pieces (optional)
Capers (optional)
Fresh parsley, minced (optional)
Parmesan or Romano cheese, freshly grated

DRESSING
Salt and coarsely ground black pepper
1 part high-quality wine vinegar
3 parts Italian olive oil

"This recipe has always been a favorite with our family. Now it is a tradition at an Italian dinner we have annually during the Desert Classic. The salad can be served as a first course or even as a main dish. We like it with lots of hot crusty bread."

Tear lettuce into bite-size pieces and arrange as a bed in a large chilled salad bowl. Arrange individual salad ingredients in wedge-shaped sections on top of lettuce (if using a clear bowl, layer the ingredients). Do not toss. Bring to the table to show off the colorful arrangement. Add salt, pepper and vinegar and toss lightly. Add oil and toss salad again.

MRS. BOB HOPE
North Hollywood, California

Bean Sprout Salad

½ cup mayonnaise
2 tbsp. soy sauce
1 tsp. curry powder
1 tsp. lemon juice
½ lb. fresh bean sprouts
½ cup thinly sliced celery
2 tbsp. minced green onion
Toasted slivered almonds
Lettuce leaves

SERVES 4

Blend mayonnaise, soy sauce, curry powder and lemon juice. Combine bean sprouts, celery and onion. Toss with the dressing and sprinkle with almonds. Arrange on lettuce leaves.

Delicious accompaniment for a fresh crabmeat dish.

MRS. JUSTIN DART
Los Angeles, California

Caesar Salad

1½ cups garlic-flavored croutons
¾ cup salad oil
2 small cloves garlic
1 large head iceberg lettuce
1 large head romaine
¼ cup grated Parmesan cheese
1 tbsp. Worcestershire sauce
¾ tsp. salt
¼ tsp. freshly ground black pepper
1 can (2 oz.) anchovies, mashed
2 lemons
Coddled egg (optional)

SERVES 4–5

Mix croutons with ¼ cup of the oil. Press garlic cloves and add to croutons and oil.

Tear greens into bite-size pieces and place in a wooden salad bowl. Add croutons and sprinkle with cheese. Blend remaining ½ cup oil with Worcestershire sauce, salt and pepper. Drizzle over greens, then toss gently until each leaf glistens. Add anchovies. Squeeze lemons and strain juice through a linen napkin; add to salad and toss again. (Add coddled egg at this time, if desired.) Serve salad immediately.

ALICE MARBLE
Palm Desert, California

Spinach Salad

About 1 lb. tender spinach leaves
6 slices lean bacon
½ cup simple syrup*
½ cup vinegar
1 medium red onion, cut into thin slivers
1 tsp. salt
2 tsp. sugar
½ tsp. fresh cracked or coarsely ground black pepper
1 tsp. Worcestershire sauce

SERVES 4

Rinse and dry spinach leaves. Tear and place in a large salad bowl.

Cut bacon into pieces about 1 inch square. Fry until cooked but not crisp. Stir in simple syrup and vinegar; keep warm. Toss spinach with the onion. Sprinkle with salt, sugar, pepper and Worcestershire sauce; toss again. Pour contents of skillet (bacon and seasoned drippings) over spinach and toss lightly, just enough to coat leaves.

* SIMPLE SYRUP: Combine 3 parts sugar and 1 part water. Boil 5 minutes, then cool.

MRS. ELLSWORTH VINES
La Quinta, California

Spinach Salad Oriental

- ½ lb. (or more) fresh spinach
- ½ cup fresh bean sprouts, rinsed and drained
- ½ cup water chestnuts, diced
- 2 hard-boiled eggs, diced
- ¼ lb. bacon, crisply fried and crumbled
- ¼ onion, diced
- ¼ cup vinegar
- ¼ cup salad oil
- ¼ cup catsup
- 2 tsp. salt
- 1 tsp. sugar

SERVES 2

Rinse spinach well and pat dry. Tear into bite-size pieces. Place in a bowl with bean sprouts and water chestnuts. Chill.

Just before serving, combine eggs, bacon and onion with the chilled ingredients. Blend vinegar, oil, catsup, salt and sugar; toss with salad ingredients.

MRS. ROBERT P. HOLLISTER
Conneaut Lake, Pennsylvania

Margo's Italian Rice Salad

- ¼ cup cold water
- ¼ cup bottled Italian dressing
- ½ cup instant rice
- 1 cup cooked peas
- ½ cup mayonnaise
- ¼ cup drained canned sliced mushrooms
- ¼ cup chopped cucumber
- 2 tbsp. chopped green onion
- 2 tbsp. chopped ripe olives

SERVES 4–6

Combine water and dressing in a saucepan and bring to a boil. Remove from heat and stir in rice. Cover and let stand 5 minutes.

Fluff rice with a fork and turn into a bowl. Add remaining ingredients and stir gently. Chill before serving.

MRS. CHALLEN F. LANDERS
Palm Desert, California

Tabbouleh Salad

3 cups boiling water
1½ cups bulgur wheat
2 large tomatoes, finely chopped
1 cup finely chopped parsley
½ cup chopped green onions
½ cup olive oil
½ cup lemon juice
2 tbsp. minced fresh mint
½ tsp. salt
¼ tsp. pepper
Romaine leaves

SERVES 8

Pour boiling water over bulgur wheat. Cover and let stand 1 to 2 hours, until light and fluffy. Combine with tomatoes, parsley, onion, oil, lemon juice, mint, salt and pepper. Chill thoroughly. Serve on romaine leaves.

MRS. FRANK LONG
Federal Way, Washington

Peanut Slaw

2 cups shredded red cabbage
2 cups shredded white cabbage
1 cup thinly sliced celery
½ cup sour cream
½ cup high-quality mayonnaise
½ cup chopped cucumber
¼ cup thinly sliced green onions (include some of the tops)
¼ cup finely chopped green pepper
1 tbsp. lemon juice
1 tbsp. prepared horseradish
½ tsp. prepared mustard
½ tsp. salt
¼ tsp. freshly ground black pepper
½ cup chopped dry-roasted peanuts

SERVES 12–16

Mix cabbage and celery. Chill (in a bowl or plastic bag) until ready to serve. Combine sour cream, mayonnaise, cucumber, onions, green pepper, lemon juice, horseradish, mustard, salt and pepper. Mix well and chill.

Just before serving, place cabbage mixture in a serving bowl. Pour sour cream dressing over cabbage and sprinkle peanuts on top.

JEAN M. BENSON
Palm Desert, California

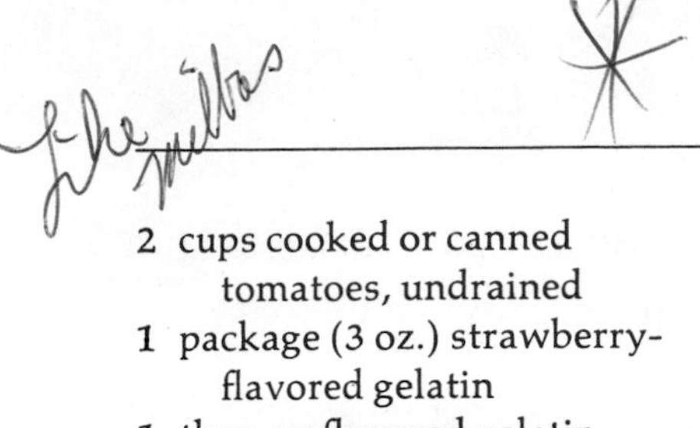

Red Crest Tomato Aspic

2 cups cooked or canned tomatoes, undrained
1 package (3 oz.) strawberry-flavored gelatin
1 tbsp. unflavored gelatin
2 tsp. prepared horseradish
1½ to 2 tsp. grated onion
1½ tsp. salt
Dash of cayenne pepper or a few dashes of Tabasco sauce
Mayonnaise

SERVES 4–6

Heat tomatoes until warm. Add flavored and unflavored gelatins and stir until dissolved. Stir in horseradish, onion, salt and cayenne pepper. Force mixture through a sieve and pour into a 2- to 4-cup ring mold or individual molds. Chill until firm.

To serve, unmold and garnish with mayonnaise.

MRS. GEORGE L. RATCLIFFE
Palm Desert, California

Coleslaw Soufflé Salad

2 packages (3 oz. each) lemon-flavored gelatin
2½ cups hot water
1 cup mayonnaise (do not use prepared salad dressing)
¼ cup sweet pickle vinegar
1 tsp. salt
Dash of pepper
Few drops green food coloring (optional)
4 cups grated or finely chopped cabbage
½ cup chopped celery or 1 tsp. celery seed
4 tbsp. chopped green pepper
2 tbsp. grated onion or 1 tsp. onion powder
¼ cup grated carrots or 2 tbsp. chopped pimiento-stuffed olives (optional)
Chopped parsley
Parsley sprigs or lettuce leaves
Pitted ripe olives
Cherry tomatoes

SERVES 12

Dissolve gelatin in hot water. Cool a little, then stir in mayonnaise, vinegar, salt, pepper and food coloring. Blend with beater. Chill until slightly thickened (the consistency of egg white). Beat until fluffy.

Combine cabbage, celery, green pepper, onion, carrots and a little chopped parsley. Fold into gelatin mixture. Pour into a 6- to 8-cup ring mold and chill until firm.

Just before serving, unmold onto a bed of parsley sprigs. Fill center of ring with pitted ripe olives and cherry tomatoes.

MRS. TONY WHAN
Rancho Mirage, California

Salad Spectacular—To start a meal in style, Dolores Hope's Antipasto Salad (page 164) is unbeatable.

A Luncheon Meeting—A delicate layering of Cheese-Spinach Crêpes (page 130) and a simple green salad.

Molded Artichokes in Consommé

- 1 tbsp. unflavored gelatin
- 1/4 cup cold water
- 2 cans (10 1/2 oz. each) condensed consommé
- 6 tbsp. fresh lemon juice
- 1/2 tsp. salt
- 1/8 tsp. pepper
- 6 drops Tabasco sauce
- 2 cans (about 16 oz. each) artichoke hearts, drained (4 cups)
- Mayonnaise
- Light cream
- Crisp greens

SERVES 6

Soften gelatin in cold water. Heat consommé, add softened gelatin and stir until dissolved. Stir in lemon juice, salt, pepper and Tabasco sauce. Chill until slightly firm. Cut artichoke hearts into quarters and stir gently into gelatin mixture. Turn into a 1 1/2-quart mold and chill until firm.

Make a dressing by thinning mayonnaise with cream. Unmold salad onto a bed of crisp greens and serve with the dressing.

MRS. DONALD F. McDERMOTT
Palm Springs, California

Beet Salad Mold

- 2 1/2 cups canned diced beets, drained (reserve liquid)
- 2 packages (3 oz. each) lemon-flavored gelatin
- 2 tbsp. vinegar
- 2 1/2 cups canned crushed pineapple (including juice)
- 1/2 cup chopped pecans
- Sour cream

SERVES 12–16

Add enough water to reserved beet juice to equal 2 cups liquid. Bring to a boil and pour over gelatin. Let cool, then stir in vinegar, diced beets, pineapple (including juice) and pecans. Pour into individual molds or an oblong dish about 2 inches deep. Chill until firm.

When ready to serve, unmold or cut into squares. Serve with sour cream.

Especially good with turkey.

MRS. DONALD F. MACPHERSON
Palm Springs, California

 Make ahead

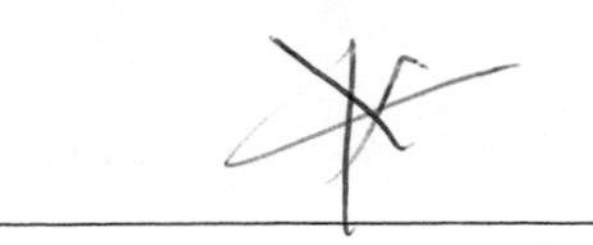

Copper Carrot Pennies

2 lb. carrots, scraped and sliced
1 medium onion, sliced*
1 small green pepper, sliced
1 can (10¾ oz.) condensed tomato soup
½ cup salad oil
1 cup sugar
¾ cup cider or wine vinegar
1 tsp. prepared mustard
1 tsp. Worcestershire sauce
½ tsp. salt
¼ tsp. pepper

MAKES 1 QUART

"This unusual recipe 'came from Missouri.' As is, it can be served as an appetizer or salad. Or it can be mixed with salad greens to take on a different look. It may even be included in a dieter's regimen by substituting an artificial sweetener for the sugar and safflower oil for salad oil."

Cook carrots until crisp-tender. *Do not overcook.* Drain well and cool. Separate onion slices into rings. Alternate layers of carrots, pepper rings and onion rings in a bowl. Combine remaining ingredients and beat until smooth. Pour dressing over vegetables and refrigerate, covered, until ready to serve.

This salad keeps beautifully for at least 2 weeks.

*Two jars (3½ oz. each) cocktail onions and their liquid can be substituted for the sliced raw onion.

MRS. FRANCIS W. ST. PIERRE
Thousand Palms, California

Danish Tomatoes

Tomatoes
Dark brown sugar
Vinegar
Salt and pepper

Slice tomatoes. Place a layer in a serving dish and sprinkle with brown sugar. Continue to layer tomatoes and brown sugar. Add vinegar, salt and pepper to taste. Chill at least 2 hours before serving.

MAMIE DOUD EISENHOWER
Gettysburg, Pennsylvania

John's Favorite Orange Salad

6 oranges
1 clove garlic, minced
1 tbsp. oregano, crumbled
Salt and pepper
½ cup vegetable oil
Juice of 1 orange (about ½ cup)
2 to 3 tbsp. chopped parsley

SERVES 6–8

Peel oranges and cut thin crosswise slices. Arrange in a large serving dish. Sprinkle with garlic, oregano and salt and pepper to taste. Pour oil and orange juice over fruit. Sprinkle with parsley. Cover and chill before serving.

MRS. JOHN CURCI
Newport Beach, California

Avocado and Bacon Salad

½ cup sour cream
½ cup olive oil
Juice of 2 limes
Salt and pepper
Tabasco sauce
1 head lettuce, or a mixed variety
2 avocados
12 slices bacon, crisply fried and crumbled

SERVES 4

Blend sour cream, oil, lime juice and seasonings. Let stand 2 hours.

Tear lettuce into bite-size pieces. Peel and slice avocados. Add to lettuce along with the bacon. Toss with the dressing and serve.

MRS. KENT HAYES
Palm Springs, California

Papaya-Fruit Molded Salad

- 1 can (12 oz.) papaya juice
- 1 package (3 oz.) lemon-flavored gelatin
- 1 tbsp. lemon juice
- 1 can (11 oz.) mandarin orange sections, drained
- 1 can (about 8 oz.) seedless grapes, drained (1 cup)
- 1 cup sour cream

SERVES 6

Heat papaya juice. Add gelatin and stir until dissolved. Stir in lemon juice. Chill until slightly thickened.

Combine orange sections, grapes and sour cream; fold into gelatin. Pour into a 4-cup mold and chill until firm.

MRS. RICHARD L. CRUTCHER
Palm Desert, California

Lemon-Cherry Mold

- 1 package (3 oz.) lemon-flavored gelatin
- 1 cup boiling water
- 1 can (about 8 oz.) crushed pineapple, drained (reserve liquid)
- 1 package (3 oz.) cream cheese, softened
- 1/3 cup chopped nuts
- 1 package (3 oz.) cherry-flavored gelatin
- 1 cup boiling water
- 1 1/2 cups canned Bing cherries, drained (reserve liquid) and cut in half

SERVES 8–10

Dissolve lemon-flavored gelatin in 1 cup boiling water. Add enough cold water to reserved pineapple liquid to equal 1 cup. Stir into gelatin. Chill until slightly thickened.

Whip cream cheese. Mix with crushed pineapple and nuts. Fold into gelatin. Pour into a 5-cup mold and chill until firm.

To make second layer, dissolve cherry-flavored gelatin in 1 cup boiling water. Stir in 1 cup of the reserved cherry liquid. Chill until slightly thickened. Stir in cherries. Pour mixture onto firmly-set gelatin in mold. Chill until firm.

MRS. ARTHUR F. BURNS
Washington, D. C.

Stuffed Tomato Salad

1 package (3 oz.) cream cheese, softened
1 package (3 oz.) pimiento cream cheese, softened
¼ cup chopped pickled watermelon rind
6 medium tomatoes, peeled and chilled
½ tsp. salt
Lettuce cups
Mayonnaise
Carrot curls
Watercress

SERVES 6

Blend cheeses thoroughly. Add chopped watermelon pickle and mix well. Chill.

Taking care not to slice through bottom, cut each tomato into 6 sections. Spread sections apart and sprinkle with salt. Place tomatoes on lettuce cups and stuff with cheese mixture. Top with a dollop of mayonnaise. Garnish with carrot curls and sprigs of watercress.

This is an excellent entrée for a salad luncheon.

MRS. HORACE W. McCURDY
Mercer Island, Washington

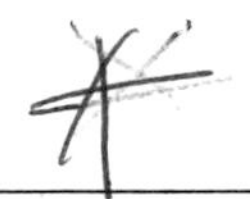

Greek Slaw

1 small head cauliflower
1 cup mayonnaise
Juice of 1 lemon
½ tsp. salt
¼ tsp. pepper
¼ tsp. hot pepper sauce
12 pimiento-stuffed olives, sliced
1 green pepper, seeded and chopped
1 onion, chopped
1 lb. or 3 cans (5 oz. each) cooked shrimp, drained
½ cup cooked rice
Lettuce leaves
Alfalfa sprouts (optional)

SERVES 4–6

Separate cauliflower into small flowerets. Blend mayonnaise, lemon juice, salt, pepper and hot pepper sauce. Mix with olives, green pepper and onion. Toss with shrimp, rice and cauliflower.

Line a salad bowl with lettuce leaves. Add shrimp mixture and garnish with alfalfa sprouts, if available.

MRS. RICHARD NELSON
Kansas City, Missouri

Thousand Island Ring Mold with Crab or Shrimp

2 tbsp. unflavored gelatin
½ cup cold water
1½ cups mayonnaise
1 cup chili sauce
½ tsp. sugar
¼ tsp. salt
¼ tsp. Tabasco sauce
6 hard-boiled eggs, sliced
1 cup thinly sliced celery
½ to 1 cup sliced ripe olives
1 to 1½ lb. cooked crabmeat or shrimp, chilled

SERVES 8

Soften gelatin in cold water. Dissolve, stirring, over hot water. Blend with mayonnaise, chili sauce, sugar, salt and Tabasco sauce. Chill until slightly firm. Fold in eggs, celery and olives. Pour into an 8-cup ring mold and chill until firm.

Unmold onto a serving platter. Fill center and garnish sides with crab or shrimp.

MRS. NATHANIEL S. ROGERS
Seattle, Washington

Shrimp Mold

2 cans (10¾ oz. each) condensed cream of tomato soup
1 package (8 oz.) cream cheese
2 tbsp. unflavored gelatin
½ cup cold water
1 cup mayonnaise
2 tbsp. lemon juice
1 cup each chopped celery, green pepper and onions
1 package (7 to 9 oz.) frozen small shrimp, cooked and diced

SERVES 10–12

Heat soup. Add cheese and stir until melted. Dissolve gelatin in the water and stir into soup mixture. Let cool, then blend in mayonnaise and lemon juice. Chill until slightly firm. Add vegetables and shrimp and mix.

Lightly rub a 6- to 8-cup copper fish-shaped mold or ring mold with mayonnaise and fill with shrimp mixture. Chill until firm.

This is delicious served with hot buttered asparagus, herbed bread and a strawberry dessert.

MRS. DON L. GRANTHAM
Lake Forest, Illinois

Pressed Chicken Mold

1 stewing chicken (5 lb.), cut up
4 whole chicken breasts
2 tbsp. unflavored gelatin
1 cup celery hearts, finely chopped
3 hard-boiled eggs, finely chopped
1 green pepper, finely chopped
½ lb. almonds or pecans, finely chopped
¾ cup chutney (Major Grey's), minced
Juice of 1 lemon
Salt
Cayenne pepper
2 heads lettuce
Papaya slices
Avocado slices
Cherry tomatoes
Curried mayonnaise

SERVES 10

Cover stewing chicken and breasts with water and simmer slowly, covered, about 1 hour. Remove chicken and reserve. There should be about 1 cup of broth remaining; if not rich enough, add some butter or chicken stock base. Dissolve gelatin in a little cold water and stir into broth.

Bone and skin the chicken. Put through a meat grinder, using coarse plate. Mix together with reserved broth, the celery, eggs, green pepper, nuts, chutney, lemon juice, salt and cayenne pepper. Pack into an 8-cup mold and chill about 12 hours.

Unmold onto a bed of lettuce leaves. Surround with papaya and avocado slices and small cherry tomatoes. Accompany with curried mayonnaise, lettuce leaves and, if desired, more chutney.

MRS. RALPH WAYCOTT
Oceanside, California

Chicken Salad

4 whole chicken breasts, steamed, skinned, boned and diced
½ cup water chestnuts, sliced
½ cup chopped pecans
½ cup seedless grapes
¼ cup finely chopped celery
1 tsp. finely minced candied ginger
¾ cup mayonnaise
2 tbsp. wine vinegar
1 tbsp. soy sauce
2 tsp. minced onion
½ tsp. curry powder
Canned pineapple slices

SERVES 6

Mix chicken, water chestnuts, pecans, grapes, celery and ginger. Blend mayonnaise, vinegar, soy sauce, onion and curry powder. Toss dressing with chicken mixture. Chill.

To serve, spoon onto pineapple slices.

MRS. F. CLARENCE GOODWIN
San Diego, California

Promenade Salad Dressing

2 large cloves garlic, crushed
1 tsp. sugar
1/2 tsp. paprika
1/2 tsp. basil
1/8 tsp. tarragon
Salt and pepper
3 tbsp. red wine vinegar
3 tbsp. cider vinegar
2 tbsp. Maggi liquid seasoning
3/4 cup sesame seed oil

MAKES ABOUT 1 1/3 CUPS

Blend garlic with sugar, paprika, basil, tarragon, salt and pepper. Beat in vinegars and liquid seasoning, then oil.

Excellent served over bibb lettuce and small bay shrimp.

MRS. KAY GOLDIE
Palm Desert, California

Piquant Salad Dressing

1 cup salad oil
1/2 cup sugar
1/3 cup catsup
1/4 cup vinegar
1/4 cup grated onion
Juice of 1 lemon
1 tsp. salt
1 tsp. paprika

MAKES ABOUT 2 CUPS

Combine all ingredients and mix in a blender (or shake thoroughly).

This is a tart, oniony dressing and is especially good on greens. Store in the refrigerator.

MRS. JEFF MINCKLER
Indian Wells, California

Slaw Dressing

1/2 cup sour cream
2 eggs
4 tbsp. sugar
1 tbsp. butter, melted
1/2 tsp. dry mustard
2 tbsp. vinegar
1 tsp. salt

MAKES ABOUT 1 CUP

Thoroughly beat sour cream, eggs, sugar and butter. Dissolve mustard in vinegar and stir into sour cream mixture.

Pour into the top of a double boiler and heat, stirring, over hot water until it thickens (do not let it boil). Remove from heat and stir in salt. Let cool before serving.

MR. and MRS. WILLIAM P. ROGERS
New York, New York

For Sure *

Hot Salad Dressing for Mixed Greens

4 thick slices bacon, cut into small pieces
1/4 cup butter
1/2 cup light cream
2 eggs, beaten
1/4 cup cider vinegar
1 tsp. each salt, pepper and paprika
1 heaping tbsp. sugar
Mixed greens

MAKES ABOUT 1 CUP

Fry bacon and drain. Pour off half the drippings; reserve the remainder.

Put butter and cream in another skillet and warm over low heat. Stir in beaten eggs, vinegar, salt, pepper, paprika and sugar. Increase heat and cook, stirring constantly, until mixture thickens. Pour desired amount of hot dressing over greens. Add bacon and reserved bacon drippings. Toss gently and serve at once.

MOLLIE PORTER CULLUM
La Quinta, California

Sweet Salad Dressing

1/2 cup sugar
1/4 cup vinegar
2 to 4 tbsp. chopped onion (for a pink dressing, use red onion)
1 tsp. prepared mustard
1/2 tsp. celery seed
Dash of salt
Dash of pepper
1 cup salad oil

MAKES ABOUT 1 1/2 CUPS

Place all ingredients except salad oil in a blender. Slowly add oil, blending until thick.

This dressing is particularly good with fresh fruit salads.

MRS. LUCIUS E. DIXON
Indian Wells, California

Honey-Lime Dressing

- 1 can (6 oz.) frozen limeade concentrate, slightly thawed
- ¾ cup salad oil
- ½ cup honey
- ¼ tsp. salt
- 2 tsp. celery seed

MAKES 2 CUPS

Put limeade, oil, honey and salt in a blender and whirl a few seconds. (If a blender is not available, beat or shake to mix well.) Stir in celery seed.

MRS. LESTER HUNTER
Portland, Oregon

Dressing for Fruit Salad

- ½ cup confectioners' sugar
- 1 tsp. dry mustard
- 1 tsp. salt
- 1 tsp. paprika
- 1 tsp. celery seed
- ¼ tsp. onion juice
- 1 cup salad oil
- 4 tbsp. cider or white vinegar

MAKES 1½ CUPS

Mix together sugar, mustard, salt, paprika and celery seed. Add onion juice. Very slowly add oil and vinegar, a little at a time. Beat with silver fork until well blended and thick.

Store in refrigerator. This dressing will never separate.

MRS. SCOTT MILNE
Indio, California

Ambrosia Fruit Salad Dressing

- 1 cup mayonnaise
- 1 cup sour cream
- ¼ cup pineapple juice
- ⅓ cup maraschino cherry juice
- 1 tsp. lemon juice
- 2 tbsp. honey
- 2 tbsp. confectioners' sugar
- ⅓ cup chopped pecans
- ¼ cup chopped maraschino cherries

MAKES ABOUT 4 CUPS

Blend mayonnaise, sour cream, fruit juices, honey and sugar. Fold in pecans and cherries.

Store covered in refrigerator. Will stay fresh for several days.

MRS. MILTON GARD
Rancho Mirage, California

BREADS

Traditions for Tomorrow

Whatever the form or flavor, nothing smells quite so good
in the making—or carries such pride in the serving—
as a home-baked bread. Perhaps it's a freshly risen loaf,
piquant with herbs. Or golden corn sticks
or a stand of rich bran muffins. Maybe it's a sunny
coffee cake to go along with the morning meal.
Take your choice of these good ideas from yesterday, and
bake them when the fancy strikes. Help to spread
the special warmth that comes with breads . . . homemade.

Olive Oil and Beer Bread

1 package dry yeast
1 cup tepid beer (Coors or any light beer)
4 scant cups sifted flour
1½ tsp. salt
4 tbsp. olive oil

MAKES 1 LARGE OR 2 SMALL LOAVES

Dissolve yeast in beer. Mix flour and salt; add dissolved yeast and olive oil and mix to a soft dough. (Add an additional spoonful of beer if dough seems too stiff.)

On a lightly floured board, knead dough until it appears slick, smooth and very elastic (12 to 15 minutes). Place in an oiled bowl and cover with a towel. Put in a warm place until doubled in bulk.

Punch down dough or knead 2 minutes. Form into two loaves and place in greased loaf pans. (Or, if preferred, place in one large loaf pan.) Let rise again, covering with a towel. Bake in a preheated 375° oven 40 to 45 minutes. When done, bread will be brown and will make a hollow "thump" when tapped.

Turn out of pans onto the towel. If you like a soft crust, brush hot loaves with butter. Let cool.

MRS. MAX THOMPSON
Palm Desert, California

Dilly Bread

1 package dry yeast
¼ cup lukewarm water
1 cup cream-style cottage cheese, warmed
1 tbsp. dried onion flakes
2 tbsp. sugar
1 tbsp. margarine
2 tsp. dill seed or dill weed
1 tsp. salt
½ tsp. baking soda
1 egg
2½ cups flour
Melted butter
Coarse salt

MAKES 1 LOAF

Dissolve yeast in lukewarm water. Add to warmed cottage cheese. Add onion flakes, sugar, margarine, dill, salt, soda, egg and flour; stir well. Knead dough on a lightly floured board. Let rise 2 hours.

Place dough in a greased 10-inch casserole or shape into a loaf and place in a greased loaf pan. Let rise 1 hour. Bake in a preheated 350° oven 40 to 50 minutes. When done, brush warm loaf with butter and sprinkle with coarse salt.

This bread freezes well.

MRS. WILFORD GONYEA
Eugene, Oregon

Herb Bread

2 packages dry yeast
1¼ cups warm water
¼ cup powdered nondairy creamer
¼ cup sugar
¼ cup salad oil
2 tsp. salt
2 eggs
4½ to 5 cups sifted flour
½ tsp. nutmeg
¼ tsp. basil, crumbled
¼ tsp. thyme
¼ tsp. oregano
Melted butter

MAKES 2 LOAVES

Dissolve yeast in ¼ cup of the warm water. Add powdered creamer, sugar, salad oil, salt, eggs, the remaining warm water and 2 cups of the flour. Beat until smooth. Add nutmeg and herbs and beat well. Beat in remaining 2½ to 3 cups flour to make a soft dough.

Knead 5 minutes on a lightly floured board. Place dough in an oiled bowl and brush with melted butter. Cover and let rise 1 to 1½ hours. Punch down dough. Divide in half and let rest 10 minutes. Shape into loaves and place in oiled loaf pans, about 9x5x3 inches. Let rise 1 hour. Bake in a preheated 375° oven 35 to 40 minutes.

MRS. JOSEPH SHEFFET
Indian Wells, California

Beer Biscuits

2 cups biscuit mix (Bisquick)
2 tsp. sugar
¼ tsp. salt
½ can beer

MAKES ABOUT 10

Mix all ingredients thoroughly. Drop by spoonfuls into greased muffin cups, filling them about half full. Bake in a preheated 450° oven 10 minutes or until biscuits rise and are golden. Serve hot, straight from the oven.

MRS. JAMES LING
Dallas, Texas

Popovers

2 tbsp. butter
4 eggs
1¾ cups milk
2 scant cups flour
½ tsp. salt
1 tsp. fresh lemon juice

MAKES 1 DOZEN

Put ½ teaspoon butter in each of 12 glass custard cups. Arrange cups on a cookie sheet and place in a preheated 375° oven until butter melts and cups are very hot.

Meanwhile, beat eggs until frothy. Using an electric mixer, add 1 cup of the milk slowly at low speed. Sift flour and salt into egg mixture; mix slowly. Add the remaining milk and lemon juice. Beat at high speed (the mixture will be thin).

When mixture is well beaten, quickly pour into the hot custard cups, filling them half full. Bake 35 minutes or until popovers double in size and are lightly brown. Serve piping hot, with lots of butter.

MRS. DEAN W. PHILLIPS
Palm Desert, California

Southern Cornbread

1 tsp. baking powder
4 cups buttermilk
3 egg yolks
2 tsp. sugar
1 tsp. salt
4 cups white cornmeal
¼ cup bacon fat or oil

SERVES 10–12

Add baking powder to buttermilk; then add egg yolks, sugar and salt. Combine with cornmeal and stir well.

Heat bacon fat in a heavy iron ovenproof skillet. Add cornmeal mixture and stir well. Place skillet in a preheated 450° oven and bake 30 minutes.

MRS. NORMAN PHILLIPS
La Jolla, California

Corn Sticks

- 2 eggs
- 2 cups milk
- 3 tbsp. melted shortening
- 2 tsp. salt
- 1 tsp. sugar
- 2 cups sifted cornmeal
- 3 tsp. baking powder
- ½ tsp. baking soda

MAKES 2 DOZEN

"Having been born and raised in Georgia, I am naturally fond of Southern cornbreads. The following recipe for corn sticks is one of my favorites. Note that no flour is used—good Southern cornmeal is fine enough to hold the bread together."

Beat eggs until light. Add milk, shortening, salt and sugar. Add cornmeal and beat until smooth. (Be careful adding the cornmeal, as meal varies and the batter should be a medium consistency.) Sift in baking powder. Dissolve soda in a spoonful of cold water and add to mixture. Stir well and pour into greased and heated corn stick pans. Bake in a good hot oven (400°) until brown and crusty, 25 minutes.

MARION B. FOLSOM
Rochester, New York

Spoon Bread

- 2 eggs, separated
- ½ cup cornmeal
- 1 cup boiling water
- ½ tsp. salt
- 1 tbsp. butter
- 1 cup milk

SERVES 3–4

Beat egg whites until stiff. Beat egg yolks. Set both bowls aside.

In a large saucepan, slowly add cornmeal to the boiling water, stirring constantly until thick. Remove from heat and add salt and butter. Stir in milk and beaten egg yolks. Fold in stiffly beaten egg whites.

Turn into a greased shallow baking dish, about 10x7x2 inches. Bake in a preheated 375° oven 30 to 40 minutes.

EDWARD DURELL STONE
New York, New York

Foolproof Spoon Bread

6 cups milk (made by diluting two 13-oz. cans Pet evaporated milk with hot water)
1½ cups yellow cornmeal
¼ cup margarine
1½ tsp. salt
6 eggs, separated

Add enough hot water to evaporated milk to make a total of 6 cups liquid; mix well and pour into a large saucepan. Warm diluted milk slowly and gradually add cornmeal. Cook until mixture is the consistency of mush. Remove from heat and add margarine and salt.

Beat egg yolks and add to cornmeal mixture. Beat egg whites until stiff and fold in. Pour into a greased deep ovenproof glass casserole. Bake in a preheated 400° oven until brown, about 40 minutes.

This recipe can be cut in half.

MRS. GEORGE G. MOORE
Bellaire Shores, Florida

Frances Moore is Mamie Eisenhower's sister.

Mexican Spoon Bread

1 can (20 oz.) cream-style corn
¾ cup milk
½ cup salad oil
2 eggs, beaten
1 cup cornmeal
½ tsp. baking soda
1 tsp. salt
1 can (about 2 oz.) chopped green chiles, drained
1 cup grated cheddar cheese

SERVES 6–8

Mix corn, milk, oil and eggs. Stir in cornmeal, soda and salt. Gently fold in chiles and cheese.

Pour into a buttered 2-quart casserole. Bake, uncovered, in a preheated 400° oven 45 minutes.

MRS. HUGH B. MANSON
Ormond Beach, Florida

Start the Day Right—With fresh juice, applesauce-filled German Pancake Omelet (page 125) and coffee.

Stylish Snacking—Set the stage for a friendly get-together with cheesy La Gougère (right) and aperitifs.

La Gougère
BURGUNDIAN CHEESE PASTRY

2 cups milk or water
2 tsp. salt
¼ tsp. pepper
½ cup butter
2 cups sifted flour
8 eggs
10 oz. Swiss cheese, grated
1 egg yolk, beaten with a little milk
Additional grated Swiss cheese

MAKES 2 RINGS

Combine milk, salt and pepper in a large saucepan. Add butter and heat, stirring, until butter melts and mixture is boiling. Remove from heat and add flour all at once, stirring briskly with a wooden spoon. Return to heat and cook over low heat, continuing to beat vigorously until mixture "detaches" itself from the side of the pan and forms a compact mass. Remove from heat and let cool a few minutes. Beat in eggs one at a time. (It is important to work energetically so that as much air as possible is incorporated with the beating of the eggs. This gives the pastry its lightness.) When the dough is shiny and smooth, mix in cheese. Let cool.

Butter two baking sheets. Divide dough in half. With a tablespoon, scoop out an oval of dough about the size of a small egg from one half. With a rubber spatula, push dough off the spoon onto one of the baking sheets. Continue in this manner, arranging the ovals so that they touch and form a circle, leaving a space in the middle about 2½ inches in diameter. Make another circle around the first. With a teaspoon, scoop out smaller ovals and arrange a circular "crown" on top of the first two circles, midway between the outer and inner edges.

On the other baking sheet, repeat procedure with remaining half of dough to make another crowned ring.

Brush with beaten egg yolk mixture and sprinkle with additional grated cheese. Bake in a preheated 375° oven 45 minutes or until brown, puffed and crusty. (Do not open oven door while pastry is rising.) The ring is served whole (hot, warm or cold), and pieces are broken off.

NOTE: Rounds of dough may also be arranged in a tube pan or a large flan ring. (If using a flan ring, place cookie cutter or custard cup in center.)

MRS. HARRY WALDMAN
Palm Springs, California

Fruit Bran Muffins

1 cup sifted flour
1 tsp. baking powder
½ tsp. baking soda
½ tsp. salt
¼ cup brown sugar
1 cup bran
1 egg, beaten
2 tbsp. molasses
2 tbsp. butter, melted
2 tbsp. buttermilk
1 cup sliced bananas
1 cup grated apples
1 cup chopped dates or raisins
1 cup chopped nuts

MAKES ABOUT 2 DOZEN

Sift together flour, baking powder, soda, salt and sugar. Stir in bran. Mix egg, molasses, butter and buttermilk and beat well. Add dry ingredients to buttermilk mixture and mix until dampened. Add fruit and nuts. Spoon into greased muffin cups. Bake in a preheated 375° oven 30 minutes.

ELISABETH E. STEWART
Pasadena, California

Pumpkin Bread

5 cups flour
4 cups sugar
4 tsp. baking soda
2 tsp. cinnamon
1 tsp. salt
1 tsp. ground cloves
1 can (about 29 oz.) pumpkin
1 cup salad oil
1 cup chopped nuts

MAKES 2 LOAVES

Blend flour, sugar, soda, cinnamon, salt and cloves. Add pumpkin and salad oil; stir well. Add nuts. Pour into two greased loaf pans, about 9x5x3 inches. Bake in a preheated 350° oven 1¼ hours or until dry when tested with a pick.

This bread keeps very well.

MRS. GENE BOSCACCI
Palm Springs, California

Lemon Bread

1½ cups sugar
⅓ cup butter, melted
3 tbsp. lemon extract
2 eggs
1½ cups sifted flour
1 tsp. baking powder
1 tsp. salt
½ cup milk
Grated rind of 1 large lemon
½ cup chopped pecans
Juice of 1 large lemon

MAKES 1 LOAF

Grease a standard loaf pan with shortening and line bottom and sides with waxed paper.

Mix 1 cup of the sugar, the butter and lemon extract. Beat in eggs. Sift together flour, baking powder and salt; add to sugar mixture alternately with milk. Beat just enough to blend. Fold in grated lemon rind and nuts. Pour into the prepared pan. Bake in a preheated 350° oven 1 hour. (A crack will form in the top of the loaf.)

While warm, remove bread from pan. Combine lemon juice and the remaining sugar; mix well. Drizzle over top and into crack of warm loaf. Wait 24 hours before cutting.

Wrapped in foil, this loaf will keep for 3 months in the refrigerator or for 1 year in the freezer.

MRS. GODFREY KING
Covina, California

Cranberry Nut Bread

2 cups flour
1 cup sugar
1½ tsp. baking powder
½ tsp. baking soda
½ tsp. salt
1 egg, beaten
2 tbsp. melted shortening
½ cup orange juice
2 tbsp. hot water
½ cup chopped nuts
1 cup chopped fresh cranberries
Rind of 1 orange, chopped

MAKES 1 LOAF

Sift together flour, sugar, baking powder, soda and salt. Add egg, melted shortening, orange juice and hot water. Combine just until dry ingredients are moistened. Fold in nuts, cranberries and orange rind. Pour into a greased loaf pan, 8½x4½x2½ inches. Bake in a preheated 325° oven about 1 hour and 10 minutes. Cool. Refrigerate 24 hours before serving.

MRS. MATT ZAPP
Cathedral City, California

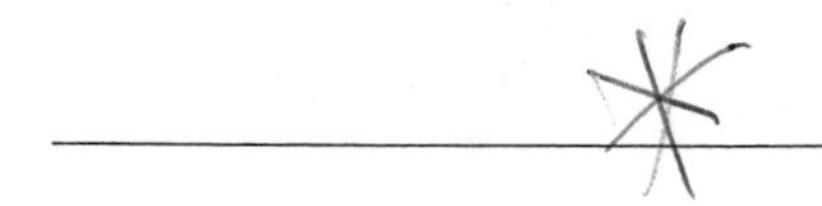

Applesauce Loaf

1 1/4 cups applesauce
1 cup sugar
1/2 cup cooking oil
2 eggs
3 tbsp. milk
2 cups flour
1 tsp. baking soda
1/2 tsp. baking powder
1/2 tsp. cinnamon
1/4 tsp. salt
1/4 tsp. nutmeg
1/4 tsp. allspice
1/2 cup chopped nuts (preferably walnuts)

NUT TOPPING
1/2 cup chopped walnuts
1/4 cup brown sugar
1/4 cup cinnamon

MAKES 4 LOAVES

Thoroughly mix applesauce, sugar, oil, eggs and milk. Sift together flour, soda, baking powder, cinnamon, salt, nutmeg and allspice. Stir into applesauce mixture and beat well. Pour into four greased small foil loaf pans.

Combine Nut Topping ingredients and sprinkle mixture over batter. Bake in a preheated 350° oven 20 minutes or longer (depending on size of pans). Loaves should be golden brown when done.

MRS. JOHN CURCI
Newport Beach, California

Edna's Banana Bread

1/2 cup shortening
1 1/3 cups brown sugar, firmly packed
1 tsp. vanilla
1/2 tsp. banana flavoring
1/2 tsp. black walnut flavoring
1/4 tsp. butter flavoring
2 eggs
2 cups sifted flour
1 tsp. baking soda
1/2 tsp. salt
1/4 cup buttermilk
1 cup mashed ripe bananas
1/2 cup chopped nuts

MAKES 1 LOAF

Cream shortening and brown sugar thoroughly. Add flavorings and blend well. Beat in eggs one at a time. Sift together flour, soda and salt; then sift again into creamed mixture. Stir in buttermilk and bananas, mixing just until blended. Stir in nuts.

Pour batter into a greased and floured loaf pan, 9x5x2 1/2 inches. Let stand in pan 20 minutes. Bake in a preheated 350° oven 1 hour. (If using smaller foil pans, bake about 45 minutes.) Test for doneness with a pick. Let stand in pan on a wire rack 10 minutes. Remove loaf from pan and place on rack. Cover with a light cloth and cool completely.

JOEL E. CARLSON
Boone, Iowa

Mr. Carlson is Mamie Eisenhower's uncle.

Vermont Blueberry Johnnycake

- 1 cup cornmeal
- ½ cup flour
- ½ cup sugar
- 2 tsp. baking powder
- ¼ tsp. salt
- 1 egg, well beaten
- ½ cup milk
- 2 tbsp. melted shortening
- 1 cup dry blueberries (if frozen, thaw and drain well)

SERVES 6–8

Sift together cornmeal, flour, sugar, baking powder and salt. Add beaten egg, milk and shortening, mixing lightly. Stir in blueberries. Pour batter into a greased baking pan, 8x8x2 inches. Bake in a preheated 450° oven 20 minutes.

NOTE: Johnnycake may be baked in a pie pan, if you prefer. To serve, cut into wedges.

MRS. CARL W. WENTWORTH
Palm Desert, California

Danish Puff

* Like Marie Sorensons

- 2 cups sifted flour
- 1 cup butter, softened
- 2 tbsp. water
- 1 cup water
- 1 tsp. almond flavoring
- 3 eggs
- Confectioners' sugar icing
- Chopped nuts

MAKES 2 COFFEE CAKES (EACH SERVES ABOUT 4)

Measure 1 cup of the flour into a bowl. Cut in ½ cup of the butter. Sprinkle with the 2 tablespoons water and mix with a fork. Round up into a ball and divide in half. With hands, pat each half of dough into a long strip, 12 x 3 inches. Place strips 3 inches apart on an ungreased baking sheet.

Mix the remaining butter and 1 cup water in a saucepan. Bring to a rolling boil. Add almond flavoring and remove from heat. Stir in the remaining flour immediately to avoid lumping. When mixture is smooth and thick, add eggs one at a time, beating until smooth after each addition. Spread half the mixture evenly over each strip of pastry. Bake about 50 minutes or until topping is crisp and nicely browned.

Frost with a confectioners' sugar icing and sprinkle generously with nuts.

MRS. GEORGE VAN WAGENEN
Edina, Minnesota

Sour Cream or Yogurt Coffee Cake

- ½ cup butter or margarine, softened
- 1 cup sugar
- 2 eggs
- 2 cups flour
- 1 tsp. baking powder
- 1 tsp. baking soda
- ½ tsp. salt
- 1 cup sour cream or unflavored yogurt
- 1 tsp. vanilla

TOPPING

- ⅓ cup brown sugar
- ¼ cup granulated sugar
- 1 tsp. cinnamon
- 1 cup chopped nuts

MAKES 1 COFFEE CAKE

Cream butter and sugar. Beat in eggs one at a time. Sift together flour, baking powder, soda and salt; add to the butter mixture alternating with sour cream, beginning and ending with flour mixture. Add vanilla. Pour half the batter into a buttered square baking pan, 9x9x2 inches, or a springform pan.

Combine topping ingredients. Sprinkle half the mixture over the batter in pan. Add remaining batter and cover with remaining topping mixture. Bake in a preheated 325° oven 40 minutes or longer.

MRS. CLOVIS P. SAUNDERS
Millbrae, California

Rich Filbert Nut Bread

- ¾ cup butter or margarine, softened
- 2¼ cups sifted flour
- 1 tbsp. granulated sugar
- 1 cake yeast, finely crumbled
- ½ cup milk
- 3 eggs, slightly beaten
- Confectioners' sugar

NUT FILLING

- 2 cups ground filberts
- ¼ cup butter, melted
- 1 cup granulated sugar
- 1 tsp. vanilla

MAKES 2 LONG ROLLS (EACH SERVES ABOUT 6)

Combine butter, flour, granulated sugar and yeast with a pastry blender. Mix milk and eggs and add to flour mixture. Work together until dough leaves the side of the bowl. Divide dough in half and wrap each in waxed paper; place in a plastic bag and refrigerate overnight.

Next day, on a board that has been covered with confectioners' sugar, roll each half of dough into a rectangular shape about ⅛ inch thick. Mix ingredients for Nut Filling and spread half evenly on each rectangle. Roll up dough as you would a jelly roll. Place on an ungreased baking sheet. Let rise 1 hour. Brush lightly with milk. Bake in a preheated 350° oven 40 to 50 minutes.

MRS. LEO PARTYKA
Indian Wells, California

Pecan Rolls

¾ cup milk
½ cup sugar
½ cup butter, melted
1 tsp. salt
1 yeast cake or 1 package dry yeast
3 eggs, beaten
3 cups sifted flour
Softened butter
3 tsp. cinnamon
½ cup raisins or currants
¾ cup chopped pecans

TOPPING
Melted butter
Honey
Brown sugar
Chopped pecans

MAKES 12–15 ROLLS

Heat milk until it starts to bubble, then pour into a medium-size bowl. Stir in ¼ cup of the sugar, the melted butter and salt. Let stand until liquid is lukewarm. Crumble yeast into liquid; stir to dissolve. Stir in beaten eggs and flour. Mix well. Cover dough and refrigerate overnight.

On a floured board, roll out chilled dough into a rectangle about 10x16 inches. Spread generously with softened butter. Mix cinnamon with the remaining sugar and sprinkle over dough. Sprinkle on raisins and nuts. Roll up dough as you would a jelly roll.

Prepare muffin cups by spooning topping ingredients into *each* cup as follows: ½ teaspoon melted butter, ½ teaspoon honey, ½ teaspoon brown sugar and 1 teaspoon chopped nuts. Cut dough into ¾-inch-thick slices and place cut side down on topping. Cover and let rise until double.

Bake in a preheated 350° oven 30 minutes. Immediately invert onto a baking sheet and let stand for a few minutes to let topping mixture run down over rolls. Remove pan.

MRS. CHARLES BORWICK
Cathedral City, California

Sour Cream Waffles

2 cups sifted cake flour
2 tsp. baking powder (Royal)
1 tsp. baking soda
1/8 tsp. salt
2 tsp. sugar
4 eggs, separated
6 tbsp. margarine, melted and cooled
2 cups sour cream
1/2 cup buttermilk

MAKES ABOUT 8 LARGE OR 12 SMALL WAFFLES

Sift together flour, baking powder, soda, salt and sugar; set aside. Beat egg whites until stiff; set aside.

Beat yolks (go right ahead and beat them—don't bother to wash the beater). Gradually add melted margarine (be sure it is cool). Add sour cream and buttermilk. (Sweet milk can be used but it's better with buttermilk.) Mix until smooth, then add flour mixture. *Gently* fold in egg whites.

Be sure waffle iron is piping hot, then spoon on batter and bake until waffle is crispy brown. Put waffle on your plate and cover with butter, maple syrup, jelly or honey. (I use all of them!)

WILLIAM DEMAREST
Palm Springs, California

George Washington's Griddle Cakes

1 3/4 cups sifted flour
2 tbsp. granulated sugar
3 1/2 tsp. baking powder
1 tsp. salt
1 egg, slightly beaten
2 cups milk
3 tbsp. vegetable oil
1 cup cherry preserves
1 tbsp. lemon juice
4 tbsp. confectioners' sugar

SERVES 4–6

Mix flour, granulated sugar, baking powder and salt. Add egg, milk and oil; blend well. Using 2/3 cup batter for each griddle cake, pour onto a hot griddle and cook until done. (Makes five griddle cakes.)

Stack the griddle cakes, spreading each layer with cherry preserves and sprinkling with lemon juice and confectioners' sugar. Keep warm. Cut into wedges to serve.

MRS. RICHARD H. ROBINSON
Palm Desert, California

PRESERVES & RELISHES

The Right Accessories

"You made this yourself?" they ask in an admiring tone.
That's the usual reaction when you hand 'round
a chutney, a relish or a conserve you've put up at home.
And here is a very select group of recipes to
augment that admiration. There are pickles and preserves
with such a ring of old-time authenticity
that they would have done Grandmother proud. Plus some
special side dishes as up-to-date as tomorrow.
Served beside hot meats, used to garnish cold plates,
even sparking up a platter of sandwiches, these
accompaniments add that plus of "something special."

Hot Curried Fruit

1 can (about 16 oz.) peach halves
1 can (about 16 oz.) pineapple slices
1 can (about 16 oz.) pears
1 can (about 16 oz.) apricots
1 jar (about 16 oz.) maraschino cherries
1 cup brown sugar
¼ cup butter
4 tsp. curry powder

SERVES 6–8

Drain fruit. Spread on paper towels and blot. Mix and arrange in a buttered 3-quart baking dish.

Mix sugar, butter and curry powder in a saucepan. Heat, stirring, until butter melts and sugar dissolves. Spread over fruit and refrigerate, covered, 24 hours. Bake uncovered in a preheated 350° oven 45 minutes to 1 hour.

May be served with a meat course or as dessert.

MRS. STANTON D. ANDERSON
Bethesda, Maryland

Mrs. Anderson is Mamie Eisenhower's niece.

Mustard Ring

¾ cup sugar
2 heaping tbsp. dry mustard
Salt
¾ cup Heinz apple cider vinegar (no substitute!)
¼ cup water
4 eggs, well beaten
1 tbsp. unflavored gelatin
1 to 2 tbsp. water
1 cup whipping cream, whipped

SERVES 6–8

Mix sugar, dry mustard and salt. Add vinegar, ¼ cup water and the eggs. Soak gelatin in 1 to 2 tablespoons water in the top of a double boiler, then dissolve over hot water. Blend in egg mixture and cook until creamy.

Remove top of double boiler from heat and let cool. Fold in whipped cream and pour into a 4-cup ring mold. Chill until firm.

MRS. GEORGE L. RATCLIFFE
Palm Desert, California

Fresh Cranberry Chutney

1 lb. fresh cranberries
1 cup water
1 2-inch stick cinnamon
½ tsp. allspice
½ tsp. salt
⅛ tsp. ground cloves
1 large unpeeled apple, cored and cubed
1 cup dried apricots, quartered
4 thin slices unpeeled lemon, seeded
1½ cups sugar
1 cup seedless grapes
1 cup sliced celery
½ cup drained bottled cocktail onions
½ cup broken unsalted cashews

MAKES 8 CUPS

Wash cranberries and put in a 2-quart saucepan. Add water, cinnamon stick, allspice, salt and cloves. Bring to a boil, lower heat, cover and continue cooking until cranberries pop (3 to 4 minutes).

Mix apple cubes, apricots and lemon slices. Add to cranberries along with sugar, grapes, celery and cocktail onions. Bring mixture to a boil, stirring gently to prevent sticking. Reduce heat, cover and simmer 30 minutes, stirring occasionally. Remove cover and continue to cook 15 minutes, watching carefully. Stir (mixture will have thickened).

Remove cinnamon stick and add cashew nuts. Cool and store, covered, in the refrigerator.

Serve cold as a relish. Particularly nice with poultry, lamb or veal.

MRS. SAMUEL JAGGAR
Portland, Oregon

Chutney Aspic

2 cups ginger ale
1 package (3 oz.) lime-flavored gelatin
1 cup chutney, lightly chopped

MAKES 3 CUPS

Heat 1 cup of the ginger ale and pour over gelatin; stir to dissolve. Add remaining cup of ginger ale. Stir and pour into an oiled 3- to 4-cup mold. Chill until slightly thickened. Stir chutney into gelatin and chill until firm.

Serve with meat or fowl.

MRS. WINSTON R. FULLER
San Marino, California

Old-Fashioned Chow-Chow

4 qt. chopped cabbage
2 qt. chopped green tomatoes (preferably cherry tomatoes)
12 green peppers, chopped
12 red bell peppers, chopped
12 onions, chopped
½ cup salt
4 tbsp. dry mustard
4 tbsp. mustard seed
3 tbsp. celery seed
2 tbsp. mixed whole pickling spices
1 tbsp. ginger
1 tbsp. turmeric
4 qt. vinegar
5 cups sugar

MAKES 16–18 PINTS

Mix vegetables with salt and let stand overnight at room temperature; then drain.

Mix spices and tie in a cheesecloth bag. Put vinegar, sugar and the spice bag in a kettle. Simmer 20 minutes. Add drained vegetables and simmer until hot and well-seasoned.

Remove spice bag. Pack hot chow-chow into hot, sterile jars and seal at once. Store in a dark place.

MRS. FRANK M. MacFALL
La Quinta, California

Carrot Conserve

2 large oranges, quartered and seeded
1 large lime or lemon, quartered and seeded
1 can (20 oz.) crushed pineapple
6 large carrots, scraped
Sugar
1 bottle (6 oz.) liquid pectin

MAKES 3½–4 PINTS

Put oranges and lime through food grinder, using medium plate. Combine with undrained pineapple and boil 10 minutes, stirring frequently. Grind carrots and add to fruit mixture. Cook until carrots are just tender, about 5 minutes. Measure mixture and add an equivalent amount of sugar. Cook, stirring constantly, about 15 minutes. Remove from heat and stir in pectin. Pour into hot, sterile jars and seal.

MRS. W. RANDOLPH BURGESS
Queenstown, Maryland

Spiced Grape Jelly

3 cups bottled grape juice
1 package (1¾ oz.) powdered fruit pectin
½ tsp. cinnamon
¼ tsp. nutmeg
3½ cups sugar

MAKES 5 CUPS

Combine grape juice, pectin, cinnamon and nutmeg in a large saucepan. Stir over high heat until mixture reaches a full, rolling boil. Stir in sugar. Bring to a full rolling boil again and boil rapidly 1 minute, stirring constantly. Remove from heat. Skim any foam and pour immediately into hot, sterile jars. Seal at once with melted paraffin.

MRS. FRANK M. MacFALL
La Quinta, California

Pepper Relish

12 green peppers
12 red bell peppers
12 medium onions
1 qt. malt vinegar
3 cups brown sugar
2 tbsp. salt

MAKES 8–10 PINTS

Put peppers and onions through a food grinder, using coarse plate. Cover with boiling water and let stand 10 minutes. Drain and put into a large saucepan. Add vinegar, sugar and salt. Bring to a boil and boil, covered, 10 minutes—no longer. Seal in hot, sterile jars.

MRS. HOWARD W. IRWIN
Portland, Oregon

Squash Pickles

12 zucchini (unpeeled)
3 large white onions
1 cup salt
4 qt. water
5 cups white vinegar
2 cups granulated sugar
1 cup water
½ cup brown sugar
5 tbsp. mustard seed
2 tbsp. celery seed
1 tsp. turmeric

MAKES 5 PINTS

Cut squash and onions into thin slices; separate onion slices into rings. Add salt to the 4 quarts water; add squash and onions and soak 12 to 18 hours. Let drain 1 hour.

Combine remaining ingredients in a large saucepan and boil 5 minutes, stirring occasionally. Add squash and onions; simmer 30 minutes. Pack into hot, sterile jars and seal.

MRS. WILLIAM GARLAND
Indian Wells, California

Saint Patrick's Pickles

1 head cauliflower
1 bunch carrots
2 green peppers
1 bunch celery
1 can (6 oz.) pitted green olives, drained
1 small jar pimientos, drained and cut into strips
¾ cup garlic red wine vinegar
½ cup salad oil
¼ cup water
2 tbsp. salt
½ tsp. oregano

MAKES 2–4 PINTS

Cut cauliflower into bite-size pieces. Cut carrots and green peppers into strips. Cut celery into small pieces. Put all ingredients in a pot and mix well. Cover and bring to a boil, stirring occasionally. Reduce heat and simmer 5 minutes. Remove from heat. Remove cover after 5 to 10 minutes. Cool, then chill 24 hours before serving.

MRS. ROBERT BREMSON
Shawnee Mission, Kansas

Crystallized Pickles

1 jar (48 oz.) whole dill pickles (Heinz genuine)
1½ lb. sugar (about 6 cups)

MAKES 1 QUART

Drain all juice from pickles. Slice crosswise into 1-inch pieces. Put a layer of pickle slices in the empty pickle jar. Cover with about ½ cup sugar. Repeat layering pickles and sugar, using all pickles and ending with sugar on top. Cover tightly and let stand at room temperature about 10 days. Turn the jar over about once a day to mix well. The pickle slices will become very clear and crisp. After 10 days, store in the refrigerator.

MRS. WANDA WALKER
Palm Desert, California

SAUCES

The Finishing Touches

A good dish or a great one . . . often it's the sauce
that makes the difference! And each of these intriguing
toppings has the makings of a great dish in it.
Crushed herbs and nuts to spice a soup,
a light white wine sauce to vary a vegetable,
a delicate whisper of anise in an Italian specialty.
These pages present unusual sauces for
many a course—including two inspirations that
turn fruit or ice cream into bravo desserts.

A Special White Sauce

4 tbsp. safflower oil
4 tbsp. unbleached flour or all-purpose flour
2 cups skim milk
Pinch of nutmeg
Pinch of white pepper

MAKES ABOUT 2 CUPS

No salt, no butter, no cream—perfect for heart patients.

Heat oil in a saucepan. Add flour and stir to make a thin paste. Add milk slowly, using a wire whisk. When thickened, stir in seasonings.

Sauce Véronique: Make White Sauce as directed above. Add 4 tablespoons sauterne and 1 cup peeled seedless green grapes. Use over broiled fish, sole fillets or haddock.

Newburg Sauce: Make White Sauce as directed above. Add ½ teaspoon paprika and 4 tablespoons dry sherry. Use as a sauce for lobster, shrimp or crabmeat.

MRS. FRED WARING
Shawnee-on-the-Delaware, Pennsylvania

Vegetable Sauce

2 cups drained miniature cocktail onions
½ cup butter
½ cup almonds
2 tbsp. brown sugar
2 cloves garlic, chopped
½ tsp. salt
½ tsp. pepper
½ cup dry white wine

SERVES 6

Rinse bottled onions (to wash away vinegar) and drain well. Combine all ingredients in a saucepan and heat gently but thoroughly.

Add sauce to any cooked vegetable of your choice. Our recommendations: green beans, spinach or broccoli.

GENERAL and MRS. WILLIAM WESTMORELAND
Charleston, South Carolina

Pesto Sauce

- 3 cloves garlic, chopped
- 3 tbsp. minced fresh sweet basil leaves (dried may be used)
- 1 tbsp. chopped parsley
- 3 tbsp. grated Italian hard cheese (Parmesan, Romano)
- 1 tbsp. chopped pine nuts or walnuts
- 1 tsp. salt
- 4 to 6 tbsp. olive oil

SERVES 2

In a mortar, work the garlic, basil, parsley, cheese, nuts and salt to a creamy paste. Still pounding with a pestle, add the oil very slowly and work mixture into a smooth sauce.

Add sauce and a pat of butter to hot pasta or soup; mix well.

MRS. HARRISON ROBERTS
Indian Wells, California

Spaghetti Meat Sauce

- 1/8 cup salad oil
- 1 onion, sliced
- 1 1/2 lb. ground round
- 1 cup tomato juice
- 1 can (about 6 oz.) tomato paste
- 1/2 tsp. chili powder
- 1/2 tsp. sugar
- 1/2 tsp. salt
- 1/8 tsp. pepper

SERVES 6

"This is one of David's favorites."

Heat oil in a skillet. Add onion and cook, stirring, until golden. Add meat and brown, stirring occasionally. Stir in tomato juice and tomato paste, then add seasonings. Simmer, uncovered, 45 minutes.

JULIE NIXON EISENHOWER
Washington, D.C.

Meat Sauce for Two

- 1/2 to 3/4 lb. ground round
- 1 small can (about 8 oz.) tomato sauce
- 1 clove garlic
- 1 small onion, cut up
- 1 tsp. oregano
- 1/8 tsp. anise seed or 2 drops anise extract

SERVES 2

Brown meat in a skillet. Drain off fat. Put tomato sauce, garlic, onion, oregano and anise in a blender and blend 10 to 20 seconds. Pour over browned meat. Simmer, uncovered, no more than 15 to 20 minutes.

Serve over thin spaghettini or vermicelli cooked *al dente.*

FRANK M. MacFALL
La Quinta, California

Italian Spaghetti Sauce

2 large cans solid-pack whole tomatoes, drained and chopped
1 can (about 8 oz.) tomato sauce
1 can (about 6 oz.) tomato paste
½ tsp. each basil, rosemary and marjoram
½ tsp. pepper
3 bay leaves
2 tbsp. Tabasco sauce
Olive oil
3 cloves garlic, minced
4 cups minced onion
3 cups minced celery
3 cups minced green pepper
3 cans (3 oz. each) sliced mushrooms
2 lb. ground beef
½ lb. sausage
1 can (4½ oz.) ripe olives, drained and chopped
1 tbsp. salt
1 tbsp. paprika
1 tbsp. chili powder
¼ tsp. cayenne pepper
1½ tbsp. oregano
1 tbsp. Worcestershire sauce

SERVES 12

In a large saucepan, warm tomatoes, tomato sauce, tomato paste, basil, rosemary, marjoram, pepper, bay leaves and Tabasco sauce. Simmer, uncovered, until meat mixture is ready.

Cover bottom of a large skillet with olive oil and heat. Add garlic to hot oil and brown. Add minced onion and brown. Stir in celery, green pepper and mushrooms and cook 10 minutes, stirring occasionally. Add ground beef, sausage, olives, salt, paprika, chili powder, cayenne pepper, oregano and Worcestershire sauce. Cook until the meat is browned and mixture is well blended. Combine meat mixture with tomato sauce; cover and simmer several hours.

This sauce freezes well.

NOTE: To cut down on the tomato flavor, add brown sugar to taste (½ teaspoon at a time). For a thinner sauce, add V-8 juice.

MRS. HAROLD HUTTON
Orange, California

Sauce Cardinal

1 cup catsup
½ cup tarragon vinegar
½ cup currant jelly
2 tbsp. butter
2 tsp. Worcestershire sauce
Salt and pepper

MAKES ABOUT 2 CUPS

"Here's a way to put a new face on yesterday's roast."

Heat all ingredients in a large skillet, stirring occasionally. Simmer leftover sliced meat in sauce 30 minutes. Especially good with leftover roast lamb.

MRS. JOSEPH E. BELL
Winnetka, Illinois

Colbert Butter

1 cup sweet butter, at room temperature
1 tbsp. lemon juice
1 tbsp. Worcestershire sauce
2 tbsp. minced parsley
1 tbsp. tarragon*
1 tsp. white pepper
1 tsp. meat extract (Bovril or B.V.), melted

Cream butter and beat in remaining ingredients. Shape into a roll and refrigerate (keeps well). Cut into slices and serve on top of fish fillets or broiled meat.

*Marinate dried tarragon in a little white wine or the lemon juice before using.

MRS. WILLIAM O. FLEETWOOD
Indian Wells, California

Beer Marinade

1 can beer
½ cup soy sauce
2 tbsp. sugar
2 tbsp. dry mustard
2 tbsp. Worcestershire sauce
Dash of Tabasco sauce
1 or 2 cloves garlic, minced

MAKES ABOUT 2½ CUPS

Combine all ingredients and mix well. Store in a tightly covered jar in the refrigerator. Use as a marinade for roasts and steaks.

MRS. GEORGE RANDOLPH HEARST, SR.
Palm Springs, California

Sweet-Hot Mustard Sauce

1 cup dry mustard (Colman's)
1 cup vinegar
1 cup sugar
2 eggs, beaten
Pinch of salt

MAKES ABOUT 2½ CUPS

Mix mustard and vinegar and let stand 2 hours. Add sugar, beaten eggs and salt. Cook over low heat, stirring until thick. Pour into sterile jars and let cool. Store in the refrigerator.

This versatile sauce can be used with all meats, although it's particularly good with steak. Thinned with mayonnaise or sour cream, it makes a fine spread for chicken or turkey sandwiches.

MRS. WILLIAM R. YANCEY
Indian Wells, California

Banana Sauce

1 cup mashed ripe banana
¼ cup sherry
½ cup brown sugar
⅛ tsp. salt
1 tsp. lemon juice
1 cup whipping cream, whipped

MAKES ABOUT 3 CUPS

Combine banana, sherry, sugar, salt and lemon juice in a saucepan; mix well. Simmer, stirring, 10 minutes. Cool and strain. Fold in whipped cream. To store, cover tightly and refrigerate (it will keep a few days).

Serve generously over fresh fruit or a fruit salad.

MRS. H. A. MOLDSTAD
Mt. Vernon, Washington

Chocolate Sauce

5 oz. unsweetened baking chocolate (Hershey's)
1½ cups sugar
⅛ tsp. salt
Pinch of cream of tartar
1 can (about 14 oz.) evaporated milk
1 tsp. vanilla

MAKES ABOUT 2 CUPS

Melt chocolate in a saucepan. Remove from heat and blend in sugar, salt and cream of tartar. Stir in evaporated milk slowly. Heat, stirring constantly, until mixture comes to a rolling boil. Remove from heat and stir in vanilla. Serve hot or cold, depending on the dessert.

This sauce will keep almost indefinitely if covered and refrigerated. (It thins down when reheated.)

BESS EMERSON
Palm Desert, California

DESSERTS

Something for Everyone

Great desserts are long remembered. And this
is a collection of greats. Even the traditional favorites have
a distinct difference all their own: coconut pudding
kissed with caramel, crêpes gilded with apricot, a mousse
made with marrons. Such special touches raise the good to grand!
From delicate soufflés to homey fruit and ice-cream treats,
these selections run a glorious gamut of flavors.
And the end result is always just a bit unique.

Crêpes à la Bidera

2 cups milk
1 tsp. vanilla
3½ tbsp. sugar
3½ tbsp. butter
2 oz. rum (preferably dark)
4 eggs, separated
3½ tbsp. quick-mixing granular flour*

SERVES 4

Scald milk with vanilla and sugar. Remove from heat; add butter and rum. Cool. Beat egg yolks with flour and dilute with the cooled milk mixture. (At this point you may set mixture aside until ready to cook the crêpes, or proceed immediately.)

Beat egg whites until stiff and fold into egg yolk mixture. Butter a well-seasoned cast-iron 6- to 7-inch crêpe pan (or use a crêpe pan with a nonstick surface). Have at hand a ladle or large spoon which holds about ¼ cup. Heat crêpe pan over moderately high heat. Just when it begins to smoke, pour in about ½ ladle of batter, tilting pan in all directions to coat the bottom with a thin film. *Cook only one side.* When crêpe is very brown and lacy on the bottom, grasp handle of pan and tilt it toward you. Lift far edge of crêpe and start *rolling* it toward you with the aid of a spatula or spoon. Roll up completely. Turn onto a warm serving plate. (By cooking the crêpe on one side only, the interior resembles an enveloped cream filling, making it unnecessary to serve a separate sauce.)

* The use of granular flour makes it possible to mix ingredients and make crêpes immediately.

MME. MARCELLE CANDEAU-PICASSO
Nice, France

Christmas 1977 1st time Made 1½ recipies, made 34 crepes

Apricot Crêpes

- 3 eggs, lightly beaten
- 1 tsp. salt
- 1½ tsp. sugar
- 1 cup unsifted flour
- 2 cups milk
- 3 tbsp. butter, melted
- Grated rind of 1 orange
- 1 jar (32 oz.) apricot preserves

APRICOT SAUCE

- 2 cans (5½ oz. each) apricot nectar
- Grated rind of 1 orange
- Juice of 2 lemons
- ¼ cup butter, melted
- 1 can (20 oz.) apricots, drained and puréed
- ⅓ cup Cointreau

MAKES ABOUT 36 CREPES

Beat eggs with salt and sugar until light. Add flour, milk and the 3 tablespoons melted butter. Stir in orange rind. Let stand at room temperature at least 30 minutes.

Butter a crêpe pan and heat over moderately high heat. Add a scant ¼ cup batter and rotate pan to cover bottom. Turn once, browning both sides. Repeat, using all remaining batter.

Spread each crêpe with apricot preserves. Roll up and place in a lightly buttered shallow casserole.

To make Apricot Sauce, combine nectar, orange rind, lemon juice, butter and puréed apricots. Cook about 5 minutes. Add Cointreau (increase amount, if desired). Spoon sauce over crêpes. Warm in oven before serving.

The crêpes may be cooked a day or two ahead. Layer between waxed paper and keep in the refrigerator or freezer.

MRS. JOSEPH HALL
San Marino, California

Salzburger Nockerl

- 6 egg whites
- 5 tbsp. confectioners' sugar
- 3 egg yolks, well beaten
- 1 tsp. flour
- 1 tsp. grated lemon rind
- 3 tbsp. sweet butter
- 2 tbsp. milk
- 1 tbsp. granulated sugar
- Confectioners' sugar

SERVES 4

"This recipe is from the Golden Hirsch Hotel in Salzburg."

Beat egg whites until stiff. Beat in 5 tablespoons confectioners' sugar; continue to beat until very thick. Fold egg yolks, flour and lemon rind into egg white mixture.

In a small shallow baking dish, combine butter, milk and granulated sugar. Heat mixture until butter melts. Scoop four large mounds of egg mixture into the butter mixture in baking dish. Bake *nockerl* in a preheated 450° oven about 6 minutes or until the tops are golden. Sprinkle with confectioners' sugar and *serve at once.*

MRS. JOHN T. HEAVEY
Palm Springs, California

Marquise Suzanne

3 packages (3 oz. each) ladyfingers
1/2 cup Kirsch
1/2 cup water
1 cup milk
1/2 vanilla bean, split lengthwise
1 egg, beaten
1 cup butter, softened
1 cup sugar
3 1/2 oz. blanched almonds, very finely ground

SERVES 6–8

Dip ladyfingers into a mixture of Kirsch and water and use them to line the bottom and side of a charlotte mold, making a petal design on the bottom. Reserve remaining ladyfingers.

Scald milk with vanilla bean (scraping seeds into milk). Add egg slowly to hot milk, stirring and cooking (do not boil) over medium heat until custard coats a spoon. Cool. Remove vanilla bean pod.

Cream butter and sugar until light and fluffy. Fold in almonds. Fold cooled custard into butter mixture. Turn into the prepared mold, filling completely. Top with remaining ladyfingers. Sprinkle with additional Kirsch. Place a plate on top and weight it down. Chill 24 hours.

Unmold on a chilled serving platter. Keep refrigerated until ready to serve. If desired, garnish with fresh strawberries, halved lengthwise and marinated in Kirsch, or a thin chocolate glaze.

MRS. HARRISON ROBERTS
Indian Wells, California

Soufflé Grand Marnier

3 tbsp. butter
1/4 tsp. salt
3 tbsp. flour
1 cup hot milk
1/4 cup sugar
4 egg yolks, beaten
4 egg whites, stiffly beaten
1/2 cup Grand Marnier

SERVES 6–8

Melt butter in the top of a double boiler. Blend in salt and flour. Gradually stir in hot milk. Stir constantly until mixture thickens, then cook 2 minutes. Cool slightly.

Add sugar to egg yolks and beat well. Pour cooled custard over this mixture. Fold in the egg whites. Add Grand Marnier and pour into a buttered and sugared 2 1/2-quart soufflé dish. Bake in a preheated 350° oven 35 to 40 minutes. Serve immediately.

MRS. JOHN F. KENASTON
Palm Springs, California

Coeur à la Crème

1 lb. small curd cottage cheese, at room temperature
2 packages (8 oz. each) cream cheese, softened
Pinch of salt
2 cups heavy cream
1 quart strawberries, sliced and sweetened
Whole strawberries

SERVES 10–12

Blend cottage cheese and cream cheese thoroughly. Add salt. Gradually add cream, beating constantly until mixture is smooth. Pour half the mixture into a blender and blend 1 minute. Blend remaining half of mixture.

Turn mixture into either *coeur à la crème* baskets lined with cheesecloth or individual heart-shaped molds (with holes for draining). Place on a deep plate and let drain overnight in refrigerator.

To serve, unmold the hearts onto chilled plates and serve with sweetened strawberries. Garnish with whole berries.

GENERAL and MRS. LAURIS NORSTAD
Toledo, Ohio

Lemon Chiffon Dessert Cake

24 ladyfingers
4 eggs, separated
Grated rind of 2 lemons
½ cup lemon juice
1 can (about 14 oz.) sweetened condensed milk
¼ cup sugar
Whipped cream

SERVES 8–10

Preheat oven to 500°. Line side of a 10-inch springform pan with ladyfingers. Crush remaining ladyfingers and sprinkle on bottom of pan.

Beat egg yolks. Add lemon rind, lemon juice and milk and beat well. Beat 2 egg whites until stiff and fold into egg yolk mixture. Pour into prepared pan. Make a meringue by beating the remaining 2 egg whites with the sugar until stiff. Cover top of dessert with meringue.

Turn off oven. Place dessert in oven for 40 minutes. Cool on a cake rack before removing side of pan. Chill. Before serving, spread whipped cream on top.

MRS. JAMES P. HEALEY
Indian Wells, California

Orange Soufflé à la Golden Dolphin

4 egg whites
¼ tsp. salt
⅓ cup sugar
⅓ cup orange marmalade

BRANDY SAUCE
½ cup sugar
⅓ cup butter
½ cup heavy cream
1 egg yolk, beaten
4 tbsp. brandy

SERVES 4

"Not only delicious, but there's hardly a calorie in a cupful!"

Beat egg whites until stiff, gradually adding salt and sugar while beating. Gently fold in marmalade. Pour mixture into the top of a double boiler. Cover and steam 1 hour over moderate heat. Serve immediately with Brandy Sauce.

To make Brandy Sauce, heat sugar and butter in the top of a double boiler. When dissolved, add cream and egg yolk. Cook over simmering water, stirring constantly, until consistency of boiled custard. Add brandy. Serve warm over soufflé.

AMBASSADOR CLARE BOOTHE LUCE
Honolulu, Hawaii

Chocolate Soufflé

⅓ cup pastry flour
⅔ cup sugar
⅓ cup cocoa
¾ tsp. salt
1 cup boiling water
3 egg yolks
1 tsp. vanilla
6 egg whites
Whipped cream
Toasted slivered almonds

SERVES 6

Sift together flour, sugar, cocoa and salt into a saucepan. Add boiling water gradually and cook, stirring constantly, over low heat 3 minutes or until thickened. Remove from heat and add to egg yolks, beating vigorously until smooth. Add vanilla and cool.

Beat egg whites until stiff. Carefully fold in cooled chocolate mixture just until blended. Pour into a buttered glass baking dish, 10x6 inches, or a lightly buttered and sugared 1½-quart soufflé dish (with collar). Bake in a preheated 300° oven 1 hour. Cool slightly before serving. Serve garnished with whipped cream and toasted almonds.

VERNON STOUFFER
Scottsdale, Arizona

Pumpkin Flan

1¼ cups sugar
1 cup canned pumpkin
¾ tsp. cinnamon
¼ tsp. ginger
½ tsp. salt
1 can (about 14 oz.) evaporated milk
4 eggs, lightly beaten
¼ cup sherry

SERVES 8

Heat 1 cup of the sugar slowly in a heavy iron skillet, stirring with a wooden spoon, until melted and caramel-colored. Pour into a 5-cup mold, rotating mold until bottom and side are covered.

Combine pumpkin, remaining sugar, the cinnamon, ginger and salt. Add evaporated milk to beaten eggs and blend into pumpkin mixture. Stir in sherry. Carefully pour into the caramel-coated mold and set mold in a pan of warm water. Bake in a preheated 350° oven 45 to 50 minutes. Do not overbake. Test center of custard with a silver knife for doneness. Remove from oven and hot water. Cool, then chill in refrigerator.

To serve, run a spatula around side of mold and turn out onto a serving dish. If desired, serve with whipped cream.

MRS. THOMAS POWER
Palm Desert, California

Marron Mousse

6 egg yolks
⅛ tsp. salt
2 tsp. rum or brandy
1½ cups pure maple syrup
4 cups whipping cream
2 jars (8 oz. each) *marrons*, drained and chopped
Whipped cream
Strawberries

SERVES 10–12

Beat egg yolks until light. Add salt and rum. Slowly stir in maple syrup. Cook in the top of a double boiler until thick, stirring constantly. Cool. Whip cream until stiff. Fold in syrup mixture and *marrons*. Pour into a mold and freeze.

To serve, unmold and garnish with whipped cream and strawberries.

MRS. HAROLD FLORSHEIM
Highland Park, Illinois

Mousse "Casiana"

2 cups whipping cream
5 tbsp. confectioners' sugar
1 tsp. vanilla
2 tbsp. sherry
1 cup finely chopped almonds or walnuts
1 cup coarsely chopped candied cherries

SERVES 8

Partially whip the cream. Add sugar, then continue to beat until stiff. Fold in vanilla and sherry. Blend well. Place in freezer for 10 minutes. Remove and fold in nuts and cherries. Turn into a wet 2-quart mold. Cover and freeze.

MRS. LEIGH BATTSON
Los Angeles, California

Chocolate Mousse

4 oz. semisweet chocolate
1 tsp. instant coffee
4 eggs, separated
1 tsp. brandy (or more)

SERVES 4

Melt chocolate in the top of a double boiler over hot water. Remove from heat and stir in coffee. Beat egg yolks until light and fluffy. Add to chocolate and beat well. Stir in brandy.

Beat egg whites until very stiff but not dry; fold into chocolate mixture. Spoon into a serving bowl or individual dessert dishes. Chill at least 8 hours before serving.

MRS. ROBERT T. STONE
Indian Wells, California

Chocolate Pots de Crème

1 cup semisweet chocolate bits
1¼ cups light cream, scalded
2 egg yolks
3 tbsp. brandy or bourbon

SERVES 4

Put all ingredients in a blender. Cover and blend until smooth. Pour into four traditional "pots" or small sherbets or even demitasse cups, filling each two-thirds full. Cover and chill at least 4 hours or until the consistency of pudding.

MRS. JOSEPH E. BELL
Winnetka, Illinois

Rachmaninoff Pudding

4 oz. bittersweet chocolate
1 cup very strong coffee
4 eggs, separated
1 tsp. vanilla

VANILLA SAUCE
3 tbsp. butter, softened
3/4 cup sifted confectioners' sugar
3 egg yolks
1/2 cup boiling water
1 tsp. grated lemon rind
1 tsp. vanilla
1 tsp. brandy

SERVES 6–8

Melt chocolate with coffee in the top of a double boiler. Beat egg yolks thoroughly. When chocolate is melted and smooth, blend in egg yolks. Remove from heat; let cool.

Beat egg whites only until they peak when beater is raised (not too stiff). Fold into chocolate mixture thoroughly, then stir in vanilla. Let stand at room temperature to set. (Or if serving immediately, put into refrigerator for a short while.) Serve with Vanilla Sauce or whipped cream.

To make Vanilla Sauce, beat butter until soft. Add sugar gradually. Blend until creamy, then beat in egg yolks. Stir in boiling water. Cool *slightly*. Put in the top of a double boiler and cook, stirring, until thickened. Remove from heat and add flavorings. Serve warm.

MRS. JOHN H. STAMBAUGH
Indian Wells, California

Sherry Pudding

1 tbsp. unflavored gelatin
1 cup medium dry sherry
1/2 cup sugar
6 egg yolks
3 egg whites, stiffly beaten
2 dozen almond macaroons, crushed
1 cup toasted slivered almonds (reserve a few for garnish)
Whipped cream

SERVES 8

Dissolve gelatin in 1/4 cup of the sherry and set aside. Beat sugar into egg yolks. Cook, stirring constantly, in the top of a double boiler over simmering water until mixture becomes a thick, smooth custard. Remove from heat and add remaining 3/4 cup sherry and the gelatin mixture. Cool slightly and fold in beaten egg whites.

When thoroughly cool, add macaroons and almonds. Pour into a 2-quart mold and refrigerate overnight until firm. Unmold on a serving plate. Garnish with whipped cream and a few toasted slivered almonds sprinkled on top.

LT. GEN. and MRS. LEONARD HEATON
Pinehurst, North Carolina

Coconut Pudding

2 tbsp. unflavored gelatin
¼ cup cold water
1 cup milk
2 cups heavy cream, whipped
2 cups grated fresh coconut
1 cup sugar

CARAMEL SAUCE
1 cup granulated sugar
1 cup brown sugar
1 cup light cream
1 tsp. vanilla

SERVES 6–8

Soak gelatin in cold water. Heat milk and stir in gelatin. Cool. Fold whipped cream into milk mixture. Add coconut and sugar. Pour into a 2-quart melon mold and chill several hours. Serve with warm Caramel Sauce.

To make Caramel Sauce, combine granulated sugar, brown sugar and cream in a saucepan. Cook until syrupy, stirring constantly. Do not overcook. Remove from heat and add vanilla. Serve warm. (This sauce is also good on rice pudding.)

MRS. F. PAUL GARDNER
Indian Wells, California

Family Lemon Pudding

2 cups fine stale bread crumbs
1 tbsp. butter, melted
4 cups milk
4 eggs, separated
1¼ cups granulated sugar
Grated rind and juice of 1 lemon
¼ cup confectioners' sugar

SERVES 6

Combine bread crumbs and butter in a large bowl; add milk. Beat egg yolks until thick and lemon-colored; gradually beat in granulated sugar. Blend into bread crumbs. Add lemon rind and juice. Pour into a buttered shallow 2-quart baking dish. Bake in a preheated 350° oven 40 minutes.

Beat egg whites until stiff but not dry. Gradually beat in confectioners' sugar. Pile meringue onto hot baked pudding. Return to oven and bake about 10 minutes longer or until meringue is delicately browned.

IVY BAKER PRIEST
Sacramento, California

Ozark Pudding

1 egg
3/4 cup sugar
2 tbsp. flour
1 1/4 tsp. baking powder
1/3 tsp. salt
1/4 tsp. baking soda
1/2 cup chopped nuts
1/2 cup diced peeled apples
Whipped cream (optional)

SERVES 3

Beat egg with sugar until light. Sift together flour, baking powder, salt and soda. Add to egg mixture and beat well. Stir in nuts and apples and pour into a buttered pie pan. Bake in a preheated 350° oven 20 to 25 minutes. Pudding will rise very high, then fall when it is almost done.

This is a very light dessert, delicious served either warm or chilled, with whipped cream.

MRS. HARRY S. TRUMAN
Independence, Missouri

Fig Steamed Pudding

2 eggs, beaten
1 cup molasses
1 cup milk
2 1/2 cups finely ground suet
2 1/2 cups flour
1 tsp. baking soda
Salt
2 cups chopped or coarsely ground dried figs

SAUCE
1 egg, separated
1/2 cup confectioners' sugar
2 cups whipping cream
Vanilla or sherry

SERVES 4–6

Add beaten eggs to molasses. Blend, then add milk and suet. Combine flour, soda and salt with figs and add to suet mixture. Mix well. Turn into a greased mold, filling it two-thirds full. Cover tightly and steam 3 hours.

To make the sauce, beat egg yolk with sugar. Beat egg white until stiff, then fold in. Just before serving, whip cream and add to egg mixture. Flavor with vanilla or sherry.

This pudding can be steamed in two containers, if desired. Serve one now, reserve the other for use later.

AMBASSADOR and MRS. JAMES SCOTT KEMPER
Chicago, Illinois

Apple Crisp

4 apples, peeled, cored and sliced
1¼ cups flour
6 tbsp. granulated sugar
6 tbsp. brown sugar
1 tsp. cinnamon
½ cup butter, softened

SERVES 6

Place apples in a buttered 8-inch glass pie plate. Mix together flour, sugars and cinnamon. Work in the butter to make a crumbly mixture. Spread over apples. Bake, uncovered, in a preheated 350° oven 30 minutes or until fruit is tender and crust is a light brown color.

Serve with whipped cream, hard sauce or softened vanilla ice cream, if desired.

MRS. BALTZER PETERSON
Atherton, California

Baked Fruit

1 can (about 16 oz.) peach halves, drained
1 can (about 16 oz.) pear halves, drained
½ cup brown sugar
2 tsp. cinnamon
6 tbsp. *pure* maple syrup (no substitute)
2 cups sour cream

SERVES 4–6

Pat fruit dry with paper towels. Arrange in a buttered shallow baking pan or dish, alternating peaches and pears in rows.

Make a sauce with sugar, cinnamon and maple syrup. Place fruit in a preheated 300° oven and bake 1 hour, basting frequently with the sauce. Serve warm, with sour cream.

MRS. TED WEINER
Palm Springs, California

The Grand Finale—A high, light and lovely Chocolate Soufflé (page 214). What could be a happier ending? For the calorie-carefree, top each serving with a dollop of whipped cream and a sprinkling of almonds.

Gift Foods—Sally's Favorite Fruitcake (page 247), St. Patrick's Pickles (page 202), Carrot Conserve (page 200), Oatmeal Cookies (page 251), Crescents (page 255), Jelly Tots (page 253), Surprise Fudge (page 263).

Fruit Thaïs

Assorted fresh and/or canned fruits: peaches, pears, apricots, pineapple, pitted Bing cherries, bananas (drain canned fruit)
Brown sugar
Shredded coconut or blanched almonds
Dry sherry (1/2 cup or more)
Crushed macaroons

Arrange fruit in layers in a buttered baking dish (the number of servings depends on the size of the dish). Sprinkle each layer with brown sugar and coconut or almonds. Pour sherry over all. Cover top with macaroon crumbs. Bake in a preheated 350° oven 20 minutes. Serve *hot*.

This dish is particularly nice after a dinner of wild game.

MRS. HAROLD L. BEHLKE
La Quinta, California

Pears Alexis

Canned pear halves, drained
Bottled caramel sauce
Chopped pecans

Place pear halves cut side down in a refrigerator tray. Place in freezer.

When ready to serve, heat caramel sauce. Place frozen pears on individual serving plates, top with hot sauce and garnish with chopped pecans.

MRS. STANLEY NEWBRANDER
Palm Desert, California

Grape Delight

1 cup sour cream
1/4 to 1/2 cup brown sugar
2 tbsp. crème de menthe
3 cups seedless grapes

SERVES 6

Mix sour cream, brown sugar and crème de menthe. Fold in grapes. Let stand overnight in refrigerator.

MRS. BEN W. VALLAT, JR.
Rancho Mirage, California

Banana Nut Torte

- 1 cup granulated sugar
- 1 tsp. baking powder
- 3 egg whites
- 12 saltine crackers, finely crushed
- ⅔ cup chopped walnuts
- 2 tsp. vanilla
- 2 to 3 ripe bananas
- 1 cup whipping cream
- 2 tbsp. confectioners' sugar
- ½ cup chopped walnuts

SERVES 6–8

Sift granulated sugar with baking powder. Beat egg whites until fairly stiff. Add sugar mixture, beating continuously. Fold in saltines, the ⅔ cup walnuts and 1 teaspoon of the vanilla. Spread evenly in a well-buttered 9-inch pie pan. Bake in a preheated 350° oven 20 to 25 minutes. (The torte will not brown on top.) Cool in pan.

When torte is cool, slice bananas generously over top. Whip cream, adding confectioners' sugar and the remaining 1 teaspoon vanilla. Beat until firm. Spread cream over bananas, covering them thoroughly. Sprinkle the ½ cup chopped nuts on top. Refrigerate until ready to serve.

Peach or Strawberry Nut Torte: Fresh peaches or strawberries may be substituted for bananas.

MRS. FRED HARDT
Indian Wells, California

Lemon Chiffon Ring

- 3 eggs, separated
- ¾ cup sugar
- Grated rind and juice of 2 lemons
- 1 tbsp. unflavored gelatin
- ¼ cup cold water

SERVES 6–8

Beat egg yolks until thick and lemon-colored. Beat in ½ cup of the sugar. Stir in lemon rind and juice. Cook in the top of a double boiler over simmering water, stirring constantly until thick. Remove from heat. Soften gelatin in cold water. Dissolve in the hot custard. Stir well and cool.

Beat egg whites until stiff but not dry; gradually beat in remaining sugar. Fold into cooled custard. Pour into a 1-quart ring mold. Chill.

If desired, garnish with raspberries, strawberries or other fresh fruit and whipped cream.

MR. and MRS. GEORGE CHAMPION
Greenwich, Connecticut

Pineapple Pavlova

4 egg whites
1 cup superfine granulated sugar
2 tsp. cornstarch
2 tsp. white vinegar
1 tsp. vanilla
1 can (about 8 oz.) crushed pineapple
3 egg yolks
Pulp of 2 passion fruit (2 bananas, sliced, may be substituted)
2 tbsp. butter
4 tsp. arrowroot
Whipped cream

SERVES 8–10

Line a large baking sheet with waxed paper; grease and dust with cornstarch.

Prepare a meringue shell by beating egg whites stiffly, gradually adding sugar as you beat. Fold in cornstarch, vinegar and vanilla. Pile into a large circle on the prepared baking sheet, building up the edge of circle to form a shell. Bake in a preheated 350° oven 1 hour. Turn off heat and let cool in oven.

To make the filling, combine pineapple, egg yolks, passion fruit, butter and arrowroot in the top of a double boiler. Bring to a boil, stirring constantly. Remove from heat. Let cool, then chill. Pile into shell and garnish with whipped cream.

Crushed strawberries and sliced bananas, added as a garnish, make this dessert even more special.

MR. and MRS. BRUCE DEVLIN
Hialeah, Florida
Bruce Devlin was the winner of the 1970 Bob Hope Desert Classic.

Apricot Fluff

⅔ cup dried apricots
1 cup water
½ cup sugar
1 tbsp. unflavored gelatin
½ cup cold water
3 egg whites
½ tsp. almond extract

SERVES 2–4

Cook apricots with 1 cup water and sugar until tender. In a blender, dissolve gelatin in the ½ cup cold water. Add hot apricots and purée. Cool.

Beat egg whites until stiff; flavor with almond extract. Fold apricot purée into egg whites. Turn into a mold and chill.

LILY PONS
Palm Springs, California

Butterscotch Freeze

- ¾ cup butter or margarine
- 4 eggs, slightly beaten
- 1½ cups confectioners' sugar
- 1 tsp. vanilla
- ¾ lb. vanilla wafers, crushed
- 3 cups heavy cream, whipped

SERVES 10

Combine butter, eggs and sugar in the top of a double boiler. Cook over boiling water, stirring constantly, until mixture thickens, about 6 to 8 minutes. Cool, then add vanilla.

Set aside half the wafer crumbs; divide the remainder between two refrigerator trays. Set aside half the whipped cream; divide the remainder between the two trays, completely covering the wafer crumbs. Spread half the custard over *each* of the two trays. Top with remaining whipped cream. Cover with remaining crumbs. Place in freezer 3 to 4 hours. To serve, cut into squares.

MRS. WALTER PROBST
Fort Wayne, Indiana

Strawberry Pie Dessert

- ½ cup margarine, softened
- ¼ cup brown sugar
- 1 cup flour
- ½ cup chopped walnuts
- 2 egg whites
- 1 cup granulated sugar
- 2 packages (about 10 oz. each) frozen sliced strawberries, partially thawed
- 1 tbsp. lemon juice
- 1 tsp. vanilla
- 1 cup heavy cream, whipped

SERVES 6–8

Mix thoroughly margarine, brown sugar, flour and walnuts. Place in a baking pan, 13x9 inches. Bake in a preheated 400° oven, stirring frequently, until golden brown (about 15 minutes). Reserve a scant cup of this mixture; spread remainder on the bottom of the pan and set aside.

In a mixing bowl, beat egg whites until frothy. Fold in granulated sugar, strawberries, lemon juice and vanilla. Beat 20 minutes. Fold in whipped cream. Turn into prepared pan and cover with reserved nut mixture. Freeze until ready to serve. (Will not become icy.)

ANGELA WARNER
Palm Springs, California

Frosted Mint Delight

- 1 tbsp. unflavored gelatin
- 2 cans (16 oz. each) crushed pineapple, drained and chilled (reserve syrup)
- ¾ cup mint apple jelly
- 2 cups whipping cream
- 2 tbsp. confectioners' sugar

SERVES 10–12

Dissolve gelatin in 1 cup of the reserved pineapple syrup. Melt jelly; stir in dissolved gelatin. Stir in chilled pineapple. Whip cream, adding sugar. Fold pineapple mixture into whipped cream. Chill in freezer until firm (do not freeze solid).

MRS. HARLOWE PERHAM
Palm Desert, California

Buttermilk Sherbet

- 1 can (about 14 oz.) evaporated milk, chilled at least 8 hours
- 4 cups buttermilk
- 1 can (about 16 oz.) crushed pineapple, drained
- ½ cup maraschino cherries, cut in half
- 1 tsp. vanilla
- 1 tbsp. sugar

SERVES 8

Whip evaporated milk until stiff. Add buttermilk gradually, beating constantly. Fold in pineapple, cherries, vanilla and sugar. (If desired, add more sugar to taste.)

Turn into refrigerator trays and place in freezer just until sherbet freezes around the edges. Stir three times, then freeze until firm.

MRS. BILLIDEAN BRADLEY
Palm Springs, California

Ice Box Cake

- 3 eggs, separated
- 2 cups confectioners' sugar
- 2 oz. unsweetened chocolate, melted and cooled
- ½ cup butter, softened
- ½ cup chopped pecans or walnuts
- 1 tsp. vanilla
- 1 box (8 oz.) vanilla wafers, crushed
- 1 qt. vanilla ice cream, softened

SERVES 8

Beat egg yolks. Add sugar, chocolate, butter and nuts. Beat egg whites until stiff, then add vanilla. Fold into chocolate mixture.

Spread half the wafer crumbs on the bottom of a metal pan, 13x9x2 inches. Cover with chocolate mixture. Spread softened ice cream on top of chocolate mixture. Top with remaining crumbs. Freeze.

MRS. GEORGE J. HESIK
Corona del Mar, California

Bombe Maison

1 qt. pistachio ice cream, slightly softened
1 oz. unsweetened chocolate
7 oz. semisweet chocolate
4 tbsp. very strong coffee
6 tbsp. dark rum
2 cups heavy cream
½ cup sugar

SERVES 12

Chill a 2-quart bombe mold and line it with ice cream, 1 to 1½ inches thick, pressing firmly against the sides. Place in freezer while preparing the filling.

Melt unsweetened and semisweet chocolate with coffee over very low heat. Cool, then beat in rum. Partially whip the cream. Add sugar and continue beating until stiff. Fold in chocolate mixture and blend gently but thoroughly. Remove bombe from freezer and fill center with the chocolate mixture. Return to freezer until chocolate is frozen. To serve, unmold and cut into slices.

WILLIAM O. FLEETWOOD
Indian Wells, California

Granny's Homemade Ice Cream

2 qt. whole milk
½ cup flour
½ cup cold water
3 cups turbinado sugar*
8 egg yolks, beaten
4 cups heavy cream
2 tsp. vanilla

Scald milk, stirring constantly. In the top section of a double boiler, mix a smooth paste of flour and cold water. Continuing to stir, slowly add scalded milk. When thickened, cook over hot water about 15 minutes. Add sugar and egg yolks and cook 2 minutes.

Strain the custard through a fine sieve. Let cool, then add cream and vanilla. Process in an electric or hand-operated ice cream freezer according to manufacturer's directions.

*Turbinado sugar is a partially refined sugar. It may be found in health food stores and some supermarkets.

MR. and MRS. BILLY CASPER
Chula Vista, California

Billy Casper won the Bob Hope Desert Classic in 1965 and 1969.

Trader Vics Champagne Apricot (from Bob Meyers book) for each drink (dessert) 1 whole peeled frozen apricot (do a whole can in ice cube trays) 1 oz Southern Comfort – 1 t. shaved ice chilled Champagne – – Place frozen apricot in chilled Champagne glass pour over it the Southern Comfort; add the shaved ice & fill the glass with champagne. Beautiful!

PIES & CAKES

High, Wide and Handsome

Hail these crowning glories—pies and cakes
you won't want to miss! Layered or loafed, chocolate-filled
or sugar-frosted, take your cake as you want it.
And the range of pies is practically perfect, too.
All the way from a cozy apple to a super-sophisticate flavored
with crème de menthe and crème de cacao.
For family or for company, these traditions of sweet success
are here for the sharing.

(To flame desserts etc.)
From Trader Vics book (Bob Meyers)

Mix 1 T pineapple & apricot preserves (or whatever kind) with 3/4 oz rum for each serving and warm the mixture before taking it to the table. Dont Cook it, but set in pan of boiling water. Take your sauce to the table in a chafing dish or heatproof glass saucepan, & then set a match to it. Your ice cream should be in serving dishes beforehand. After sauce is burning, stir it and ladle it onto good vanilla or coconut ice cream. For somthing extra special first spoon a mixture of sliced bananas, pineapple & grated coconut over the ice cream, before adding the burning rum sauce.

New York State Flat Apple Pie

CRUST
- 1/2 cup butter
- 1/2 cup margarine
- 2 cups flour
- 3 to 4 tbsp. ice water

FILLING
- 11 or 12 New York State apples (medium size)
- 1 cup sugar
- 1 tbsp. cinnamon
- Juice of 1/2 lemon
- 1/2 cup New York State maple syrup
- New York State sharp cheese

To make the crust, cut butter and margarine into flour with knife or pastry blender until texture resembles corn-meal. Add ice water gradually, working in just enough to hold dough together. Roll out on lightly floured board or marble slab to 1-inch thickness. Place in refrigerator 20 minutes. Remove and roll out a flat sheet, 10x15x1/8 inch thick. Line a baking sheet, 10x15 inches, with the pastry.

To make the filling, pare, core and cut each apple into 6 sections. Arrange in one layer on pastry. Mix sugar and cinnamon and sprinkle over apples. Sprinkle with lemon juice.

Bake in a preheated 450° oven 20 minutes, then reduce temperature to 350° and bake 30 minutes longer. Remove from oven and sprinkle with maple syrup. Serve warm, with a generous slice of cheese.

MRS. NELSON A. ROCKEFELLER
Washington, D.C.

Heavenly Pie

- 3 eggs, separated
- 1 cup sugar
- 1 tsp. vanilla
- 22 Ritz crackers, finely crushed
- 1 cup pecans, coarsely chopped
- 1 cup whipping cream
- Sugar
- Vanilla
- Semisweet chocolate

Beat egg whites until foamy. Gradually add 1 cup sugar and beat until stiff. Beat egg yolks lightly and combine with 1 teaspoon vanilla, the cracker crumbs and nuts. Fold into egg whites. Turn into a buttered pie plate. Bake in a preheated 300° oven 25 to 30 minutes. Let cool to room temperature.

For topping, whip cream with a little sugar and vanilla; spread over pie. Shave chocolate over the cream. Keep in refrigerator until ready to serve.

MRS. RANDOLPH SCOTT
Beverly Hills, California

Orange Pie

4 cups fresh orange segments
½ cup sugar
Fresh orange juice
3 tbsp. cornstarch
⅛ tsp. salt
¾ tsp. vanilla
⅔ cup apricot jam
1 10-inch baked pie shell, cooled
½ cup toasted shredded coconut

Combine orange segments and sugar; let stand 30 minutes. Turn segments into a sieve and drain, reserving the juice. Measure the juice and add enough fresh orange juice to make 1½ cups. In a saucepan, blend juice with cornstarch and salt. Cook, stirring, until it reaches the consistency of molasses. Stir in vanilla. Let cool to room temperature.

Spread jam over bottom and side of baked pie shell and arrange orange segments on jam. Pour sauce over oranges, then sprinkle with coconut.

MRS. LOUIS GOLAN
Cathedral City, California

Lemon Custard Pie

1 cup sugar
2 heaping tbsp. flour
½ tsp. salt
1½ cups milk
3 egg yolks, beaten
1½ tbsp. butter
1 tsp. grated lemon rind
Juice of 1½ lemons, or ½ cup (depending on tartness of fruit)
1 baked pie shell, cooled

MERINGUE
3 egg whites
Pinch of salt
¼ tsp. cream of tartar
6 tbsp. sugar

To make custard, mix dry ingredients together. Combine milk and egg yolks; mix with dry ingredients and pour into the top of a double boiler. Cook, stirring over hot water until thick. Remove from heat; stir in butter, lemon rind and juice. Let cool a little and pour into baked pie shell.

Put egg whites in a medium-sized bowl. Add salt and cream of tartar. Beat on medium speed until soft peaks form when beater is raised. Gradually add sugar, 2 tablespoons at a time, beating well after each addition. Continue beating until stiff peaks form when beater is raised. Spread meringue on warm filling, sealing to edge of crust. Bake in a preheated 400° oven 7 to 10 minutes or until meringue is golden.

MRS. WILLIAM R. HAYDEN
San Marino, California

Fresh Peach Pie

- 1⅓ cups finely crushed graham crackers (about 16)
- ½ cup butter, melted
- 4 egg whites
- ½ tsp. salt
- 1 tsp. vinegar
- 1 cup sugar
- 1 cup shredded coconut
- 1¼ cups heavy cream
- 2 tbsp. sugar
- 1 tsp. vanilla
- Sliced fresh peaches

Mix cracker crumbs and melted butter thoroughly. Press into a 9-inch pie pan and set aside.

Beat egg whites until frothy. Add salt and vinegar; continue to beat until very stiff. Gradually add 1 cup sugar, 2 tablespoons at a time, beating well after each addition. Spread over crust and bake in a preheated 275° oven 1¼ hours. Cool.

Toast half the coconut. Whip cream and fold in remaining untoasted coconut, 2 tablespoons sugar and the vanilla. Arrange peach slices over baked meringue. Cover with whipped cream and sprinkle toasted coconut on top. Chill.

Fresh Fig or Pear Pie: Figs or pears may be substituted for the peaches.

MRS. RANDOLPH SCOTT
Beverly Hills, California

French Silk Pie

- 25 vanilla wafers, finely crushed
- ¼ cup butter, melted
- ½ cup chopped pecans
- ¾ cup butter, softened
- 1 cup sugar
- 1 tsp. vanilla
- 2 oz. unsweetened chocolate, melted and cooled
- 3 eggs

To make the crust, mix vanilla wafer crumbs, the melted butter and pecans. Press into a 9-inch pie pan and bake in a preheated 350° oven 15 minutes. Cool.

Cream softened butter and sugar. Stir in vanilla and chocolate. Add eggs, one at a time, and beat well. Spread into crust and chill.

MRS. HALLECK C. YOUNG
Omaha, Nebraska

Strawberry Refrigerator Pie

- 2½ cups vanilla wafers, finely crushed
- 3 tbsp. butter, melted
- ½ cup butter, softened
- 2 cups confectioners' sugar
- 3 eggs, well beaten
- ½ cup chopped nuts
- 1 pint strawberries, crushed and slightly drained
- 1 cup whipping cream, whipped

Mix half the vanilla wafer crumbs with the melted butter and press into a 10-inch glass pie plate.

Cream softened butter and sugar, then beat in eggs. Spread this mixture over crumbs. Sprinkle with nuts. Spoon in a layer of strawberries, top with whipped cream and sprinkle with remaining crumbs. Chill at least 12 hours.

MRS. HERSCHEL GREEN
North Hollywood, California

Pumpkin Chiffon Pie

- 2 tbsp. unflavored gelatin
- 1 cup milk
- 1¼ cups canned pumpkin
- ½ cup brown sugar
- ½ tsp. salt
- ½ tsp. cinnamon
- ¼ tsp. ginger
- 4 eggs, separated
- ⅓ cup rum
- ½ cup granulated sugar
- 1 9-inch baked pie shell, cooled
- ½ cup toasted shredded coconut

Soften gelatin in half the milk. Combine pumpkin, brown sugar, spices, egg yolks and remaining milk in a heavy saucepan; mix well. Stir in the gelatin mixture. Cook about 10 minutes or until mixture bubbles and gelatin is dissolved. Cool to room temperature, then stir in rum. Chill until mixture has the consistency of mayonnaise.

Beat egg whites until stiff, gradually adding granulated sugar. Fold into pumpkin mixture. Turn into pie shell and top with coconut. Chill at least 2 hours before serving.

MRS. MALCOLM SHELTON
Amarillo, Texas

Blueberry Cheese Pie

1 package (8 oz.) cream cheese, softened
¼ cup milk
½ cup sugar
½ tsp. lemon juice
1 package (9 oz.) frozen whipped topping, thawed
Graham cracker crust or favorite crust
½ can (21-oz. size) blueberry pie filling

Fluff cream cheese with electric mixer. Add milk, sugar and lemon juice. Blend well to dissolve sugar. Fold in the whipped topping. Pour into crust and chill.

Spoon on blueberry pie filling just before serving.

MRS. CARL HAAGEN
Santa Barbara, California

Chris's Cold Pie

4 eggs, separated
½ cup lemon juice
½ cup water
1 tbsp. unflavored gelatin
1 cup sugar
¼ tsp. salt
1 tbsp. grated lemon rind
1 graham cracker crust (recipe on box)
Nutmeg

In a small bowl, beat egg yolks with lemon juice and water just until combined. Mix gelatin, half the sugar and the salt in the top of a double boiler. Pour in egg yolk mixture, blending well. Cook, stirring constantly, over boiling water (water should not touch top section of double boiler) until gelatin dissolves and mixture thickens. Remove top from boiling water. Stir in lemon rind. Let set 20 minutes in a bowl filled with ice cubes, stirring occasionally. Remove from ice when mixture thickens enough to mound when dropped from a spoon.

Meanwhile, beat egg whites (at room temperature) in a large bowl until soft peaks form when beater is raised. Gradually add remaining sugar, 2 tablespoons at a time, beating well after each addition. Continue beating until stiff peaks form when beater is raised. Gently fold gelatin mixture into egg whites just until combined. Turn into pie crust. Dust top with nutmeg and chill several hours. (If desired, omit nutmeg and serve topped with whipped cream.)

MRS. JOHN TRUYENS
Los Angeles, California

Grasshopper Pie

- 16 chocolate sandwich cookies, finely crushed
- 3 tbsp. butter, melted
- 14 large marshmallows
- 1/3 cup milk
- 1 cup heavy cream, whipped
- 3 tbsp. crème de cacao
- 3 tbsp. green crème de menthe

Mix cookie crumbs and melted butter and press into a pie pan.

Melt marshmallows with milk in the top of a double boiler over boiling water. Remove from heat and cool. Fold in whipped cream, crème de cacao and crème de menthe. Pour into crust and freeze at least 24 hours. Remove 15 minutes before serving. (This pie may be stored in the freezer for at least a month.)

MRS. EUGENE J. MOORE
Cathedral City, California

Frozen Lemon Pie

- 1/4 cup butter
- 1 1/2 cups finely crushed graham crackers
- 3 eggs, separated
- 2/3 cup sugar
- 3 tsp. grated lemon rind
- 1/4 cup lemon juice
- 1/8 tsp. salt
- 1 1/4 cups whipping cream

Melt butter in a heavy skillet. Add cracker crumbs and stir until thoroughly mixed. Press mixture on bottom and side of a 9-inch pie plate and smooth with the back of a spoon. Chill crust in freezer while preparing filling.

Beat egg yolks lightly. Combine with sugar, lemon rind, lemon juice and salt in the top of a double boiler. Cook over boiling water, stirring constantly, until mixture thickens. Chill.

Beat egg whites in a large bowl until they stand in stiff peaks when beater is raised. Fold in chilled lemon mixture. Whip the cream and fold in. Pour into chilled crust and freeze until firm.

MRS. HAROLD HUTTON
Orange, California

French Chocolate Cake

1½ cups sifted cake flour
1 tsp. baking powder
¼ tsp. salt
1 scant tsp. baking soda
1 cup cold strong coffee
½ cup butter or margarine, softened
1½ cups sugar
1 egg, beaten
2 oz. unsweetened chocolate, melted and cooled
2 tsp. vanilla

FROSTING
2 tbsp. butter or margarine
2 oz. unsweetened chocolate
1 box (16 oz.) confectioners' sugar, sifted
1 tsp. vanilla
Light cream

Line bottoms of two 9-inch layer cake pans with waxed paper; grease the paper.

Sift together flour, baking powder and salt. Blend soda into coffee. Cream butter and sugar. Add beaten egg and melted chocolate. Add sifted ingredients alternately with the coffee. Add vanilla and blend well. Pour into pans (batter will be thin). Bake in a preheated 350° oven 25 to 30 minutes or until cake springs back when touched lightly. Cool before frosting.

To make the frosting, melt butter and chocolate together in the top of a double boiler over hot water. Remove from heat, add sugar and blend. Stir in vanilla and enough cream to make desired spreading consistency.

This cake need not be refrigerated. It can be frozen if you like to have something on hand for emergencies.

MRS. LEWIS L. STRAUSS
Brandy Station, Virginia

Viennese Chocolate Cake

1 cup sifted all-purpose flour
¼ tsp. salt
2 tsp. double-acting baking powder
2 tbsp. butter or margarine, softened
1¼ cups granulated sugar
½ cup milk
1 oz. unsweetened chocolate, melted and cooled
½ cup chopped nuts
1 tsp. vanilla
½ cup brown sugar
¼ cup cocoa
1 cup water
Whipped cream

SERVES 6

Sift together flour, salt and baking powder. Cream butter and ¾ cup of the granulated sugar. Add sifted dry ingredients alternately with milk, stirring after each addition. Stir in melted chocolate, nuts and vanilla. Pour into a greased 1½-quart round casserole. Combine remaining granulated sugar, the brown sugar, cocoa and water. Stir to blend and carefully spoon sauce over top of the batter.

Bake in a preheated 350° oven 45 to 50 minutes. When cake is *completely* cool, turn upside-down onto a serving platter. Serve with whipped cream.

MRS. NORRIS GOFF
Indian Wells, California

Golden Cream Chocolate Cake

2 cups sifted cake flour
2 tsp. Calumet or 4 tsp. Royal baking powder
¼ tsp. baking soda
½ tsp. salt
½ cup butter, softened
1¼ cups sugar
2 eggs
3 oz. unsweetened chocolate, melted and cooled
1 cup milk
1 tsp. vanilla

GOLDEN CREAM FILLING
½ cup sugar
3 tbsp. cake flour
¼ tsp. salt
1½ cups milk
2 egg yolks, slightly beaten
1 tsp. vanilla
Yellow food coloring (optional)

CHOCOLATE FLUFF FROSTING
¼ cup butter, softened
1½ cups sifted confectioners' sugar
1 tsp. vanilla
3 oz. unsweetened chocolate, melted and cooled
¼ tsp. salt
2 egg whites

Sift together flour, baking powder, soda and salt three times; set aside. Cream butter thoroughly. Gradually add sugar and cream until light and fluffy. Add eggs one at a time, beating thoroughly after each addition. Add chocolate and blend. Add sifted dry ingredients alternately with milk, a small amount at a time, beating after each addition until smooth. Add vanilla. Pour batter into two greased 9-inch layer pans. Bake in a preheated 350° oven 30 minutes. Cool before filling and frosting.

To make Golden Cream Filling, combine sugar, flour and salt in the top of a double boiler. Add milk gradually. Cook over boiling water 10 minutes, stirring constantly. Pour a small amount of mixture into beaten egg yolks, stirring well. Add egg yolks to mixture in top of double boiler and cook 2 minutes longer, stirring constantly. Remove from heat, add vanilla and cool. If a deeper yellow color is desired, add a few drops of food coloring. Spread filling between the cake layers.

To make Chocolate Fluff Frosting, cream butter and half the sugar. Add vanilla, melted chocolate and salt. Beat egg whites until stiff but not dry. Add remaining sugar, a little at a time, beating until mixture stands in peaks when beater is raised. Fold egg whites into chocolate mixture gently but thoroughly. Frost top and sides of cake.

MRS. HOWARD D. McGREW
Laguna Hills, California

Cherry Jubilee Cake

3 cups cake flour
2 scant tsp. baking soda
1 tsp. salt
1 cup Coca-Cola syrup, at room temperature (available at soda fountains)
¾ cup buttermilk
¼ cup maraschino cherry juice (from 8-oz. jar)
⅔ cup butter, softened
2 cups sugar
2 eggs, separated
2 oz. unsweetened chocolate, melted and cooled
1 jar (8 oz.) maraschino cherries, drained and finely chopped (reserve juice)

CHOCOLATE FILLING
3 cups confectioners' sugar
⅔ cup butter, softened
1 egg (do not beat)
4 oz. unsweetened chocolate, melted and cooled
3 tbsp. Coca-Cola syrup
1 tsp. vanilla

TOPPING
About 4 cups white frosting
1 jar (4 oz.) maraschino cherries, drained and finely chopped (optional)

Line three square baking pans, 9x9x2 inches, with waxed paper and grease well.

Sift flour with soda and salt. Mix Coca-Cola syrup, buttermilk and cherry juice. Cream butter and sugar; add egg yolks and mix thoroughly. Add melted chocolate. Add sifted dry ingredients to creamed mixture alternately with Coca-Cola mixture. Beat egg whites until stiff and fold in. Gently stir in cherries. Pour batter into pans and bake in a preheated 350° oven for about 45 minutes. Cool before frosting.

To make Chocolate Filling, combine all ingredients and beat until smooth enough to spread. Use between cooled cake layers.

Frost the sides and top with your favorite white frosting recipe (preferably seven-minute frosting). For a spectacular-looking cake, swirl additional chopped maraschino cherries into the white frosting.

WILLIAM S. JUDKINS
Atlanta, Georgia

A Cake for Company—Mah-Jongg, bridge, backgammon, canasta . . . whatever your game, you're sure to win raves with the unusual blend of rich, dark chocolate and juicy cherries in Cherry Jubilee Cake (left).

Lunch at the 19th Hole—To top off any course: Cold Crab Soufflé (page 119), Asparagus Tarragon (page 149), Popovers (page 184) and Orange Pie (page 231). The drink? Cool, refreshing Folding Farrells (page 29).

Hungarian Chocolate-Walnut Torte

12 eggs, at room temperature
1 tsp. baking powder
1½ cups sugar
5 tbsp. water
1 cup ground walnuts
½ cup fine bread crumbs

ICING
1 cup whipping cream
1 can (5½ oz.) chocolate syrup, chilled
1 tbsp. orange extract
Rum
Raspberry jam

Separate eggs. Beat together egg yolks, baking powder and sugar. Add water gradually and beat until thick and lemon-colored. Beat egg whites until stiff but not dry. Mix together walnuts and bread crumbs. Fold egg yolk mixture into egg whites. Add nut mixture a little at a time, mixing lightly. Pour into four greased baking pans, 9x9x2 inches. Bake in a preheated 375° oven 15 to 20 minutes. Cool.

To make the icing, whip the cream. Add chocolate syrup and orange extract, mixing lightly. Sprinkle each cake layer with rum and cover lightly with raspberry jam. Fill between layers and frost outside of cake with chocolate mixture.

To store, cover cake and keep in refrigerator. (Torte can be frozen. Remove 30 minutes before serving.)

MRS. ANDREW ALLEN
Atherton, California

Chocolate Butter-Rum Torte

1 package (6 oz.) semisweet chocolate bits
½ cup sour cream
½ cup confectioners' sugar
¼ tsp. salt
1 tsp. vanilla
1 10-inch angel food cake (unfrosted)
3 generous tbsp. rum
1 cup heavy cream, whipped (use 2 cups for a more generous frosting)
½ cup slivered blanched almonds

SERVES 14

Melt chocolate bits over hot (not boiling) water. Stir until smooth. Remove pan from water and blend in sour cream, sugar, salt and vanilla. Beat until smooth.

Cut cake crosswise into four layers. Sprinkle layers with rum. Reassemble cake, with chocolate filling between the layers. Frost top and side with whipped cream and decorate with almonds. Use a serrated cake knife to slice.

This cake may be frozen. Let stand at room temperature about 40 minutes before slicing.

MRS. CLIFTON H. PIERCE
Indio, California

Potato Cake

1½ cups flour
2 tsp. baking powder
1 tsp. cinnamon
1 tsp. ground cloves
1 tsp. nutmeg
1 cup butter, softened
2 cups sugar
½ cup milk
4 oz. unsweetened chocolate, melted and cooled
4 eggs, beaten
2 cups chopped nuts
1½ cups mashed potatoes (do not use "instant" mix)

MILK ICING
1 cup sugar
5 tbsp. light cream
1 tsp. butter
1 tsp. vanilla

"This was one of my mother's favorite recipes—and now it's one of mine."

Sift together flour, baking powder and spices and set aside. Cream butter and sugar. Mix in milk, melted chocolate and eggs. Combine with sifted dry ingredients. Add nuts and mashed potatoes; stir well. Pour into a greased and floured 10-inch tube pan. Bake in a preheated 300° oven 60 to 70 minutes. Cool before frosting.

To make Milk Icing, combine sugar, cream and butter in a saucepan. Cook over high heat until mixture spins a thread. Remove from heat. Add vanilla and beat until creamy. (If icing commences to sugar, add a little cold milk or cream.)

MRS. RALPH BUSCH, JR.
Ventura, California

Pecan Cake

2 cups butter or margarine, softened
2 cups sugar
6 eggs
1 tbsp. lemon juice
1 tsp. grated lemon rind
1 tbsp. vanilla
4 cups chopped pecans
1½ cups golden raisins
3 cups sifted flour
1 tsp. baking powder
¼ tsp. salt

Line the bottom and side of a 10-inch tube pan with waxed paper; grease the paper.

Cream butter and sugar until fluffy. Beat in eggs one at a time. Add lemon juice, rind and vanilla. Mix pecans and raisins with ¼ cup of the flour. Sift together remaining flour, baking powder and salt. Alternately fold sifted dry ingredients and nut mixture into butter mixture. Spoon into prepared pan. Bake in a preheated 300° oven 1 hour and 50 minutes.

This cake needs no icing.

MRS. SAMUEL R. McDANIELL, JR.
Longwood, Florida

Old-Fashioned Hickory Nut Cake

- 2/3 cup butter, softened
- 1 1/3 cups sugar
- 2 cups sifted cake flour
- 1 tbsp. baking powder
- 1/4 tsp. salt
- 3/4 cup milk
- 1/2 cup (2 oz.) hickory nuts, coarsely chopped (pecans or walnuts may be substituted)
- 1/2 tsp. vanilla
- 4 egg whites (1/2 cup), at room temperature, stiffly beaten

HICKORY NUT FROSTING

- 1/4 cup butter
- 1/8 tsp. salt
- 4 cups sifted confectioners' sugar
- 1 tsp. lemon juice
- 1/4 tsp. vanilla
- 1/3 cup light cream, heated
- 1/2 cup (2 oz.) hickory nuts, coarsely chopped

Line two 9-inch layer cake pans with waxed paper; butter the paper.

Using an electric mixer, cream butter at high speed 5 minutes. Add sugar gradually and cream thoroughly at high speed. Sift together flour, baking powder and salt three times. Add to butter-sugar mixture alternately with milk, beginning and ending with flour mixture. Stir in nuts and vanilla. Fold in egg whites. Pour batter into prepared pans. Bake in a preheated 350° oven 30 minutes. Cool before frosting.

To make Hickory Nut Frosting, cream butter, then add salt and half the sugar. Beat until smooth. Add lemon juice and vanilla and mix well. Alternately add remaining sugar and the cream, beating until fluffy and smooth. Add hickory nuts and mix well. Spread 3/4 cup frosting between the layers and remainder over top and sides of cake.

VERNON STOUFFER
Scottsdale, Arizona

Sour Cream Pound Cake

- 1 cup butter
- 3 cups sugar
- 6 large eggs, separated
- 3 cups sifted flour
- 1/4 tsp. salt
- 1/4 tsp. baking soda
- 1 cup sour cream
- 1 tsp. vanilla or almond extract

Cream butter and sugar. Beat egg yolks well and add to butter mixture, mixing thoroughly. Sift flour with salt and soda and add to creamed mixture alternately with sour cream. Add flavoring. Beat egg whites until stiff and fold into mixture.

Pour into a large greased and floured tube pan. Bake in a preheated 325° oven 1 1/2 hours.

MRS. ROGER ADDINGTON
Tampa, Florida

Banana Cake

2 cups sifted cake flour
2 tsp. baking powder
1 tsp. baking soda
¼ tsp. salt
¾ cup butter, softened (or margarine or a combination)
1½ cups sugar
2 eggs
1 cup mashed bananas (about 2 large or 3 small)
½ cup buttermilk
1 tsp. vanilla
½ cup chopped pecans (optional)

Grease and flour two 9-inch layer cake pans or one oblong pan, 12x9 inches.

Sift together flour, baking powder, soda and salt; repeat one or more times. Using an electric mixer, cream butter and sugar at medium speed 2 minutes, until light and fluffy. Add eggs and beat 2 minutes, scraping down around side of bowl. Add bananas and beat 2 more minutes, until well blended and fluffy. Beating 1 minute, alternately add sifted dry ingredients, buttermilk and vanilla. Beat 1 minute longer to ensure a good mixing. Nuts may be folded in at this point or reserved to sprinkle on top of batter in pans. Turn batter into prepared pans and bake in a preheated 375° oven 40 minutes or until cake springs back when touched lightly.

Top individual servings of cake with whipped cream. Or if you prefer to frost the cake, use a light coating of confectioners' sugar icing rather than a heavy, rich frosting. A light sprinkling of coconut on the icing will enhance the delicacy of the cake.

MRS. C. L. ANDERSON
Banning, California

Fresh Apple Cake

½ cup butter, softened
1½ cups sugar
2 eggs
2 cups flour
1 tsp. baking soda
1 tsp. baking powder
½ tsp. salt
4 cups sliced peeled apples
Whipped cream or ice cream

Cream butter and sugar. Beat in eggs one at a time. Sift together flour, soda, baking powder and salt; beat by hand into butter mixture (batter will be very thick). Fold in apple slices. Turn into a buttered baking pan, 13x9x2 inches. Bake in a preheated 350° oven 40 minutes.

Top individual servings with whipped cream or ice cream.

MRS. NICHOLAS COSCARELLI
Desert Hot Springs, California

Carrot Cake

2 cups sugar
4 eggs
3 cups flour
2 tsp. cinnamon
1½ cups vegetable oil (Wesson)
2 tsp. baking soda
⅓ cup buttermilk
1 tsp. lemon extract
⅛ tsp. salt
1 cup chopped pecans
3 cups grated carrots

Beat sugar and eggs together. Sift flour with cinnamon and add alternately with oil to sugar-egg mixture. Combine soda and buttermilk and add to flour mixture with lemon extract, salt, nuts and carrots. Mix well. Pour into a greased and floured tube pan. Bake in a preheated 300° oven 1½ hours.

MRS. JOSEPH LINSK
Palm Springs, California

Queen Elizabeth II Cake

1 cup boiling water
1 cup chopped dates
1 tsp. baking soda
½ cup butter, softened
1 cup sugar
1 egg, beaten
1½ cups sifted flour
1 tsp. baking powder
½ tsp. salt
½ cup chopped nuts
1 tsp. vanilla

ICING
6 tbsp. brown sugar
5 tbsp. light cream
2 tbsp. butter
Chopped nuts or shredded coconut

It is said that the Queen uses this recipe in her own kitchen.

Pour boiling water over dates. Add soda and let stand while mixing remaining ingredients.

Cream butter and sugar. Add beaten egg. Sift together flour, baking powder and salt. Stir into butter mixture along with nuts and vanilla. Add dates and mix. Pour into a greased and floured baking pan, 12x9 inches. Bake in a preheated 350° oven 35 minutes. Cool before frosting.

To make the icing, combine brown sugar, cream and butter in a saucepan. Boil 3 minutes. Spread on cake and sprinkle with chopped nuts or coconut.

MRS. STANLEY NEWBRANDER
Palm Desert, California

Jack's Favorite Prune Cake with Sauce

2 cups flour
1½ cups sugar
1 tsp. baking soda
1 tsp. salt
1 tsp. cinnamon
1 tsp. nutmeg
1 cup vegetable oil (Wesson)
½ cup buttermilk
3 eggs
1 cup stewed pitted prunes
1 cup chopped pecans
1 tsp. vanilla

SAUCE
1 cup sugar
½ cup butter
½ cup buttermilk
1 tsp. baking soda

Sift together flour, sugar, soda, salt, cinnamon and nutmeg. Add oil, buttermilk and eggs; mix well. Stir in prunes, nuts and vanilla. Pour into a greased and floured baking pan, 13½x9 inches. Bake in a preheated 350° oven 35 to 40 minutes or until done.

When cake is done, make the sauce. Combine all ingredients in a saucepan and bring to a boil, stirring. Pour sauce over each serving of cake.

MR. and MRS. JACK NICKLAUS
North Palm Beach, Florida

Jack Nicklaus was the winner of the 1963 Bob Hope Desert Classic.

Fruitcake

2 lb. large whole pecans
1½ lb. (about 4½ cups) pitted dates, chopped
1 lb. candied cherries, cut in half
1 lb. candied pineapple, cut in half
2 cups sifted flour
2 tsp. baking powder
½ tsp. salt
4 eggs
1 cup sugar

Line two loaf pans, 10x5x3 inches, with heavy brown paper; grease and flour the paper.

Mix pecans, dates, cherries and pineapple. Sift together flour, baking powder and salt. Wearing rubber gloves to protect your hands from the citric acid in the fruit, work sifted dry ingredients into fruit mixture until thoroughly coated. Beat together eggs and sugar. Add to fruit mixture and mix well, coating fruits and nuts thoroughly. Press cake mixture into prepared pans with your hands. Bake in a preheated 275° oven 1¼ hours. (Have a pan of water in the bottom of the oven throughout the baking period.)

MRS. JOHN MARSHALL SOUERBRY
Palm Desert, California

Sally's Favorite Fruitcake

- 1 lb. (3 cups) pitted dates, cut in half
- ½ cup red candied pineapple, cut into chunks
- ½ cup green candied pineapple, cut into chunks
- ½ cup whole red candied cherries
- ½ cup whole green candied cherries
- 2 cups whole Brazil nuts (cut in half, if you prefer)
- 2 cups black walnuts
- 1 cup sifted flour
- 1 cup sugar
- 1 tsp. baking powder
- ¼ tsp. salt
- 4 eggs, well beaten
- 1 tsp. vanilla or rum extract

PINEAPPLE GLAZE

- ½ cup light corn syrup
- ¼ cup unsweetened pineapple juice

Line two loaf pans, 8½x4½x2½ inches, with heavy brown paper; grease the paper.

Combine dates, candied pineapple, whole cherries and nuts. Sift together dry ingredients and add to fruits and nuts, stirring to coat well. Stir in beaten eggs and vanilla. Pour batter into prepared pans. Bake in a preheated 325° oven 1 hour or until done. Cool.

To make Pineapple Glaze, combine corn syrup and pineapple juice in a small saucepan. Quickly bring to a rolling boil. Remove from heat. Using a pastry brush, immediately brush about half the glaze over cooled fruitcake. Let this set, then repeat.

Store cake in an airtight container in refrigerator or freezer.

MRS. NORMAN G. HOLLER
Vista, California

Hawaiian Wedding Cake

BASE

- ½ cup butter, softened
- 1 cup flour

FILLING

- 2 eggs
- 1½ cups brown sugar
- 2 tbsp. flour
- 1 tsp. baking powder
- ½ tsp. salt
- ½ cup shredded coconut
- 1 cup chopped walnuts
- 1 tsp. vanilla

ICING

- 2 tbsp. butter, softened
- 1½ cups confectioners' sugar
- ¼ cup lemon juice (more or less, to taste)

To make the base, cream the ½ cup butter with 1 cup flour. Press into a greased loaf pan, 9x5x3 inches. Bake in a preheated 350° oven 10 to 15 minutes. Let cool.

To make the filling, beat eggs thoroughly. Add brown sugar, flour, baking powder, salt, coconut, walnuts and vanilla; mix well. Spread filling over the cooled base. Return to a 350° oven and bake 15 to 20 minutes longer. Let cool.

To make the icing, blend butter and confectioners' sugar. Stir in lemon juice to make an easy spreading consistency. Spread icing over cooled cake.

DR. and MRS. ROBERT MORREY
Rancho Mirage, California

Lemon Cheesecake

CRUST
- 3/4 package zwieback, finely crushed
- 1/2 cup butter, melted
- 1/4 cup sugar
- 1 tsp. cinnamon

FILLING
- 4 eggs, well beaten
- 1 cup sugar
- 4 packages (8 oz. each) cream cheese, softened
- 1 tbsp. lemon juice
- 1/8 tsp. salt

TOPPING
- 2 cups sour cream
- 1/4 cup sugar
- 1 tsp. vanilla

SERVES 14 OR MORE

Mix all crust ingredients. Press three-fourths of the mixture on the bottom and side of a 10-inch springform pan. Reserve remaining crumb mixture.

To make filling, beat eggs with sugar until thick and lemon-colored. Add cream cheese, lemon juice and salt to egg mixture. Using an electric mixer, beat until smooth. Pour into crust. Bake in a preheated 375° oven 20 minutes. Remove cheesecake from oven and set aside to cool. Meanwhile, make topping by blending sour cream, sugar and vanilla.

Raise oven temperature to 475°. When oven reaches that temperature, spread topping evenly over cheesecake. Sprinkle with reserved crumb mixture. Bake 10 minutes. Cool, then refrigerate for several hours. The cheesecake will keep 5 days in the refrigerator.

MRS. FRANCIS J. SULLIVAN
Long Beach, California

Cheesecake Deluxe

CRUST
- 18 graham crackers, finely crushed
- 1/2 cup butter, softened

FILLING
- 2 packages (8 ounces each) cream cheese, softened
- 5 eggs, separated
- 1/2 cup sugar
- 1 tsp. vanilla

TOPPING
- 2 cups sour cream
- 3 tbsp. sugar
- 1 tsp. vanilla
- 5 drops almond extract

SERVES 10–12

To make the crust, mix crackers and butter. Press onto the bottom and side of a deep 10-inch springform pan.

To make the filling, beat cream cheese until smooth. Add egg yolks, sugar and vanilla. Mix well. Beat egg whites until stiff and fold in. Turn into crust and bake in a preheated 350° oven 30 to 40 minutes. Cool *thoroughly* before adding the topping.

To make the topping, combine sour cream, sugar, vanilla and almond extract. Mix well and spread on cooled cheesecake. Bake in a preheated 350° oven 20 minutes. Cool at room temperature, then refrigerate.

MRS. GLENN R. SIMMONS
Rancho Mirage, California

COOKIES & CANDIES

Those Petite Sweets and Treats

"Good things come in little packages," or so the saying goes. And maybe that's why cookies and candies are ever-popular. Their pleasure comes in tidbit portions— to tuck into a lunch box or picnic basket, to fill out a tea table, to sweeten up after-dinner coffee and cognac. And who of us, at any age, can resist the temptation of a brimful cookie or candy jar? Rich with good, fresh ingredients, homemade sweets make the happiest kind of memories.

Almond Crisp Cookies

- 1/4 cup sifted flour
- 1/4 tsp. salt
- 1/2 cup sugar
- 1/2 cup butter
- 2 tbsp. light cream
- 2/3 cup slivered almonds

MAKES ABOUT 3 DOZEN

"These are lacy, rich and crisp. Good with ice cream, in a sort of a sandwich."

Sift together flour, salt and sugar into a small saucepan. Add butter and cream; cook over low heat, stirring occasionally, until bubbly. Remove from heat and stir briskly 30 seconds. Stir in almonds.

Drop dough by a *teaspoon* (no larger than that) onto a greased cookie sheet about 4 inches apart. Bake in a preheated 375° oven 5 minutes. Cool cookies slightly before removing with a pancake turner. Finish cooling on a waxed-paper-covered rack.

MRS. FRITZ TAVES
Palm Desert, California

Chocolate-Coconut Macaroons

- 1 package (6 oz.) semisweet chocolate bits
- 1/2 cup sugar
- 2 egg whites
- 1/4 tsp. salt
- 1/2 tsp. vanilla
- 1 can (about 3 1/2 oz.) shredded coconut

MAKES 2 DOZEN

Slowly melt chocolate bits in the top of a double boiler over simmering water. Remove from heat and let cool. Gradually adding sugar, beat egg whites until they stand in peaks. Gently stir egg whites and sugar into melted chocolate. Add salt, vanilla and coconut.

Using a small teaspoon, drop mixture onto a cookie sheet covered with brown paper. Bake in a preheated 325° oven 15 minutes. Remove from paper immediately.

MRS. LAWRENCE C. MILLS
Hinsdale, Illinois

✳ *Old-Fashioned Oatmeal Cookies*

1½ cups confectioners' sugar
3 eggs, separated
2½ cups old-fashioned oats
1 tsp. baking powder
1 tsp. butter, melted
1 tsp. vanilla

MAKES ABOUT 3½ DOZEN

"This recipe came down to me from my grandmother. My father, Chief Justice Hughes, was brought up on these cookies and loved them dearly, as does our entire family."

Add sugar to egg yolks and work together until mixture is smooth and thin. Stir in the oats, baking powder, butter and vanilla. Beat egg whites until stiff and fold in. For each cookie, drop a teaspoon of batter onto a greased cookie sheet. Bake in a preheated 350° oven 10 to 12 minutes, watching carefully. Lift quickly off sheet.

ELIZABETH HUGHES GASSETT
Bloomfield Hills, Michigan

Oatmeal Cookies

½ cup butter, softened
1 cup light brown sugar
½ cup granulated sugar
1 tsp. vanilla
2 eggs and ¼ cup water, well beaten
1 tsp. salt
1 cup sifted flour
½ tsp. baking soda
About 1 cup quick-cooking oats
Chopped nuts (preferably walnuts)

MAKES ABOUT 5 DOZEN

Mix all ingredients in the order listed. Drop dough by spoonfuls onto a greased cookie sheet. Bake in a preheated 400° oven 7 to 8 minutes. Then run under the broiler to brown.

NORMAN ROCKWELL
Stockbridge, Massachusetts

Potato Chip Cookies

- 1 lb. butter, softened (do not use margarine)
- 1 cup sugar
- 3½ cups sifted flour
- 2 tsp. vanilla
- 2 cups crushed potato chips

MAKES ABOUT 3½ DOZEN

Cream butter and sugar. Stir in remaining ingredients. Drop dough onto an ungreased cookie sheet; flatten with a fork. Bake in a preheated 350° oven 12 minutes. Keep in an airtight container.

MRS. PAUL JENKINS
Bermuda Dunes, California

Sesame Crisps

- ½ cup butter, softened
- 1 cup brown sugar
- 1 tsp. vanilla
- 1 egg
- ½ cup sesame seed, toasted
- 1 cup sifted flour
- ¼ tsp. baking powder
- ¼ tsp. salt

MAKES ABOUT 4 DOZEN

Cream butter, sugar and vanilla. Beat in egg, then stir in sesame seed. Sift together flour, baking powder and salt; add to the creamed mixture and mix well.

Using a teaspoon, drop dough in rounds onto a well-greased cookie sheet. Bake in a preheated 375° oven 8 to 10 minutes. Let cool a minute before removing from cookie sheet.

MRS. ALLEN KERR
Indian Wells, California

Jelly Tots

- 2 cups sifted flour
- ½ tsp. baking powder
- ¼ tsp. salt
- 1 cup butter or margarine, softened
- ½ cup sugar
- 1 egg yolk
- 2 tbsp. water
- 1 tsp. vanilla
- About 1¼ cups finely chopped nuts
- Jelly

MAKES ABOUT 3 DOZEN

Sift together flour, baking powder and salt. Cream butter, sugar and egg yolk. Add water, vanilla and sifted dry ingredients; mix well.

Form dough into balls the size of a small walnut. Roll balls in chopped nuts and place on a greased cookie sheet. Bake in a preheated 350° oven 5 minutes. Remove from oven and make an imprint in the top of each ball with the top of a small thimble. Return to oven and bake 8 to 10 minutes longer. When cool, fill impression with the jelly of your choice.

MRS. JOHN B. SUGGS
Palm Desert, California

Ranger Cookies

- ½ cup butter, softened
- ½ cup margarine
- 1 cup granulated sugar
- 1 cup brown sugar
- 2 eggs
- 2 cups sifted flour
- 1 tsp. baking soda
- ½ tsp. baking powder
- ½ tsp. salt
- 1 tbsp. vanilla
- 2 cups quick-cooking oats
- 2 cups Rice Crispies
- 1 cup shredded coconut

MAKES ABOUT 6 DOZEN

Cream butter, margarine and sugars. Add eggs and mix well. Sift together flour, baking soda, baking powder and salt; add to creamed mixture. Add vanilla, oatmeal, cereal and coconut and mix well.

Form dough into balls about the size of a walnut. Place on a greased cookie sheet and flatten with a fork. Bake in a preheated 350° oven 10 to 12 minutes.

MR. and MRS. TOM NIEPORTE
Boca Raton, Florida

Tom Nieporte was the winner of the 1967 Bob Hope Desert Classic.

Kolachki

1 cup butter, softened
1 package (8 oz.) cream cheese, softened
4 egg yolks, beaten
2½ cups sifted flour
¼ tsp. salt

FILLING
1½ lb. walnuts
4 egg whites
¾ cup sugar

MAKES ABOUT 3½ DOZEN

"These delicacies were served to us in Leningrad in 1959, right after Sputnik was launched."

Cream butter and cream cheese until light and fluffy. Add beaten egg yolks and continue to cream. Gradually add the sifted flour and salt, mixing well after each addition of flour. Mix until a dough is formed which does not cling to the side of the bowl. Separate dough into 3 equal parts and flatten out in the palm of your hand. Wrap each part separately and store in the freezer while making filling.

To make filling, crush small amounts of walnuts (using a rolling pin) until all are crushed. Beat egg whites with sugar until stiff peaks form when beater is raised. Add the crushed walnuts to egg whites and fold in thoroughly. Store in refrigerator until ready to use.

Roll out dough ⅛ inch thick, using confectioners' sugar as if it were flour. (Work fast so that the dough does not stick.) Cut dough into 2- or 3-inch squares, depending on how large a cookie you want. Put a heaping teaspoonful of filling in center of square; raise one corner over filling to meet opposite corner, sealing filling in. Bake in a preheated 350° oven about 15 minutes or until filling expands and dough is lightly browned.

MRS. JAMES W. ALLEN
Alpine, New York

Pecan Crescent Cookies

2 cups flour
1 cup butter, softened
1½ cups diced pecans
¼ cup granulated sugar
½ tsp. salt
¼ tsp. baking powder
Confectioners' sugar

MAKES ABOUT 5 DOZEN

Mix all ingredients except confectioners' sugar. Form into crescents by squeezing dough in the palm of the hand. Place on an ungreased cookie sheet. Bake in a preheated 350° oven 12 minutes or until light brown. While still warm, roll crescents in confectioners' sugar.

AMBASSADOR and MRS. LEONARD K. FIRESTONE
Brussels, Belgium

Lemon Log Cookies

1 cup butter, softened
¾ cup brown sugar
1 egg, separated
½ tsp. salt
1 tsp. grated lemon rind
1 tbsp. lemon juice
2⅓ cups sifted flour
1 cup chopped nuts

MAKES ABOUT 4 DOZEN

Cream butter, sugar and egg yolk together. Add salt, lemon rind, lemon juice and flour; beat well.

Shape dough into fingerlike rolls. Dip into slightly beaten egg white and roll in nuts. Place on a lightly greased cookie sheet and bake in a preheated 375° oven 10 minutes.

MRS. SPIRO T. AGNEW
Indian Hills, Maryland

Danish Audreens

1 cup butter, softened
½ cup confectioners' sugar
2 cups sifted cake flour
¾ cup chopped nuts
1 tsp. vanilla

MAKES 4–5 DOZEN

Cream butter and sugar. Stir in flour and nuts. Add vanilla and mix well. Chill dough until easy to handle. Form into very small balls and place on a greased cookie sheet. Bake in a preheated 350° oven 20 minutes. While still warm, roll balls in additional confectioners' sugar.

MRS. KAY OLESEN
Palm Desert, California

Peanut Butter Refrigerator Cookies

- 1/2 cup peanut butter
- 1/2 cup shortening
- 2 cups brown sugar (firmly packed)
- 1 tsp. vanilla
- 2 eggs
- 2 1/4 cups sifted flour
- 2 tsp. baking soda
- 1 tsp. salt
- 1 cup raisins, finely chopped
- 2 cups quick-cooking or old-fashioned oats
- 1/2 cup chopped nuts

MAKES 4–5 DOZEN

Cream peanut butter with shortening thoroughly. Add sugar and vanilla. Continue creaming until fluffy. Add eggs and beat well.

Sift together flour, baking soda and salt; add to peanut butter mixture with raisins, oats and nuts. Shape dough into long rolls. Wrap rolls in waxed paper and chill well.

When ready to bake, unwrap rolls and cut into 1/2-inch slices. Place on an ungreased cookie sheet and bake in a preheated 350° oven about 15 minutes.

GENERAL OMAR N. BRADLEY
Los Angeles, California

Double Chocolate Brownies

- 1/2 cup butter (do not use margarine)
- 2 squares unsweetened chocolate (Baker's)
- 1 cup sugar
- 2 eggs, well beaten
- 1/8 tsp. salt
- 1/2 cup sifted flour
- 1/2 cup chopped nuts
- 1 tsp. vanilla

FROSTING

- 1 1/2 tbsp. butter
- 2 squares unsweetened chocolate
- 2 cups confectioners' sugar
- 3 1/2 tbsp. milk
- 1/2 tsp. vanilla
- Pinch of salt

MAKES ABOUT 2 DOZEN

Melt butter and chocolate in the top of a double boiler. Remove from heat. Add sugar and stir well. Add eggs and salt. Mix flour and nuts and stir into chocolate mixture. Stir in vanilla.

Spread in a well-greased baking pan, 11 1/2x8 1/2 inches. Bake in a preheated 350° oven 20 minutes. Remove from oven and cut into squares; take out of pan immediately. Let cool before frosting.

To make frosting, melt butter and chocolate in the top of a double boiler; remove from heat. Mix sugar and milk and stir until creamy. Stir into chocolate mixture, then add vanilla and salt. Spread over cooled brownies, adding an extra dab on top.

MRS. ROGER ADDINGTON
Tampa, Florida

Brownies

- ¾ cup sifted cake flour
- ½ tsp. double-acting baking powder
- ¾ tsp. salt
- 2 eggs
- 1 cup sugar
- 1 tsp. vanilla
- 2½ oz. unsweetened chocolate
- ½ cup soft shortening
- 1 cup chopped nuts

MAKES 16

Sift together flour, baking powder and salt; set aside. Beat eggs, then add the sugar and vanilla. Melt chocolate with shortening, then add to the eggs and sugar mixture. Stir in sifted dry ingredients, then add nuts. Pour into a greased baking pan, 8x8x2 inches. Bake in a preheated 350° oven 30 to 35 minutes or until done. Cool slightly, then cut into 2-inch squares.

MARY JEAN EISENHOWER
Phoenixville, Pennsylvania

Miss Eisenhower is Mamie Eisenhower's granddaughter.

Chewy Brownies

- ⅓ cup butter or margarine, softened
- 1 cup light brown sugar
- ½ cup chocolate syrup
- 2 eggs
- 1 tsp. vanilla
- ¾ cup sifted flour
- 1 tsp. baking powder
- 1 cup chopped nuts

MAKES 32

Grease and flour two baking pans, 8x8x2 inches. Cream butter, sugar and chocolate syrup. Add eggs and vanilla and stir well. Sift flour with baking powder and add to chocolate mixture. Stir in nuts.

Spread in prepared pans. Bake in a preheated 350° oven 25 to 30 minutes. Cool slightly before cutting into 2-inch squares.

MRS. JOHN FRAIM
Indian Wells, California

Chocolate-Marshmallow Fudge Cakes

1 cup sugar
2 eggs
½ cup flour
2 oz. unsweetened chocolate
½ cup butter
1 tsp. vanilla
1 cup chopped pecans
Large marshmallows

MAKES ABOUT 16

Cream sugar, eggs and flour. Melt chocolate and butter together and add to creamed mixture. Add vanilla and nuts.

Pour into a greased baking pan, about 11½x7 inches. Bake in a preheated 350° oven 18 minutes. Remove from oven and cover top with large marshmallows. Return to oven until marshmallows are lightly browned. Cool slightly, then cut into bars.

MRS. ROBERT E. HIBBERT
Houston, Texas

Coconut and Nut Bars

CRUST
½ cup butter, softened
½ cup brown sugar
1 cup sifted flour

TOPPING
2 tbsp. flour
½ tsp. baking powder
¼ tsp. salt
1 cup chopped walnuts
2 eggs
1 cup brown sugar
1 tsp. vanilla
½ cup shredded coconut

MAKES ABOUT 2½ DOZEN

To make crust, mix butter, the ½ cup sugar and the 1 cup flour to a crumbling mass. Press into buttered baking dish, 13x8 inches. Bake in a preheated 350° oven 8 minutes. Remove from oven and let cool.

To make topping, sift the 2 tablespoons flour, baking powder and salt over walnuts; set aside. Beat eggs. Add sugar and vanilla, then walnuts and coconut. Spread evenly over baked crust and return to oven for about 15 minutes. Do not overbake. Cut into squares while still a bit warm.

MRS. CHARLES H. SPARKS
Eugene, Oregon

Toffee Bars

- 1 cup butter or margarine, softened
- 1 cup brown sugar
- 1 tsp. vanilla
- 2 cups sifted flour
- Dash of salt
- 1 package (6 oz.) semisweet chocolate bits
- 1 cup chopped walnuts

MAKES ABOUT 3 DOZEN

"With three children around, we usually try to keep the cookie jar filled for after-school snacks. And these Toffee Bars are one of their favorites. People usually think I've made a mistake and left out the liquid — but honestly, there isn't any!"

Cream butter, sugar and vanilla in a mixing bowl until light and fluffy. Add flour and salt and mix well. Stir in chocolate bits and walnuts. Spread in a greased jelly roll pan, 15½x10½x1 inch. Bake in a preheated 350° oven 20 minutes. While warm, cut into bars. Cool in pan.

MRS. BING CROSBY
Hillsborough, California

Noëls

- 2 tbsp. butter
- 2 eggs
- 1 cup brown sugar (packed)
- 5 tbsp. flour
- ⅛ tsp. baking soda
- 1 cup chopped nuts
- 1 tsp. vanilla
- Confectioners' sugar

MAKES ABOUT 16

Melt butter in a baking pan, 9x9x2 inches, over low heat or in the oven. Beat eggs slightly. Combine brown sugar, flour, baking soda and nuts and stir into beaten eggs. Add vanilla.

Pour mixture over melted butter but do not stir into butter. Bake in a preheated 350° oven 20 minutes. Turn out of pan onto a cake rack to cool. Cut into squares and dust with confectioners' sugar.

MRS. JAMES WILSON
Palm Desert, California

Date and Nut Squares

2 eggs
½ cup granulated sugar
½ tsp. vanilla
½ cup sifted flour
½ tsp. baking powder
½ tsp. salt
2 cups finely cut-up dates
1 cup chopped walnuts
Confectioners' sugar (optional)

MAKES 16

These squares are chewy and rich, rather like the Bishop's Bread served to the circuit preachers of earlier days.

Beat eggs until foamy. Beat in granulated sugar and vanilla. Sift together flour, baking powder and salt; stir into egg mixture. Mix in dates and nuts. Spread in a greased baking pan, 8x8x2 inches. Bake in a preheated 325° oven 25 to 30 minutes or until the top has a dull crust. Cut into 2-inch squares; cool in pan. If desired, dip in confectioners' sugar.

MRS. WILLIAM J. YOUNG
Cathedral City, California

Graham Cracker Dream Bars

Graham crackers
1 cup butter (or half butter and half margarine)
1 cup sugar
½ cup milk
2 eggs, slightly beaten
1 cup shredded coconut
1 cup chopped walnuts
½ tsp. vanilla
1 cup fine graham cracker crumbs

FROSTING
2 cups confectioners' sugar
¼ cup butter, softened
Juice of ½ large lemon (a lot of lemon juice makes the difference!)
Light cream

MAKES 3–4 DOZEN

Grease the bottom of a baking dish, 11x8 inches. Line the bottom of the dish with whole crackers, filling in the edges with broken pieces. Melt butter in a saucepan. Add sugar, milk and eggs and bring to a rolling boil (stir to prevent sticking). Stir in the coconut, walnuts, vanilla and crumbs. While still hot, pour over the crackers in the dish. Add a top layer of whole crackers. (Press them down on the mixture so they will adhere.) Let cool before frosting.

To make frosting, mix sugar, butter and lemon juice. Stir in enough cream to make spreading consistency. Spread over graham crackers. Refrigerate overnight. To serve, cut into small bars.

An excellent choice for teas.

MRS. ALBERT J. LILYGREN
Kirkland, Washington

Chinese Candy-Cookies

- 2 packages (6 oz. each) butterscotch bits
- 2 cups chow mein noodles
- 1 cup roasted peanuts

MAKES ABOUT 2½ DOZEN

Melt butterscotch bits in the top of a double boiler. Remove from heat and add noodles and peanuts; mix well. Using a teaspoon, drop mixture onto waxed paper and let cool.

MRS. JOHN TRUYENS
Los Angeles, California

Peanut Butter Creams

- 1 cup crunchy peanut butter
- ½ cup butter
- 2 cups confectioners' sugar
- 1 tsp. vanilla
- 1 cup chopped walnuts
- 1 package (6 oz.) semisweet chocolate bits
- 2 tbsp. paraffin

MAKES ABOUT 6 DOZEN

Blend peanut butter, butter, sugar and vanilla. Mix in walnuts. Shape mixture into small balls and chill until firm. Melt chocolate with paraffin.

Drop peanut butter balls into chocolate. Lift out with a fork and cool on waxed paper. Store, covered, in the refrigerator.

MRS. ROY D. ADAMS
Indian Wells, California

Spiced Nuts

- 1 cup sugar
- 1 tsp. salt
- 2 rounded tsp. cinnamon
- 1 tsp. nutmeg
- 1 tsp. ground cloves
- 1 tbsp. light corn syrup
- ½ cup water
- 1 tbsp. butter
- 3 cups walnuts

MAKES ABOUT 3½ CUPS

Cook and stir sugar, salt, cinnamon, nutmeg, cloves, corn syrup and water until mixture reaches the soft ball stage. Remove from heat. Add butter and let it melt gradually. Stir until mixture is creamy. Then add the walnuts and stir until nuts are well mixed and thoroughly coated. Pour onto waxed paper and spread to dry.

MRS. WALKER SMITH
Newport Beach, California

Wonderful Peanut Brittle

- 2 cups sugar
- 1 cup light corn syrup
- ½ cup water
- 2 cups raw peanuts
- 1 tbsp. butter
- 1 tsp. vanilla
- 2 heaping tsp. baking soda

MAKES ABOUT 3 POUNDS

Spread a large sheet of foil on a board or slab and butter it well. Set aside.

Cook and stir sugar, corn syrup and water in a large iron skillet until mixture spins a thread. Add peanuts and cook over medium heat, stirring occasionally, until the color is a light gold. Remove from heat. Stir in butter and vanilla, then add soda (the mixture will foam). Quickly pour onto buttered foil and let cool. Break into pieces.

MRS. LESLIE HUNCKE
Leawood, Kansas

Italian Creams

- 1 cup milk
- 3 cups sugar
- 1 heaping tbsp. butter
- 1 tsp. vanilla
- ¾ cup chopped walnuts

MAKES ABOUT 3 DOZEN

Heat milk and 2 cups of the sugar in a large heavy saucepan, stirring occasionally; allow mixture to boil gently. Add butter.

Meanwhile, heat remaining 1 cup sugar in a heavy skillet (without any water), stirring gently so that the sugar will dissolve without burning. When sugar in skillet is completely dissolved, remove sugar and milk mixture from heat and stir in the dissolved sugar. (If not removed from heat, the mixture will boil over when the dissolved sugar is added.) After combining, return to heat and cook, stirring gently, until mixture reaches the soft ball stage. Remove from heat and beat by hand until mixture thickens. Add vanilla and walnuts. Pour into a buttered pan and let cool. When firm, cut into squares, as you would fudge.

MRS. ROBERT C. BOOTH
Pomona, California

Creamy Pecan Pralines, Mexican Style

- 3 cups sugar
- 3/4 cup milk
- 1/2 tsp. baking soda
- 2 tbsp. butter
- 2 cups pecan halves
- 1 1/2 tsp. vanilla

MAKES 2 1/2–3 DOZEN

Cook sugar, milk, baking soda and butter over low heat, stirring occasionally, until mixture reaches the very soft ball stage.

Remove from heat. Add pecans and vanilla and beat until it loses the "glossy" look. Working fast, drop by spoonfuls onto waxed paper and let cool.

MRS. MICHEL T. HALBOUTY
Houston, Texas

Surprise Fudge

- 2 cups granulated sugar
- 1 cup brown sugar
- 2 tbsp. instant coffee
- 1 1/4 cups milk
- 2 tbsp. light corn syrup
- 1/4 cup butter
- 1 tsp. vanilla
- 3/4 cup chopped dried figs
- 3/4 cup chopped walnuts

MAKES 3 POUNDS

Mix sugars, coffee, milk and corn syrup in a heavy saucepan. Cook over medium heat, stirring constantly, until sugars dissolve. Cook to 236° on a candy thermometer, or until mixture reaches the soft ball stage.

Remove from heat and add butter. Cool to lukewarm *without stirring.* Add vanilla, figs and walnuts and beat until mixture begins to thicken. Drop from a teaspoon onto waxed paper and cool until firm (or spread in a greased pan; when firm, cut into squares).

MRS. WILLIAM H. ADAMS, JR.
Fort Worth, Texas

INDEX

C

D

E

Q

R

S

T

V

W

Y

Z